Echoes from the Ozarks

Echoes from the Ozarks

Memories of the Missouri Hills

By Mark D. Meadows

Foreword by Aaron Elkins

Literature should illuminate life.
If it doesn't, it's not literature, it's litter.
                    ~John G. Neihardt

Echoes from the Ozarks: Memories of the Missouri Hills
by Mark D. Meadows

Published by Mark D. Meadows

Copyright © 2022 by Mark D. Meadows

Cover design by Philip Meadows at xenopixel.com
Text formatted by Aaron C. Meadows

Library of Congress Control Number: 2022913388

ISBN: 979-8-8396-3766-5 (print)

First Edition

1 3 5 7 9 10 8 6 4 2

Dedication

to the cherished memory of

Christopher Edward Meadows

1973-2020

"Mr. Christer"

That little boy called Mr. Christer
Had brothers, but not any sister.
When asked how denied
He felt, he replied,
"Not knowing her, I haven't missed 'er!"

Foreword

In his introduction to this collection, Mark Meadows implies that anybody, given patience, and perseverance, could write a book like this one. "Everybody's life is filled with humorous and interesting events and associations," he says. "Most people simply do not write them down."

Well, he's wrong—or more likely, overly modest. Meadows is a one-of-a-kind, a throwback to Mark Twain, a keen observer who views the world through a prism that reveals gleams of humor, sentiment, and gentle irony where others see, well, nothing much, or at least nothing to write home about. On top of that, the man is a first-rate writer. His style is simple, coherent, witty, and eminently readable.

In today's world of humor, "edgy" is the in-word, and sarcasm—ridiculing others by parodying their quirks and foibles —is the genre's reigning mode. Not so in this book, I'm happy to say. Whatever else you might find Mark Meadows to be, you won't come up with "sarcastic." Or "edgy." Or "nasty." "Ironic?" Well, yes, here and there, but always good-hearted, never with malice.

In other words, these brief slices of life are old-fashioned, in the very best sense of the term. You can even find *morals* in them, but you have to look for them yourself. As with Aesop— also one of his literary forebears—Mark prefers anecdote to explication, and crisp descriptions rather than in-your-face moralizing.[*]

I wish you a good time leafing through these congenial tales. Read. Relax. Enjoy.

Aaron Elkins
Sequim, Washington

---

[*] The morals that we now associate with Aesop's fables were tacked onto them centuries after their first appearance.

Acknowledgements

Aaron Elkins

I am forever grateful to Aaron Elkins, friend and favorite author. Without his pushing, I would never have summoned the moxie to collect my chronicles in book form. He has given me insights into good writing and sage advice as to the means to publish. I am thankful to Aaron for the kindly kick in the pants he gave me to start this project. If you enjoy the book, you should be thankful to him as well.

Judy Meadows

I am perpetually beholden to Judy, my wife of fifty-six years, for a lifetime of love and support. Her mind is quick and practical. She is willing to share her discernment and advice with me whenever I ask her guidance. Whether I am cooking, writing, or building a bookshelf, her recommendations insure a better end result. She has been eternal in encouragement and patient in proofreading. Her counsel in composing this book has been invaluable.

Everyone Else

The list of those who have encouraged my writing during my long lifetime is almost endless. I appreciate every single one. I cannot list them all, but only a few who made special contributions.

My nephew **Philip Meadows**, a gifted artist and architect, designed the book cover. Our sons, **Chris, Aaron, and Alex**, have been unswerving in their support. **Aaron Meadows** was tireless and patient in formatting the text. My brother **Roger Meadows** taught me so much about publishing that my head swirled. **Larry Quinalty** enlightened me in some finer points about punctuation and grammar. Friends **Darrell Ledenham** and **Lydia Rufleth** helped me decide whether certain tricky tales should make the cut.

Introduction

In 1983, I resigned from my job at Arkansas State University, so that Judy and I could move to southwest Missouri with our three young sons, Christopher, Aaron, and Alexander. Our two dogs Gypsy and Babe came with us. We bought a run-down, rocky, eighty-five acre farm in Barry County about twelve miles from where I grew up. Every building on the property cried out for the bulldozer. The dilapidated old house did not have indoor plumbing, but hardly needed it since the ancient well was dry!

As the years rolled by we drilled a new well, replaced the outbuildings, and built an addition with kitchen, bathroom, and laundry room—everything that required running water. We lived in that terrible old house for twenty-five years, raised our sons there and saw them off to college. In 2008, we erected a new house on the same property and happily saw the old house bulldozed.

Through our years here in the Ozarks, I ran a mail order clock parts business for eight years and then repaired clocks. Judy was a school librarian.

Everybody's life is filled with humorous and interesting events and associations. Most people simply do not write them down. I have written about some of the situations we have experienced, and I hope that you will find these tales entertaining. Some of the names are real, but some are fictitious —especially when a character's behavior is eccentric or less than admirable.

~Mark D. Meadows
Cassville, Missouri
author@ozarkmark.com

Table of Contents

Tony's Troubles

During a twenty-four hour period in July 1997, Tony Washeck suffered three traumatic events. On Friday the twenty-second, he was driving his truck when a bee got behind his glasses. While trying to rid himself of the bee, he flipped his glasses out the window. In a display of quick thinking, he threw a red bandana out the window to mark the spot, so found the glasses. At a square dance that night, his upper denture leapt from his mouth and skated across the floor, much to his embarrassment. Tony fell off his tractor the next morning. He was injured to the extent that he could not attend the dance at his home square dance club that night in Aurora, Missouri.

Tony was president of the Aurora Grand Squares Club. Georgene, the vice-president, asked me to do a roast at their Christmas dance, including jokes and a poem about Tony. I barely knew Tony at that time and did not know whether I could write a respectable poem. I said that I would do the roast if I was able to write a poem. Luckily, I became ill with flu the next day and was confined to bed. As I lay there, rhymes, couplets, and ideas began to come to me. Finally, I got up and got a clipboard, so I could write them down.

A few days before the Christmas party and dance, Peggy, Georgene's kind-hearted sister-in-law, told me that if I knew what was good for me, I would not dare do a poem about Tony. "You'll be in big trouble," she said. "You don't know Tony, but

1

he has a terrible temper, and he may break you in half." This warning gave me pause, as Tony was a big, muscular man. However, at this point, it was too late to back out.

At the dance, I stood to speak and was chagrinned that the emcee had Tony stand right beside me! A friend had lent me a huge set of pretend false teeth made from cow's teeth. I used them as a prop while telling some jokes before reading my poem. As I nervously began my poem, I kept one eye on Tony, towering and glowering over me, and one eye on the nearest exit. I wondered how fast Tony could run. Here is my poem:

The Great Denture Adventure

Have you met Tony Washeck, that big square-dancing fellow?
Things that would kill a lesser man just make Tony mellow.
He's faster than a speeding bullet, mighty as a train.
Sometimes he does such crazy things, his friends think he's insane.

I have three things to tell you; I'll tell the last one first.
Impartial logic tells me this one might have been the worst,
But of the three disasters, this one took the smallest toll;
This one traumatized his body; the others tried his soul.

I've ridden horses long enough to know bluff is a factor;
I didn't know the same was true of riding on a tractor.
One Saturday when Tony got his tractor out to work,
The tractor threw him on the ground by starting with a jerk.

Oh, he could have been hurt badly or killed himself instead,
But this time luck was with him, and he landed on his head.
Disasters often come in threes, and this was number three.
The first two came the day before, as you are soon to see.

Both the windows on his truck were open all the way,
As Tony sped along the road one happy July day.
We all have had that feeling: "Someone's here with me."
Tony had that feeling, and that someone was a bee.

This bee had poor eyesight, but he wasn't wearing glasses.
Tony's specs would let the bee see how the landscape passes—
Or so he thought, and so he flew right into Tony's eye.
The truck swerved wildly; Tony thrashed; the bee thought he might die.

A mighty battle followed; who'd win was nip and tuck.
The final outcome wasn't based on skill, but only luck.
While down the highway sped the truck, the two fought mightily,
Till out the window Tony flung his glasses—and the bee.

Tony had gone into town to buy some underwear;
To mark the spot he jettisoned a brightly-colored pair.
A lady motorist behind thought Tony had undressed,
And passed his truck to look inside, but drove on unimpressed.

Tony got the truck slowed down and turned the other way
To where his underpants were waving in the breezy day.
The way the sun shone on his specs he saw them at a glance,
A bit of luck—he'd want his glasses that night at the dance.

We danced that night at Everton, I'm glad that I was there,
As Tony danced so flawlessly around within his square.
He turned his head to Margie, as if to say a word,
But when he opened up his mouth, a great event occurred.

Out shot Tony's upper teeth and flew across the room!
Some folks saw them coming and thought they'd met their doom.
The teeth winged seven dancers and bounced against the wall,
Then knocked the caller off his feet in the middle of a call.

After one more ricochet, their flight path grew unstable:
They dented in the coffee urn and landed on the table.
They took a bite out of a pie and would have eaten more,
But now their energy was spent, and they slid out on the floor.

Tony towered tall and straight, just like a mighty oak,
And looked around the tumbled scene of chaos, then he spoke.
But Tony is quick-witted, (I swear that this is true.)
He loudly said, "Don't worry, Marge! I'll get them back for you!"

If you drive up to Everton and bribe the touring guide,
He'll unlock the dancing hall and let you slip inside.
He'll show you teeth marks on the wall, a chewed up coffeepot,
And other ample evidence. Will you believe or not?

All of these disasters gave Tony's friends a scare;
They wouldn't stand beside him outside or in a square.
Oh, they still loved the big guy; the thought to them was frightening
Of knowing they might not survive if he got struck by lightning.

But I have quite a different view: I take it as a sign
That after these catastrophes, he feels and looks just fine.
In lightning, hail, or earthquake, I'll trust in his endurance.
Standing right by Tony's side's as good as life insurance!

As I read the poem, the audience hooted and laughed, but I noticed that Tony, towering over me, looked grim and never cracked a smile. I manfully read on and on. When I finished the poem, the audience applauded, but Tony grabbed me! I didn't have a chance to run, and my life flashed before my eyes. Tony did not break me in half; he gave me a bear hug and said, "That is the best poem I have ever heard."

He thanked me warmly and ever afterward looked upon me as one of his best friends. I gave Tony an elegant copy of the poem in a binder. Tony's wife Margie read the poem to every family gathering from then on.

Omar and the Mountain

Our mare Mocha's first foal was a black-bay colt born April 24, 1991. We named him Omar, his full registered name being Omar ibn Azur. My horse was Mocha's brother Adhem, but when Omar was old enough and trained, he became my horse. He grew to 16.1 hands and gradually lost his dark color to become a beautiful flea-bitten grey horse.

Omar was the most trusting horse I ever rode. He totally believed in me, and if I had ridden him to a tree and told him to climb it, he would have given it a try. He would go anywhere I told him, even places that looked daunting and dangerous, because he trusted my judgment.

I rode Omar for several years, but in 2003 he developed a hoof problem, and since 2004 he was retired to the pasture, only ridden now and then by a visiting tenderfoot. There is a sad saying, but a veracious one: "No hoof no horse." Omar's impaired hooves prevented his use as a horse, but he enjoyed a well-fed, happy existence in our pasture and lived a long life.

In November 2012, the gentle Omar got his near front leg broken when kicked by a neighbor's horse. He limped and hopped, favoring that leg, but we knew there was nothing that could be done. A veterinarian lived just a mile down the highway, and eventually I asked him to look at Omar when he was passing by. The vet stood around in the yard talking to us for five or ten minutes and charged us seventy-five dollars! No, he would never stand in our yard again. The vet twenty miles away would have charged less than half that to come.

The seventy-five dollar advice the vet gave us was, "If that horse doesn't get better in six weeks, you'd better have him put down." Omar, standing nearby, overheard him and made a remarkably fast recovery!

Thinking back to those trail-riding days on my tall horse, I will relate one story that still gives me a chuckle.

On May 24, 2003, we rode with a group of trail riders near the Buffalo National River in the Boston Mountains of Arkansas. We met the group at a farm owned by the father of one of the riders. The farm bordered the national land associated with the Buffalo River.

When Judy and I unloaded Mocha and Omar from our trailer, we were subject to good-natured teasing by the group of quarter horse riders. They felt our Arabians might not be up to snuff. They made fun of the Arabians' "thin little legs" and wondered if they could keep up with their stout quarter horses.

It was beginning to rain by the time we got our horses saddled, but one of the group was a country weather prophet, and he assured everyone that this rain would not amount to anything. I have forgotten his arcane reason for this certainty. Judy and I donned hats with plastic covers and our Australian outback coats, while the other riders also fitted themselves with semi-waterproof gear.

Our plan was to ride out the top of a nearby ridge that stretched miles to the south. We hoped to find a forgotten trail that led down the end of the mountainous ridge and joined a well-traveled trail in the Buffalo National River system. We started south across a beautiful, green valley in the rain, and then onto a long ridge.

When we came to any little irregularity in the terrain, any diminutive draw or ditch, somebody would say something like, "Think them A-rabs can get acrost that?" And they all would guffaw and laugh up their sleeves.

We never found the trail, as we never reached the end of the ridge. We got several miles down river, though never in sight of the river, as we were riding south along the open top of a high ridge. By this I mean that it was open pastureland without trees. The sky got as dark as . . . well, it wasn't quite as dark as the inside of a coal mine at midnight, but it was rightly dark and ominous. Thunder rolled and lightning flashed, and it began to rain much harder. The weather prophet could not understand it, but he acknowledged defeat. The head guides of the group knew the country and said, "If we go back the way we came, it will take forever, and we'll get soaked and more exposed to lightning. There is an old road down at the base of this mountain that would take us back by a lot shorter route and be in the woods. We would be safer from lightning, but I do not know if we can get down to it."

We all rode over to the forest on our right, which marked the edge of the mountain. We looked down. The hillside was very steep, almost straight down in places. It was heavily forested with tall trees, and was brushy and rough, filled with ravines, boulders, underbrush, and vines. The overcast sky and pouring rain made the wet forested hillside look almost as dark as night, so even more scary than it would on a bright, sunny day.

Every one of the people on quarter horses tried to urge and force their horses through the brush and down the dangerous declivity. Not one of their horses would venture to set foot on the dark descent. The riders concluded, "I guess we have no choice but to go back the way we came."

I told Judy, "Come on!" I rode Omar up to the edge and over it and started down the long mountainside with Judy on Mocha right behind me. Omar was always good to put his head down and examine the trail—or lack of it—in rough terrain, so as to find the best footing. With Omar and Mocha leading the way, all the careful quarter horses were willing to follow. We fought our way part way down the hill through the dense vegetation to an old fence. I skirted along the fence on Omar and found a place where it was down. Omar and Mocha stepped gingerly over the wire, and the other riders dismounted and carefully led their horses over the fallen fence.

After we crossed the old fence, we confronted the worst part of the steep downhill mountain slope. We broke through brush, climbed over fallen trees, jumped rivulets and ditches, and finally made it to the old road at the base of the mountain. The road was overgrown and washed out, but I rode Omar north up the old road along the river, overcoming every hazard and leading the way for Mocha and all the pusillanimous ponies behind her.

When we got back to the trailers, the head man of the quarter horse riders told me, "Oh, my gosh! That Omar is one impressive horse."

It was amusing and satisfying for me to see him have to eat crow, after being so skeptical and scornful of our Arabians. I thought I saw the gallant Omar wink at me, but it might merely have been a raindrop hitting his eye.

Bad Neighbors Make Bad Fences

Leann, Missouri, was named after a girl, Leann Thomas, sometime in the nineteenth century. By the time I was born in the 1940s, Leann had lost its federal post office status. The stamp window and small bank of post office boxes still existed in the Leann Store, those boxes crammed with bills, accounts, and sundry other papers by the old storekeeper.

During my childhood, Leann consisted of a country store with a muscle-powered gasoline pump, a one-room school, and three or four houses. The community extended into the hills a mile or two in all directions from the store, encompassing twelve or fifteen farmhouses.

Henry Allmon's Leann Store was the hub where families encountered each other and old men sat and gossiped beside the iron coal stove in winter and the cold stove in summer. Not everyone in the community had the humility, honesty, and compassion of the old storekeeper. I now realize that my father had an uncanny understanding of those Ozark characters. But then, he was an Ozark character himself.

Delmar Whittaker lived up the hill north of the Leann Store. Delmar was a show-off and liked to acquire conveniences that ordinary people did not have, so that he could boast about them. He was a big man—bald, fat, and probably even bigger, because of being puffed up with pride.

When the first riding lawnmowers became available, Delmar bought one. It was just a small one, but still, it was a riding mower, and nobody else in the community had one. Daddy felt well equipped to have a power mower and several sons to push it. Once when I went with Daddy to the Leann Store, Delmar Whittaker was there. He said to Daddy, "Hey, Lester, I saw you drive by and wave the other day when I was mowing. What did you think of my new riding mower?"

Daddy said, "Oh! I saw you scooting across the yard, but I didn't realize there was a riding mower under you."

One time, a hound showed up at our place. Hounds are usually friendly and easy to catch, so one can read the name on the collar and return the dog to its owner. This one was not. The dog hung around for a couple of weeks, an unwelcome guest, always lurking in the sidelines. Sometimes he did something obnoxious, like tearing a sheet on the clothesline or getting into the chicken house, scaring the chickens, and eating eggs. Daddy and we kids all tried to catch it, but it always slunk away, just out of reach. Daddy alternated between trying to catch the dog and trying to chase him down the road, hoping he would go home.

During the daytime the stray dog haunting our home was a minor annoyance, but we could have lived with that. He even slept sometimes, but if someone came near him, the coy dog awakened and avoided contact.

This dog was a night owl. As soon as the house was quiet and all the family were asleep, the hound began to bay. All night long, he stayed right outside the house and kept up a racket. Periodically Daddy would step outside and scold the dog to be quiet, but as soon as he was back in bed, dozing off, the dog set up his nocturnal chorus again.

Daddy put up with this dog-induced insomnia for a couple of weeks, but his patience was not limitless. One early, grey dawn, after Daddy spent a night of dog-troubled dozing, our old frame house rattled to the boom of the twelve-gauge shotgun. A baying spree was cut off with a final yelp. We kids jumped out of bed and looked down from the upstairs windows to see Daddy in his underwear approach the dog's finally approachable form with a flashlight and read the tag on the collar.

The dog belonged to Delmar Whittaker! After breakfast Daddy took the collar and drove the two miles to Delmar's home to apologize for shooting his dog. Delmar graciously told Daddy, "You did us all a good turn. That dog wasn't worth shooting."

Delmar Whittaker once ran for state representative. He went around the district electioneering and passing out cigars or pencils or combs with his name on them, as office seekers did in those days. When the primary election returns were printed in the newspaper, my parents were amused to note that the other candidates for representative got vote tallies ranging from 87 to 354 votes, but Delmar Whittaker got three votes, presumably his own, his wife's, and his mother-in-law's.

Shortly after the election, Daddy was in a doctor's waiting room in nearby Aurora, and Delmar Whittaker was there also. A man came into the room and said, "Hey, Delmar, I see you ran for office."

Delmar said, "Yup, that's right."

"But you didn't win, did you?" said the man.

"No, I didn't win," Delmar replied, "but I sure gave them a run for their money."

-o-o-o-o-o-o-o-o-o-o-o-

The Galliwegs were another old Leann family, who lived a couple of miles from the store. Daddy liked all the Galliweg brothers, with one exception. He felt that Jasper was shifty and sneaky. Some of the other brothers had done time in the slammer for petty larceny, such as chicken stealing, a popular crime in those days, but Daddy could forgive plain, honest dishonesty like that. He simply could not excuse sneaky, underhanded dishonesty that tried to look honest.

Jasper's wife was honest, gregarious, and hard-working. My parents felt that she had married beneath herself. While his wife was working and earning money for the family, Jasper somehow got himself put on a disability income, though he seemed as able-bodied as the next man.

In the 1970s, after I had left home and married, my father took up the hobby of beekeeping and had several hives. Local people became aware that he always had honey for sale, and his most regular customer was Jasper Galliweg. Jasper bought two quarts of honey at a time for $6.00 the pair. Every few weeks, like clockwork, Jasper brought back the two empty jars and bought two full ones.

One time when Jasper came to buy two quarts of honey, he said, "Oh, I'm sorry! All I have is a twenty. Do you have change, Lester?"

Daddy said, "Don't worry about it. Just pay me double the next time you come for honey."

After Jasper left with his half gallon of honey, Daddy told Mama, "He'll never come back again, because he owes me that six dollars."

Sure enough, for the rest of his life, Daddy never laid eyes upon Jasper Galliweg again.

-o-o-o-o-o-o-o-o-o-o-o-

In 1948, power poles and lines began creeping their way northward up Highway 39, and out the rural dirt roads on either side. Electric power reached our house in July 1949. My parents, as well as all the other farm families, had to get their old farmhouses wired for electricity. There were incompetent, itinerate electricians who followed the progress of power and made themselves available to wire existing houses. They usually put one ceiling fixture and one or two ungrounded outlets in each room. My father lamented all his life the sloppy job they had done on our house.

As part of the electrification process, all the farms had a "pole light" installed. This consisted of a 300-watt incandescent bulb roofed by a reflector to protect it from the rain. It was mounted high up on one of the power poles to illuminate the farmyard when switched on from inside the house. Daddy bought a brand new wooden extension ladder that he could use to change the bulb. He had wanted a good ladder anyhow, and this was his excuse to buy one, but most of the families in the area did not have the means to plunk down for a fine ladder.

Our neighbor, Elmer Evers, somehow learned that Daddy had a tall ladder, and when his pole light bulb burned out, he came and asked to borrow Daddy's ladder. Daddy told Elmer, "It's hanging out there in the barn. Just help yourself, and put it back when you're done."

A few days later Elmer returned the ladder to our barn from whence he had taken it. Next time Daddy had to use the ladder, he noticed that the top rung was broken. He told the family about it at supper, "I know how he broke the ladder. He raised it up and let it slam against the light pole, and that broke the rung. I wish he had been polite enough to tell me about it. I know what his problem was. He doesn't have the money to offer to buy me a new ladder, and he's not handy enough to replace the rung. So he was in a fix, but I wish he'd said something to me."

It is quite a job to put a new rung in a ladder. The two heavy wooden rails have a series of holes drilled partway through them, and the rungs are fitted into those holes. Then a nail is driven into each rail through each end of each rung to hold the ladder together. Daddy made a new rung out of a piece of two-by-four, which he ripped with a handsaw, then dressed down with drawknife and plane to make it round and perfect, and exactly the same size as the broken one. Daddy had to pull the nails out of one end of the top four or five rungs, then use a jack to pry the rails apart enough to insert the new rung. He let off the jack, putting all the rungs back in their holes. Next he drove the nails back in and gave the ladder a new coat of white paint. No one could ever have discerned that it had been damaged.

A couple of years later Elmer's bulb burned out again, and he asked to borrow the ladder. Daddy said, "Just get it out of the barn, but you know, you have to be mighty careful when you put a ladder against a pole, or you'll break the top rung. You have to let it against the pole real easy."

Elmer said, "Oh, I didn't know that. You can trust me, I'll be awful gentle."

So the ladder was never broken again. Elmer and his wife later lost their farm, and Elmer spent his remaining career as a school janitor. Daddy was always glad that he had been neighborly to Elmer.

-o-o-o-o-o-o-o-o-o-o-o-

Soon after we got electricity in 1949, Daddy traded for a used electric motor and rigged up a power grinder on which he sharpened his mower's sickle bars in hay season. That task of holding up the other end of the sickle bar as Daddy meticulously sharpened each section or point was daunting to a child. Daddy would grind a bit, orange sparks spraying upward, then flip the sickle bar over to look at the sharpened side. The bar holder, who was one of us kids, had to be on his toes not to let a section cut him during this flipping back and forth, especially when Daddy got to the middle, and the kid had to switch to the sharp end.

Ira Bucket was a scrawny, stingy old man who lived a mile or so from our home. Somehow, Ira learned that Daddy had an electric grinder, while Ira was still using an old pedal grinder— being too cheap to buy an electric one. He began bringing his sickle bars over, two at a time, and getting Daddy to sharpen them. That is asking a lot, as it takes some time to go down the bar and sharpen both edges of each section. As usual, one of us kids had to hold the end of the bar. To make matters worse, all the sections on Ira's sickle bars were worn out and should have been replaced with new sections. This made sharpening them harder and slower, and this was hay season, when Daddy could not handily spare the time.

Daddy commented, "These sickle blades are really hard to sharpen when they're worn down like these are."

Ira said agreeably, "That's what I've done fount out a'ready."

Ira stood patiently watching the progress, occasionally removing his hat to wipe the sweat from his bald head with a frayed bandana handkerchief. After Daddy finished the job, Ira would ask, "What do I owe you?"

Daddy would say, "Oh, that's all right! You don't owe me anything."

And Ira would say, "Well, thanks, till you're better paid!" and happily (if he was ever happy) depart with his keen sickle bars.

After four or five times of this madness, Daddy was fed up. The next time he sharpened the sickle blades for Ira and was asked the perennial question, "What do I owe you?" Daddy said, "Oh, how 'bout twenty-five cents?"

Ira pulled out a leather purse, snapped it open, allowing a couple of moths to escape, and dug a quarter from among a few threadbare bills. He hesitantly handed Daddy the coin. Ira never came back again to get his sickle bars sharpened.

One time Ira told my parents about one of his cows getting caught in a fence. Eventually his corpulent wife Cora happened along and assisted in freeing the cow. As Ira solemnly told the story, my parents could barely refrain from laughing at his confusing use of pronouns.

"I fount that cow all caught up in the fence, and wore myself out tryin' to get her loose. Finally Cora, she come out and hepped me. She come and tried to get aholt of her, and she kicked her a good one and knocked her down in the mud, and she was wallerin' around trying to get up. She had one piece of bob-wire wrapped plumb around her leg, but she was kicking so much I couldn't get it loose, and she said, 'Get a rope on her,' and she was threshing around so much I picked up a board and hit her a good one to settle her down, and she said to get a rope on her again, so I looped a rope around her hind leg and tried to tie her to a young tree, but she said, 'We need slack. Give me that rope, and give me some slack, so I can wrap it around this here tree,' and I give her a good shove in the back, and she thrashed around some more, and she kicked her again, so I hit her again with that board, and she finally got that rope wrapped around the tree, so we could get her tied down and get her loose. I was about ready to get my gun and shoot her, so it was lucky she come out when she did."

Leann is on Highway 39, which was a gravel road in the 1950s. To get from Leann to our home a mile east and a quarter mile south, we had to ford Jenkins Creek. There was no bridge in those days. When rain had swollen the creek to a rush of roiling brown water, we had to drive all the way south to Highway 248, another gravel highway which was called Highway 44 in those days, and follow it several miles northeast, and then go down a small country road a couple of miles to get to our home "the back way."

If there had been enough rain to swell the stream, but not engorge it, we could still ford it on "the upper crossing," which was a rock shelf about a foot high and a few feet upstream from the regular ford. Sometimes Daddy crossed the upper crossing when prudence would have sent him the long miles around the back way. Before my parents bought a brand new Chevrolet in 1950, we had a rattletrap Ford that the water flowed right through, and we kids in the back seat had to raise our feet up when we forded the high water.

Once, Ira Bucket was angry with Daddy for some reason I cannot recall. This grudge coincided with the only extended vacation trip my family ever took. We were gone about two weeks and returned late one night. It had been raining, and Jenkins Creek was up. We could have negotiated the upper crossing and gone home, but the headlights revealed a shiny new barbed-wire fence all the way to the ford, blocking the upper crossing.

Ira Bucket owned the land on the north side of the ford, but always made his fence corner several yards north of the ford, so that his neighbors could use the upper crossing when they needed to. Now, out of spite, he had fenced across the upper crossing, and we had to drive many nighttime miles on gravel roads to get home the back way.   Ira's grudge was also punishing our neighbors.

When the creek went down Daddy went to see Ira and ask him to move the fence. He came home later and told Mama, "He says he'll take down that fence."

As a child, I thought my daddy could do almost anything, and this episode certified that belief.   He had only to say, "Mr. Bucket, tear down that fence!" to make it so. Many years later, I pondered Daddy's amazing powers of persuasion and wondered how he could possibly convince a mean old man to tear down his bright new fence and move it.   "He certainly must have had a golden tongue!" I thought.

Long after Daddy was dead and gone, I asked Mama about it. She said, "Oh, Daddy had something on him. He had seen Ira where he shouldn't be with somebody else's wife."

The conversation had gone something like this:

Ira: "That fence is staying right where it is, and you can put that in your pipe and smoke it!"

Daddy: "I was just remembering once several years back when I saw you and Elvira slipping in the back door of that old Johnson house. I never did tell anybody about that."

Ira: "That fence is coming down tomorrow."

Blackmail is an incomparable tool for moving negotiations along quickly.

17

Calton's Fiddle

On May 21, 2010, Judy and I sat with my mother at the book signing in the Barry County Museum for Volume 11 of the "Lifetimes of Memories" series. We helped her find page 133 where her autobiography began in each copy, as she autographed books for a long stream of people. Many interesting individuals came and chatted with us. Possibly the most interesting was Buck Calton, who is featured in Volume 2 of that series.

Buck and I discussed the old Calton Mill at Tom Town, which his great grandfather first built in the 1840s, and which has been rebuilt several times, but is now in ruins. We talked of Calton Cemetery and those who lie there.

I remembered the name Calton from my childhood, when a thin, grey-haired old man named Porter Calton used to come now and then to visit with my parents. They always welcomed him and gave him lemonade or coffee to encourage him to tell a few interesting yarns. Porter Calton was a courtly old gentleman, who always lifted his hat to my mother. He would never dream of cursing or uttering an oath, yet some of his stories involved rough hill folk who would "cuss a blue streak." In telling tales about those people, Porter thought nothing of quoting them verbatim. Thus, a string of blue oaths that would curl a sailor's hair would issue from his otherwise unsullied lips.

Porter Calton was a wolf hunter, meaning mainly that he enjoyed hunting coyotes, which people in those days called wolves. Coyotes were a bane to farmers, in killing their animals and fowl. They also killed the rabbits that otherwise might grace the table, fried up beside a bowl of gravy. Part of the time the county offered a bounty on coyotes to encourage people to kill them. Porter always had a great string of dogs, and engaged in buying, selling, and trading dogs as part of his wolfish pastime.

Porter was an innocent in the ways of the world and could barely take care of himself after his wife died. Kathleen Marbut, a close relative who frequently visited him, soon tumbled to the fact that Porter was buying cans of soup, but pouring them through a sieve to strain out the broth before cooking the former soup. He explained, "I didn't know what kind of stuff might be in that juice or whether it was good for a person."

At the book signing, I asked Buck if he was kin to Porter Calton. Buck said, "I am, and that reminds me of another person who asked me that very question."

Buck Calton and his wife lived for many years at Peoria, Illinois, but when he retired, they moved back to the village of Washburn, Missouri. Their house was down a lane, and they had their name on the mailbox. One day Buck was in the yard, and looked to see a pickup, coming lickity-split down the lane, raising a cloud of dust behind it. The pickup flew up into the yard, screeched to a stop, and a man climbed out. "Are you kin to Porter Calton?" he asked.

Buck said, "Yes, he's my cousin."

The man said, "I bought a dog from him once, and it wasn't worth a damn!" He climbed back in his pickup without another word, slammed the door, and took off down the lane pursued by a swirl of dust.

Buck said that Porter fancied himself a proficient fiddle player. Year after year he carried his fiddle to every gathering he attended, hoping that someone would ask him to play. At one event that Buck and his wife visited, there was a man who had moved to the Ozarks from the east coast. He had played the violin in the symphony orchestra of one of the eastern metropolises. When Porter Calton came hopefully into the party with his fiddle and bow, the easterner's eyes lit up. He said to Porter, "May I play your instrument?" and Porter graciously handed it over.

The stranger tuned the strings, rosined the bow, and began to play. He played sweet and moving strains of classical music such as had never echoed from those rural walls before. Porter listened enrapt to such pieces as The Second Waltz of Shostakovich and Mendelssohn's Violin Concerto No. 2. Moisture formed in Porter's eyes, and finally he was weeping a great flood of tears. At last he exclaimed through sobs, "I never dreamed my old fiddle had such music as that in it!"

It Isn't the Cough

My mother liked to say, "It isn't the cough that carries you off; it's the coffin they carry you off in." Yet at one time or another, most of us have had a cough so severe that we felt it would carry us off.

Nowadays there are various nostrums and cough suppressants that may or may not help relieve the cold and cough, but in my youth we used home remedies. When the need arose, Dr. Mama would treat us children with coal oil and grease. I'm not sure if coal oil is exactly the same as kerosene, but certainly it is a close relative. Mama would melt some bacon grease or lard in a squat tin can on the wood heating stove, then mix in a dollop of coal oil. She painted the solution on her victim's chest and throat with a paint brush. It was very warm, almost hot, and it felt good. She often commented, "I want to put in as much coal oil as I can, because that's what does the good. But if I get too much, it'll blister your skin, so I have to be careful."

My skin turned vivid pink, but never blistered, so I guess she had a good feel for how to mix it. Next, she pinned some soft cloth, like an old tee shirt, around the neck to hang down over the chest to keep it warm. This also kept the grease from soiling the shirt or other garment. The warmth of that treatment penetrated the chest and throat, loosening up the phlegm and helping to cure the cough and cold.

Lou Stapleton, my old friend who lived to be 105, told me of her mother's method for making cough syrup. Lou's mother would slice an onion and put the slices, one by one, in a cup, with a layer of sugar between each slice. She set the cup aside for a time and let the sugar draw the onion juice out of the slices. Eventually, she would have Lou drink the sweetened juice off of the onion slices as a cure for her cough.

My friend, the late Colonel Ken Eggleston told me, "My father's remedy for cold and cough was to drink a half pint of whiskey and rub the bottle on his chest." Indeed I have sometimes found that a swallow of straight whiskey will stop that tickling feeling that causes non-productive coughs. The same treatment, a big swallow of whiskey, is also an infallible cure for the hiccups.

Jim McCarty, another friend, tells of his great-grandfather Patrick McCarty from Limerick, Ireland, who had a sure fire cure for colds and coughs: "Strain just the juice from a fifth of whiskey. Hang your hat on the bedpost. Get in bed and drink the juice until you see two hats."

My older brother Roger asked me, "Do you remember the absolutely horrible-tasting, but effective cough medicine called Glessco?"

I replied that I did not, and he said, "Then you must be lucky enough never to have tasted it, because you'd remember it."

Roger was referring to Dr. Drake's Glessco Cough Relief, which is known by all who ever imbibed it as the nastiest, vilest, and most vomitous taste ever invented by man. The children's version even showed a picture of Mother Goose on the label to beguile innocent children into a willing acceptance of their first dose. That first taste triggered a loss of innocence, and the fight was on ever to dose the child again.

The old two-story farmhouse where I grew up was called "The Nathan Thomas Place" after the man who built it in 1904. When my parents bought the farm in late 1943, the upstairs was unfinished, with only oak studs demarcating the rooms to be. The outside walls had no insulation—just oak studs with clapboards nailed to the outside of them. Downstairs the situation was little better, with quarter-inch painted paneling inside the rooms, but not one speck of insulation between that and the outside clapboards. My father smoked Lucky Strike cigarettes in those days, and if it was a windy day, he had to cup the match in his hands to light a cigarette inside the house.

In the early 1950s, my father finished the upstairs by adding some insulation in the outside walls and putting up wallboard to form bedrooms. Then he took out a partition downstairs to enlarge the living room by incorporating the west downstairs bedroom. After that, all of us kids slept in bedrooms upstairs, but before this remodeling, my brother Roger and I slept in that west downstairs bedroom. It jutted out from the main part of the house, and our bed was against the outside north wall, with me on the inside, next to the wall.

On a frigid night in the dead of winter, when I was four or five years old, the north wind was howling and shaking the old frame house. I was coughing and coughing and coughing, and my chest was sore from the strain. I suddenly came wide awake, as Daddy was in the room carrying a lighted kerosene lamp to check on me, this being before 1949 when rural electric power reached us. Daddy said, "I'll be right back."

He left the lamp in our room and departed. In a couple of minutes I heard the kitchen door shut and knew Daddy had lit a lantern and gone outside to one of the outbuildings for some reason that I could not imagine. I dozed off. Next thing I knew Daddy was bustling into the room wearing his coat and cap and carrying a full sheet of thick plywood.

Daddy leaned the plywood against the doorframe and took off his coat. He had me get up and he wrapped me in a blanket and set me in the living room by the big Warm Morning wood heating stove. I could see orange flame flickering in the mica windows of the stove and hear its breath, so knew that Daddy had opened the draft and damper to awaken the wood fire. He told me, "You just sit here a minute and get warm. That north wind is blowing right through that wall, and I'm going to slip that plywood down by the bed to shut off some of that wind."

Indeed, with not a smidgeon of insulation of any kind in that old house, we could feel the icy tongues of winter licking at us through fissures in the wall. Daddy suited action to word, and I heard him pull the bed out from the wall. Roger must have continued to sleep, as I did not hear anything out of him. I heard Daddy drive a couple of nails into the wall to hold the plywood upright and slide the bed back against the wall.

Next Daddy took the lamp into the kitchen and came back with a little glass of whiskey with sugar in it. Daddy always kept a bottle of whiskey in the cabinet, though I never saw him drink any of it. He stirred the whiskey with a spoon to dissolve the sugar and said, "Drink this right down!"

I did so, and it seemed to burn a path all the way down to my toes, but did make my throat feel better. Daddy tucked me back in bed, and laid a coat or robe over the covers on my side of the bed. That plywood cut off those frigid tendrils of wind, and I was soon snug and in dreamland. I don't think I coughed any more that night, but it's too long ago to remember for sure.

Daddy did not have much "bringin' up" and was not even allowed to finish high school. Yet he was self-reliant, had wonderful common sense, and demonstrated great capabilities in knowing just what needed to be done in any situation. That cold night so long ago, he may very possibly have kept the cough from carrying me off.

The Every Day Shirt

I found an old picture of myself wearing my ED shirt. Judy scolded me about that shirt. I had two blue dress shirts exactly alike, except that one had a little hole in the belly region, probably from its former owner's cigarette ash. I was forever getting that one from my closet, putting it on with my bow tie, and then noticing the hole and having to go to all the trouble of taking off my tie, changing shirts, and re-tying my tie. Finally, I solved the problem by using a permanent marker to write "ED" on the pocket of the holey one.

When Judy saw me wearing it, she demanded, "Where did you get that shirt?"

"Out of my closet," I replied.

She asked, "Well, who wrote Ed on the pocket?"

"I did," I admitted.

She asked, "Why did you write 'Ed' on your pocket? Your name's not Ed!"

I replied, "That doesn't say 'Ed.' Those are the initials E. D. This shirt has a hole in it, so I'm taking it for Every Day wear."

She said spiritedly, "No sensible person writes a big ED on the pocket of his everyday shirts!"

I replied, "I did, and I'm sensible."

She said, "I'm beginning to think that's debatable!"

"And," I said sanctimoniously, "I did write it in blue ink, so it matches the shirt."

She ordered, "After this, if you want to write ED on your everyday shirts, write it inside the collar where it won't show. Do not write it on the pocket!"

I *always* insist on having the last word in any argument.

"Yes, Dear." I concluded, "Whatever you say, Dear."

Up Above the World So High

When I was a kid of a boy, my big brother Roger built a tree house way up in an old oak tree in the edge of the woods near our home. I do not know how he got the boards up there, but he was five years older than me and capable of wonderful feats. The tree house was really just a platform of boards nailed across two big limbs that stuck out from the trunk at the same level. My brother Denis was three years younger than me, and we pined to climb up into that tree house, but both Mama and Roger had strictly forbidden it.

One day when Roger was away from home, maybe gone with Daddy to the feed mill or on some other errand, Denis and I happened to wander near the tree house as we played. We looked longingly at it and thought how great it would be to view the world from such a height. I decided that I could quickly nip up the tree, take a look down on the world for a few minutes, and sneak back down, with no one the wiser. Roger had driven big spike nails into the tree, protruding about three inches to form climbing steps, since there were no low limbs on the big trunk. It was actually easier than I expected to shinny up on those spikes, and I was soon atop the tree house platform. It was great!

Then I looked down. . .

From the ground, the tree house appeared to be about twenty-five feet high, but when I looked down from the platform, I could see that it was actually closer to a quarter of a mile above the earth. A cloud or two drifted between me and the ground, and my brother Denis looked like an ant. I wanted to climb down, but I was too terrified even to begin. My whole life flashed before my eyes, and young as I was, that did not take long. I wondered if I would have to spend my life up there, if we could find a long enough rope to send food up to me, and how I could meet a wife and raise a family there when I grew up. There was only one thing to do, and I did it.

"Go to the house and get Mama!" I yelled to Denis.

That shows how desperate I was. In the first place, my crime would be found out. Even more to the point, I knew in my heart that Mama could not do anything. She was too heavy and unathletic to climb the tree, and even if she could climb it, she certainly could not carry me back down with her. However, Mama did come, and Mama *did* get me down. I am not typing this remembrance in a tree house. Do you know how she did it? She *talked* me down. I don't remember what she said, but she talked enough of my fear away to get me to follow her step-by-step instructions about where to hold on and where to put my foot to find the first spike, so that soon I was safely beside her. Through my disobedience I got myself into a fix that I could not get out of, and Mama extricated me purely by the power of her words.

This was a signal event that I have thought of many times. It was an early lesson in the might of words and the power of the spirit. I thought my rescue required a physical agent that could lower me to the ground, but I was saved by non-physical means, by nothing but vanishing words and the spirit of the mother's love behind them. The course of history has been changed for good or ill innumerable times by words written or spoken. Words can bring to safety the man on the ledge or the airplane with a disabled pilot. They can break or mend a family or a friendship. Words can stir us to war and soothe us in peace. I got some inkling of the power of words long ago in a tree house.

There was another lesson to be learned, something about getting into trouble through disobedience. I'm still working on that one.

The Enigmatic Mr. Good

An antique clock is considered to be more valuable when it has a pristine paper label attached to it. Inside some old weight clocks, the label covers the entire back. Many times those labels are fragmented and disintegrated, not only from wear, but also from acid used in the papermaking process. However, now and then, those large labels are in beautiful, almost immaculate condition. The label contains the brand name of the clock, such as "Seth Thomas" or "New Haven." It has directions for setting up and maintaining the clock, and it commonly has a little advertising hype in the form of the slogan: "Warranted Good."

This is an amusing bit of understatement indicative of a simpler and more honest age. The maker probably felt he was stretching humility to the limit in boasting that his clock was good.   Heaven forbid that he should claim anything so extravagant as warranting the clock to be the best on the market or even of superlative quality. It is simply warranted to be good. And yet those modestly "warranted good" clocks are still running and keeping time after 150 years and more of service. They may be a little better than good.

When I see the words "Warranted Good" emblazoned on a clock label, I smile partly in acknowledgement of the understatement, but also because it reminds me of Art and Nan Clarke from Kansas City. The Clarkes planned occasional trips to southwest Missouri several years ago, as this area held three attractions for them. They always came to see Judy and me in our clock supply shop, so they could pick up some parts and information to feed Art's clock-tinkering hobby. They went to Branson, Missouri, to take in a couple of shows, and they visited Bass Pro, the famous outdoor-sports store in Springfield.

Art and Nan were a genial and likable couple, but afflicted by a lamentable want of knowledge and discernment. Art was a master of nonsensical nomenclature. When he asked for the clock parts he needed, he called each one by a misnomer he had invented, so had to undergo interrogation before we could supply his needs: "I need the weight for a Secession clock."

"Oh, you mean a Sessions clock," I said.

Art replied, "Yes, that's right, a Secession kitchen clock."

"But kitchen clocks don't run on weights," I declared. "They run on mainsprings."

Art countered, "I mean the ticky-tocky weight that swings back and forth."

"Oh! You mean the PENDULUM!" I would exclaim.

"That's right," he said. "And I also need a new whizzergig for this clock."

"A whizzergig!" I said, completely puzzled.

Art replied, "Yes, the dingy-dongy bangs too fast because somebody cut the ears off the whizzergig."

"Oh my goodness!" I exclaimed. "You mean that the clock strikes too fast because somebody trimmed the FLY."

And so it went with every part that he needed, as he called each by a fanciful sobriquet.

The Clarkes were not quietly ignorant, but tended to broadcast their condition. A favorite topic was Bass Pro, but they always inverted that name and any other convenient name they uttered. "We took a different route this time and stopped at Pro Bass before your place. We usually come here first and then go to Pro Bass, but we thought we'd get Pro Bass out of the way first this time. Then we stopped and ate fish and hush doggies at John's Long Silver before we came on down."

As it turned out, all the talk about "Pro Bass" and "John's Long Silver" was simply the apex of a mountain of ignorance. On one occasion Art brought along a Gilbert clock for which he needed to buy a new glass, and he prattled on volubly in a most foolish and oblivious vein:

"I thought this was a Gilbert clock, because it says Gilbert on the label. But then I noticed that it says 'Warranted Good' too, so I'm not sure whether Gilbert or Warranted Good made it. If Gilbert made it, why does it have Warranted Good's name on it too? What did Warranted Good have to do with it anyhow? Did Warranted Good actually make it? My theory is that maybe Gilbert made it and Warranted Good distributed it, but I could be wrong. I simply don't understand why they'd put Warranted Good's name on the label too. We know Warranted Good must have been involved somehow, but we simply don't know how. I looked in several of the clock books for Warranted Good, but couldn't find any listings, so he must not have been a well-known maker. I keep coming back to the question, did Gilbert make it or did Warranted Good make it?"

Judy and I stared at each other with mouths agape. We had just seen the Guinness record for denseness broken before our eyes.

Check In Cheap

When Judy and I visited her family in Columbia, Missouri, in the 1990s, we usually stayed at a fairly economical motel, such as Econolodge or Super-8. It cost about $55 per night. Once when we decided to go with only a week's notice, I phoned for reservations, and found both these motels fully booked. An Internet web site showed several motels in Columbia, and the Really Reasonable Inn sounded appealing. I tried to use their Internet reservation system, but it always malfunctioned, so I telephoned 1-800-GO-CHEAP and reserved a single room for $37.95 plus tax—the last room available. That price sounded wonderful, and I was lucky to get the last room. At least, I thought I was lucky. . .

There were a few surprises when we checked in, aside from the peeling paint and general run down appearance of the lobby. The Really Reasonable Inn proved to be a very large facility, with more rooms than some of the more famous motels in Columbia. The apathetic young man behind the desk said, "The computer shows two singles reserved for you."

I said, "That's an error. I always share a room with my wife, so we reserved one double."

He gave us a room with two double beds, as it was the only double he had. A bonus was that he charged me only $34.09 including tax. We were saving $20, compared with our regular accommodations!

The clerk did not have me fill out the usual form with name, home address, and license number of our car. We were registered anonymously. Instead of handing me a new-fangled plastic electronic door key, he gave me a real brass key with a plastic tab inscribed "110," which was our room number. He also handed me a television remote control so matter-of-factly that I was slow to realize that I had never received a remote at the check-in desk before. Some of their absent-minded guests must have carried away remotes when they left the motel.

I picked up a brochure in the office, which described the Really Reasonable Inn as "a memorable place to stay." It revealed that the Really Reasonable Inn was a nationwide confederation of motels, not all of which bore the Really Reasonable Inn name. Missouri boasted three such motels, and one of them was in our own tiny hometown. The Krummy Kourt Motor Lodge in Cassville, Missouri, was part of the chain. I felt proud.

We learned that the motel in Columbia was built by Motel 6 and operated by that franchise for many years. When "leaving the light on for you" revealed too much dilapidation to be repaired economically, Motel 6 sold the facility, and it became a Really Reasonable Inn.

When we entered Room 110, I knew there was something odd, but couldn't put my finger on it. The walls were tarnished white, but something was strange. Then I realized that there were no pictures on the walls! Those imitation paintings that motels buy by the case were nowhere to be seen. The only decorative adornments were cobwebs, which graced certain corners.

Three weak light fixtures dimly illuminated the chamber. Two were one-bulb fixtures, but the main light source was a two-bulb fixture with one bulb and one empty socket. The bulbs were 60-watt *clear* bulbs, which do not provide as much light as frosted bulbs. What light there was seemed absorbed by the dingy yellow walls that had once been white. I went back to the front desk and asked the young man, "May I have a light bulb for our room?"

"Is one burned out?" he asked.

"One is completely missing," I replied.

He said, "I'll send one over right away."

I returned to our room, carried in our luggage, and began to arrange it. Soon there was a knock at our door. A huge young man, apparently with an asbestos hand, filled the doorway. He placed in my hand a sizzling hot light bulb, which he must have robbed from some other fixture on the premises. I had to juggle the hot bulb from one hand to the other and toss it on the bed to cool. When I screwed it into the empty socket, it had little effect in alleviating the gloom.

Before worrying further about the lighting, I decided to take my shower.

When I entered the bathroom at the Really Reasonable Inn, I made the mistake of shutting the door behind me. It was a common laminated, hollow-core door, but years of moisture had de-laminated it. Someone had tacked it back together with nails little larger than straight pins, but they were loose in their moorings. When I tried to open it, the door stuck and twisted. The little nails began to pop out, and the door to come apart. I warned Judy, "You'd better not shut this door, or it may disintegrate when you try to open it."

The bathroom contained a few uncommon features. The hot and cold water controls were reversed on the lavatory, so that hot was on the right. If the faucet or shower was turned off too abruptly, there was an ominous clang of the pipes within the walls. The exhaust fan blade encountered interference with something, so that when it was turned on, it emitted a clicking sound as it revved up. "Tick---tick---tick—tick—tick-tick-tick-tickticktick-hmmmm!" And when turned off, it reversed the noise: "Tickticktick-tick-tick-tick—tick—tick—tick—tick---tick---tick---tick." I noticed that the toilet paper holder boasted only the tag end of a roll, and there was no spare!

When I took my shower, I was reminded of a story our friend Diane told me. Soon after her marriage, she went with her cowboy husband Lavern to a weekend of cattle penning events. At the end of the first day, she said, "I'm so hot and tired, I have to have a shower."

Diane had never stayed in a camper before, so Lavern instructed her, "You can take a shower, but you'll have to learn to take a cowboy shower."

"What's a cowboy shower?" she asked.

He explained, "There is a limited amount of water in our reservoir, so we need to conserve it. You turn on the shower, quickly get wet, and turn it off. You soap up, then you turn on the shower and quickly rinse off."

He explained to Diane how to operate the shower.

Lavern said, "I have to go take care of the horses, so you go ahead and shower, and I'll be back in a little while."

Diane got in the shower and pulled down on the lever. A trickle of water came out. She thought, "Lavern assigns me impossible tasks, but I always manage to do them, and I can do this too." She quickly wet herself and a washcloth with the dribble, soaped up, and then pulled the lever again. Even less water came out, but she caught it in her cloth and rinsed herself off.

As she proudly stepped out of the shower, Lavern came in and cheerfully asked, "Did you get your shower all right?"

"Yes, I did," she replied.

Lavern indicated a switch beside the shower and asked, "Didn't you turn on that switch, the way I told you?"

"Oh, I forgot about that switch," she said.

Lavern asked, "Golly! How did you shower? That switch turns on the pump to supply water to the shower head."

Diane said, "Well, there wasn't very much water."

Lavern laughed uproariously and said, "You took a whole shower with just the half cup of water that was trapped in the shower pipe."

"I guess that was a *cowgirl* shower!" Diane concluded.

36

When I took my shower at the Really Reasonable Inn, I figured that the scanty flow must be designed for cowboys. I had the control turned up all the way to full flow on hot, but only a lukewarm, skimpy squirt issued forth. The bath towels were worn and inadequate—a perfect match for the flow of water.

I emerged from the bathroom, dressed, and said to Judy, "I'm going to the grocery store!" I drove a few blocks and bought some 100-watt frosted bulbs, some toilet paper, and a carton of orange juice as a treat for Judy.

Back at the motel room, I installed all new bulbs, and we marveled at what a cheerful difference they made. Judy took a cowboy shower, and we sat in creaky chairs and enjoyed the lovely illumination as she worked on school papers and I read a few chapters in an Ellis Peters novel. From outside we heard exuberant sounds of people shouting, arguing, scolding children, and yelling back and forth. Judy said, "This is like a night in the inner city! I hope people don't keep up that noise after we go to bed."

They did. We felt as if we were in a Greek neighborhood on the eve of a holiday celebration.

We finally fell asleep, but not for long. The revelry spilling out of rooms lasted late into the night. Our bed was hard and uncomfortable, and we tossed and turned. We also suffered from some sort of allergy. We sneezed and got stuffy noses, sore throats and itchy eyes. I had noticed during the evening that there were no roaches present. I speculated that they had moved to classier accommodations. Now I wondered if heavy doses of insecticide were giving us allergic reactions. We rolled and twisted, had troubled dreams, and woke up many times. At 6:00 a.m. we finally got up with sore backs, feeling wearier than when we lay down.

"I never knew standing up could feel so good!" I exclaimed.

We arose to the sound of pouring rain. I tried to open the drapes, so we could watch the rain, but they were stuck shut. I threw open the door and looked out. The drenching downpour and baleful thunder cast a further pall of gloom over the seedy motel, which must be a depressing sight even on a sunny day.

I saw an unshaven young man stagger from his second-floor room, cigarette in hand, and spit lustily over the balustrade. His missile barely missed an unsteady young man carrying a beer cooler to his car. Neither was aware of the other's presence or the near miss.

A couple of weary women emerged from separate rooms, looking as if they might have been conducting business in their rooms overnight. I saw a furtive couple with no luggage emerge. I suspected they had rented their room for only an hour or so.

Behind me, Judy said, "I wonder if there is anything in these drawers." She opened a drawer and took out a book. It was shiny and new, and the spine made a popping sound when she opened the book. The only brand new, never-used equipment in this threadbare motel room was a Gideon Bible!

As we creakily tramped through the rain, stowing our luggage, light bulbs, and toilet paper in the car, I said, "Well, we saved $20!"

We smiled at each other a little remorsefully, then laughed. Twenty dollars suddenly seemed like small change.

Coffee Calamity

"If this is coffee, please bring me some tea; but if this is
tea, please bring me some coffee."
~Abraham Lincoln

Judy and I went to Springfield, Missouri, on March 12, 2013. We had some medical appointments and other errands which took up most of the day.

The coffee calamity began when Caspar's Chili Shack was so full that the line reached outside and down the sidewalk, so we decided to eat lunch elsewhere. We had passed the former Planet Sub at the corner of Kimbrough and Cherry on our way to Caspar's and seen that Planet Sub was gone. The building now featured the grand opening of a Chinese restaurant. Springfield can always use more Chinese restaurants. It already has more Chinese restaurants per capita than any other city in the United States. We drove back there for lunch. Judy got beef with broccoli, and I got Hunan beef. Both were good, but we would not go back because this restaurant did not serve hot tea! The lack of the normal hot tea with Chinese food left me craving a cup of hot coffee.

COFFEE NUMBER 1—Later in the day, as we went from some medical appointments towards Sam's Club, I drove into a McDonald's to buy a cup of coffee. Pulling into the lot right ahead of us was a rough pickup, which took the first parking space on the right. I started to drive on into the lot to seek a parking place, but the pickup guy began to back up as if to run into our car. I honked the horn loudly, and he pulled back into the space. I went slowly down the parking lot to look for a space, but that pickup guy was actually a psycho, and a large psycho at that. He jumped out of his pickup and ran after us down the parking lot shaking his fist and shouting, "What's wrong with you?"

I did have my heavy Colt revolver, but the concealed carry instructor quoted Psalm 34:14, which roughly translated says that it is better to avoid conflict than to shoot a nincompoop. So I sped up and went on through the lot without my coffee.

COFFEE NUMBER 2—Judy had been hankering for an ice cream cone, so after we left Sam's, I pulled across Campbell Avenue to Andy's Frozen Custard. They used to advertise that they had great coffee from freshly ground beans, and they did. I have drunk it before. I ordered Judy's frozen custard and hot coffee, but the man told me that they quit selling coffee several years ago. I said, "But you used to advertise about your great coffee." He said, "We just didn't sell enough." At least Judy got her ice cream cone.

COFFEE NUMBER 3—After we left Andy's, we went south on Campbell to Plainview Road, a shortcut on the long trail home. The shortcut passes through the village of Battlefield, named after the nearby Civil War Battle of Wilson's Creek. In Battlefield, I espied a Kum & Go convenience store, so pulled in and took my go-mug in to get coffee. Success finally! I took my coffee out to the car and took a swig. "This coffee's just lukewarm! It's not hot," I said.

Judy told me, "Take it back in and heat it in the microwave."

I suited my actions to her words. I told the lady at the counter, "This coffee is just lukewarm. I want to heat it up in the microwave."

I put my mug in for forty-five seconds, but when I took it out, there was a rim along the top of that tiny microwave that snatched the cup out of my hand and shot it down to the floor where the lid came off and all the coffee spilled. I told the lady at the counter, and she came with a mop. I said, "Maybe God didn't want me to have a cup of coffee," and walked out a dollar poorer with my empty cup.

As I drove home, bereft of coffee, I said philosophically, "Oh well, we'll be in Cassville tomorrow. McDonald's makes good coffee and I often get a cup there."

Judy said, "Oh! Did I forget to tell you? Day before yesterday the Cassville McDonald's burned to the ground!"

Trading Stamps

It is ironic that little acts of kindness often have untoward side effects. There is an old saying that "no act of kindness goes unpunished," but often Nemesis visits her retribution upon some completely innocent sap, who had nothing to do with the original act of wanton goodwill.

When Mama moved into an apartment at Ozarks Methodist Manor, a retirement and nursing complex for the elderly, she unpacked and shuffled through her bounteous possessions. In so doing, she discovered a little fund of outdated postage stamps. I say they were "outdated," but of course, no unblemished United States postage stamp ever loses its value. It took limitless errands and missions to keep Mama up and running. One of the assignments she charged to me was buying appropriate supplementary stamps to bring all these old stamps up to current first class postage, which at the time was 39¢. Accordingly, I jotted down the denominations I needed and headed for the local Marionville Post Office.

Marionville is a small town where everybody knows everybody else. Consequently, the Marionville Post Office is a little shirttail institution that does not stand upon ceremony. I told the postmistress, "I need six four-cent stamps, seven three-cent stamps, and nine two-cent stamps."

She replied, "We don't even have all those denominations. What are you trying to do?"

I told her, "My mother found a batch of old stamps, and she wants to bring them all up to today's postage."

She said, "Does your mother live at Methodist Manor?"

"Yes," I admitted, knowing that she had theorized an ancient mother, based upon my own apparent vintage.

She said, "I'll tell you what. We aren't supposed to take back old stamps, but just as a favor, you tell her to put all those stamps in an envelope with her name on it and send it over by the lady that comes to get their mail. I'll give her the equivalent in new stamps. I'll just use up her old stamps in mailing things here at the post office."

I exclaimed, "Oh, thank you! That is so nice of you."

"No problem!" she said. "This will be much simpler for everybody."

That's what *she* thought! She was not going to be punished for her act of kindness, but someone else was.

Several months later Mama was pawing through some of her chattels when she came upon a veritable gold mine of outmoded postage stamps. This was the harvest of thirty or forty years of neglected stamps and changing postal rates. The small stockpile she had charged me with was a mere nugget compared with this mother lode of inadequate stamps. All that was wanted was a hapless victim that she could send on a fool's errand.

For a couple of weeks preceding my sister Shirley's visit from Delaware, Mama virtually placed me on standby. She would mention various items she needed, chores to be accomplished, phone calls to be made, and assignments to be executed, but when I would ask, "So, do you want me to take care of that?" she would blithely say, "Oh no, never mind. I've put it on my list of things for Shirley to do while she's here."

One day when Shirley and Mama were planning an assault upon the city of Aurora, Mama hauled out her hoard of deficient stamps. She handed the box to Shirley, saying, "I want you to take these to the Aurora Post Office and trade them in on new postage stamps."

Shirley said, "I'm sure they won't take back old stamps at the post office."

Remembering her Marionville experience, Mama said positively, as if talking to a lamentably uninformed child, "Of course they'll take them back! I've traded stamps in at the post office before, and it was no problem."

"Well, if you're sure," said Shirley doubtfully.

"Of course I'm sure!" replied Mama with no doubt whatsoever.

As Shirley drove into Aurora and approached the big post office, her feet were getting ever chillier. She tried one more time, "I just feel really apprehensive about trying to trade in those stamps."

Mama said, "My stars and stripes! You'll find it's no problem at all. Don't go looking for trouble."

She was no doubt trying to quote that old saying, "Never trouble trouble, till trouble troubles you!"

Mama waited in the car while Shirley lugged her box of stamps up the steps to the post office. When it was her turn at the window, the postal clerk greeted her pleasantly. She handed him the box, saying, "I'd like to trade these old stamps in on thirty-nine-cent ones."

"What are you trying to pull, Lady?" asked the astonished clerk, as other customers eyed Shirley dubiously, comparing her face with the nearby wanted posters. "We SELL stamps here. We do NOT trade stamps."

Shirley said defensively, "My 91-year-old mother sent me in with these. She claims she's traded in old stamps at the post office before."

"That explains it," said the clerk as he used his forefinger to draw little circles in the air near his ear. "However, I'm afraid she's mistaken. No post office in the United States will trade stamps or take them back. It's totally against regulations."

"I wonder what I should do with all these stamps," Shirley lamented lugubriously.

The clerk took pity and said, "Aw, heck, let me have a look at them."

As the line behind Shirley lengthened, and people looked at their watches, shuffled their feet, and frowned, the postal clerk helped Shirley sort all the stamps into little piles valued at thirty-nine cents exactly, or wanting certain denominations to bring them up to thirty-nine cents. "Let me see," mused the clerk. "Here are three fifteens. If we put a nine with two of them and had a twenty-four to go with the other . . ."

"Here's a six and a three that would do for the nine," said Shirley. "And here's a twenty, but we'd still need a four-center for the other."

"Here are two twos," said the clerk. "That'll work!"

After a prolonged tête-à-tête of this nature, they had the whole counter covered with little piles of stamps, some of them totaling thirty-nine cents, others lacking various amounts, which the clerk jotted down, to bring them up to thirty-nine cents. The helpful clerk tallied his figures and told Shirley how many fives, how many twos, and how many ones she must buy to turn all these stamps into current postage.

Back at the Manor, their errands complete, Shirley got out all of Mama's envelopes, both legal and note sized. She worked arduously for some length of time plastering each envelope with a colorful array totaling thirty-nine cents, and making enough envelopes to last Mama for years—barring another rise in postal rates. Her job was so taxing on the tongue that she had to consume several glasses of water to get rid of the coating of glue. When she showed Mama the tall stack of stamped envelopes, with the satisfaction of a job well done, Shirley noticed two leftover five-cent stamps.

"Hey!" she exclaimed, "He made me buy two too many five-cent stamps. I wonder if he'd let me bring them b. . ." She clamped her hand over her mouth.

Bamboozled at the Bamboo House

One cold, bright day in January 2013, Judy and I joined my brother Denis for lunch at the Bamboo House Chinese Restaurant in Marionville, Missouri. We chose a table and started to remove our warm coats, but the charming little oriental proprietress admonished us, "No, no! You must prace order, then serect table."

We leapt back from the table as if it were a dangerous animal and went to the counter to order. The daily specials were about a half dozen choices similar to Cashew Chicken—that is chicken dishes using the deep fried white chicken chunks but with a particular sauce for each different dish.

Denis made his choice first: Bamboo Chicken. Wow! That sounded so good. We all love bamboo shoots. Judy actually started to order that too, but then decided on Sesame Chicken, just to be different. I always order something hot and spicy. If there had been hot sauce on the table, I would have ordered the Bamboo Chicken and spiced it up, but instead I ordered General Chicken, which had red warnings of hotness on the menu.

As we waited for our food, Denis told us an amusing story about a malapropic acquaintance who kept talking about someone having a pet bamboo. Denis said, "It took me awhile to figure out that he was talking about a pet baboon."

Denis's dish arrived first, and we all stared at his plate to observe whether we could actually see the chicken or if it would be totally obscured by the smothering of bamboo shoots. There was not one single bamboo shoot in his Bamboo Chicken! It looked pretty much like Cashew Chicken without the cashew nuts and chopped green onions—just chicken chunks with a bambooless sauce on it.

When the proprietress brought Judy's and my food, Denis asked, "Why are there no bamboo shoots in my Bamboo Chicken?"

She laughed musically and said, "Oh, Bamboo Chicken lecipe do not incrude bamboo shoots. Him our house speciarty for Bamboo House Lestulant, so we name him Bamboo Chicken."

Only the inscrutable Chinese would think of doing that! Whatever my reason for naming a dish "bamboo" anything, I would make sure that it had bamboo shoots in it. I suppose the Chinese have never heard of truth in advertising—or maybe it loses something in the translation.

In spite of the paucity of bamboo shoots, we enjoyed our meal, and then the proprietress brought us a tray with three fortune cookies. I think it is uncanny how the fortunes found in Chinese fortune cookies frequently hit the nail on the head.

I told Denis, "Judy and I often find that we open each other's fortunes, but we can always tell who should get which one after we read them."

I opened my supposed fortune, and, sure enough, it described Judy to a tee: "You look pretty." No one would ever describe me as looking pretty. I took a quick look at Denis and was reassured that it was indeed Judy's fortune.

Next I opened what was to have been Judy's fortune, but of course now we knew it would be mine. Sure enough, a more perfect description of me was never put on paper: "You display the wonderful traits of charm and courtesy."

When Denis opened his fortune, Confucius raked this seemingly sedate and modest person over the coals for being such a show-off. "Confucius say: Show-off make some people mad, some people sad, nobody glad."

We supposed that Denis must have a secret life of self-aggrandizement, possibly doing such things as juggling and standing on his head to draw attention to himself.

Judy and I counseled Denis to restrain his tendencies for flamboyance and grand gestures. "Remember that you don't always have to be the center of attention," I told him.

"Yes," Judy added, "It's not all about you."

We hoped he would take our advice to heart, but how could we tell, since we never knew he was a show-off until Confucius told us? Denis always seemed to display the wonderful traits of charm and courtesy. Hey! I don't suppose I got Denis's fortune by mistake. But then . . . where does that leave me?

Owen's Last Outing

My friend Owen works too hard. Owen had a severe heart attack several years ago with resultant bypass surgery, so I think he should relax more and not drive himself so hard. He used to take time off to go on outings with me, which gave him a chance to rest and slow down. Now he always says he is too busy when I invite him to go on pleasant little trips. I believe the last time he joined me was a few years ago when we went to Springfield, Missouri, to buy chemicals for my clock repair business.

It is not easy for a one-horse operation to buy chemicals in small quantities. One chemical I needed was aqua ammonia, which is industrial-strength ammonia so strong that one whiff can incapacitate a person. It will burn the skin if you splash some on yourself. Oddly enough, I could buy a railroad tank car full of the stuff, but I had trouble finding it in small quantities. I was about to settle for a fifty-five-gallon drum from one company, when I learned that Chem-Tech would sell me a thirty-gallon drum. I also ordered five five-gallon cans of other chemicals, such as acetone and industrial alcohol.

One problem was that thirty gallons of ammonia would last me for decades, and I did not wish to have the $40 deposit tied up in the thirty-gallon drum for all those years. I decided to buy six five-gallon plastic gasoline cans from Walmart. We would siphon the ammonia into the six smaller containers, and then return the drum. I bought a length of one-inch plastic tube to use as a siphon hose. We planned to pick up the chemicals, go to our friend Lamont's nearby home, empty the drum, and then take it back for my deposit before heading home. It was a breezy day, and we would siphon outside, so the wind would disperse the hazardous fumes.

Owen drove to my home early one morning, and we started on the hour-long drive to Springfield. I had a 1978 Dodge van at that time, and I pulled my home-made, pickup-bed trailer behind it. The first minor hitch came as we drove through the village of Billings. We heard a clatter and could see in the rearview mirrors that my tailpipe was dancing in the street behind us. What good luck! If this had happened at highway speed I might have lost it. I had just bought a new muffler system, and the mechanic forgot to weld the tailpipe to the muffler. I quickly turned around and drove back. Owen jumped out and threw the tailpipe into the trailer, and we were on our way again.

We stopped at Walmart and bought the gasoline cans, then went on to Chem-Tech, where we had no difficulty in purchasing the thirty-gallon drum of ammonia and the five-gallon cans of other chemicals. We headed for Lamont's home, five miles out of Springfield. As we turned into Lamont's driveway, it started pouring rain, which spoiled our plan of siphoning outside in the open air. We opened the doors on Lamont's barn, and I backed the trailer inside.

Owen ordered, "You get clear away from here while I siphon this stuff! With your lung trouble, it would be murder for you to breathe the fumes."

I said, "Surely I could help some and run in and out."

Owen said, "No, you just run OUT!"

So I did. As I hovered under the eaves of the barn, I could hear the rattle of cans in the trailer and smell the ammonia vapors. The fumes began to hurt my nose, so I moved to a shed farther away.

"Hey, Owen," I called out, "You'd better come out and get some fresh air!"

"No," gasped the reply, "I want to stay at it and get it over with!"

After about a half hour, Owen emerged from the barn and drank in the fresh air in great gulps.

"Heck!" he exclaimed, "This plain old air is too weak. I don't think I can breathe it anymore! I'll have to take home a bottle of that ammonia to suck on, so I can taper off onto regular air!"

Owen went back into the ammonia-rife barn, loaded the six five-gallon containers of ammonia back in the trailer, and got into the van. We drove to Chem-Tech and returned the thirty-gallon drum for the deposit, then headed homeward down Battlefield Road. The normal route home, in those days, before the construction of James River Freeway, was west on Battlefield Road to Highway FF, south on FF to Highway M, west on M to Highway 60, and thence homeward.

As we headed south on FF, I said to Owen, "I have always suspected that if a person followed FF south through the town of Battlefield, it would hit an east-west highway that would provide a shortcut to Highway 60. Why don't we try that?"

"Whatever you say," said the affable Owen. "You're driving."

I suited action to word and stayed on Highway FF. We passed through the town of Battlefield and kept going. The wide-paved highway became less wide and lost its shoulders. The less-wide paved road became a gravel road. The farther we went, the less propitious the road became. Finally we were driving through close-grown woods on a dirt road with grass growing between the tracks.

All of a sudden we dived down a steep hill, which was nearly a half-mile long and slimy with the continuing rain. A quarter-mile past the bottom of the hill, we rounded a sharp corner and were confronted by a flooded bridge. Brown water roared in such a torrent that there was no question of attempting to cross it, nor did there appear to be room to turn around with my van and trailer, since the timber grew close to the road.

We sat in the van listening to the rain, thinking for a few minutes. I suggested, "If we unload all eleven of those forty-pound containers of chemicals, the trailer should be light enough for two men to turn around by hand. Then we can manhandle it out of the way to give me room to turn the van around. We'll re-hook the trailer, load all the containers back in, and Bob will be our uncle!"

Owen said amenably, "That sounds like a plan."

I said, "Before we go to that trouble, let me get out and survey the situation and see if there is any hope that I might be able to turn this thing around without all that exertion."

After reconnoitering, I got back in the van and shook the rainwater off my hat. "I think there's one gap in the trees where I might be able to force the trailer over the brush far enough that I could turn around, if I can ever get the rig positioned so that I can hit it."

I backed and turned and geed and hawed for ten or fifteen minutes, gradually rotating the rig, so that I could hit the gap in the trees, then "gave it the gas" to lunge backward over the brush. We made it! There was room enough to turn the van and head back for the hill. Owen commented, "You'd better get a good head start at that muddy hill, or you'll never make it up!"

I agreed. With as much speed as possible, we went barreling towards the hill. Up we went, sliding some, but continuing upward. When we were about halfway up, we heard a clunk and saw in our rearview mirrors that the bumper had fallen off my trailer! Doubtless, I weakened the bumper when I backed into the brush.

"I'm afraid to stop on this slippery hill!" I shouted.

Owen yelled, "Just slow down, and I'll bail out! You keep going up the hill!"

I slowed a little, Owen jumped out, and I continued sliding and spinning up the hill, feeling a great relief when I reached level ground at the top. I got out and started walking back down the hill towards Owen. I could not help but reflect on what a forlorn figure he presented, slogging up that muddy hill through the rain, dragging a bumper. But on the bright side, I thought how lucky he was to have me there, on the way down to help him drag it. We loaded the bumper, and this time we went home by the old route that we knew so well. Owen must have had a crick in his neck. When I glanced his way, I saw him silently shaking his head, as we drove along.

As Owen helped me lug all those heavy containers of chemicals into my shop, he kept saying, "I'll never forget this trip you took me on. I'll never forget this trip you took me on."

I knew he was reliving our pleasant adventures and trying to tell me how much he had enjoyed the day out. Owen must have forgotten the fun we have on outings together, as he always seems too busy to join me anymore when I invite him to go places. He really ought to quit working so hard and give his heart a rest now and then.

The Colossal Clock

My clock repair customer, George Tucker, told me an interesting story some years ago.

When George was in the military service, he was stationed in Munich, Germany. George and his wife had a station wagon, and one day George's friend Buck asked him if he would run an errand with him in his station wagon. Buck had a Volkswagen, and this task required a bigger vehicle.

When they got off duty that evening, they headed for the heart of Munich in George's station wagon. George told me, "It seemed as if we went down every narrow side street and back alley in the oldest part of Munich. I never figured out how Buck ever found the store in the first place, let alone remembered his way back."

George and Buck finally arrived at a used furniture store, and Buck proudly pointed to his purchase, a huge, ten-foot tall, antique German grandfather clock. Buck had paid $1500 for it. George said, "Are you completely crazy? What on earth are you going to do with that monster? It won't fit in any house you'll ever live in."

Buck said, "Well, I love that clock, and I'm going to ship it back home and then I'll figure out what to do with it."

They could barely haul the mammoth clock in the station wagon, but they did get it back to the base, and Buck had it crated and shipped to the United States.

Thirty years later, George happened to be passing through Tucson, and looked up Buck in the phone book and went by to see him. After an enjoyable visit, George was getting in his car to leave when he happened to think of the gargantuan clock. He said, "Hey, Buck! What did you ever do with that huge clock you bought in Munich?"

Buck said, "You kept telling me how crazy I was. See if you think I'm crazy now. I still own that clock, but it's been out in Los Angeles for years. It's on display in the largest automobile agency in L. A., and they send me a $500 rent check on it every month. People hear about that clock and come in to see it, and they try and sell them a car."

Outhouses Were In

When my grandfather, Washington Irving Meadows, came to live with us in 1952, we became a two-outhouse family.

Our primary outhouse was an old grey, barn-wood two-seater, down the hill behind our main house. Grandpa was to live in a nicely fixed up room in the original log house, which stood some twenty yards south of the main house. My father felt that the old outhouse, or "toilet," as we called it then, was too far for his elderly father to walk.

A few weeks before Grandpa's arrival, Daddy came home with a beautiful, second-hand, whitewashed, pinewood outhouse on the back of our farm truck. As an audience of his children watched, Daddy set to work with pick and shovel, digging a square hole near the back door of Grandpa's room. He poured a little concrete foundation around it and set the toilet in place over the hole. It was only a one-seater, but quite a princely privy for one old gentleman to use. Grandpa had not grown up with anything as sissified as toilet tissue, so Daddy had located a supply of corncobs, at Grandpa's special request. Daddy also made a neat little holder to contain a roll of toilet paper for the faint of bottom who might chance to use the toilet.

The finishing stroke was the ventilation holes. Whoever built the pine toilet had made it tight and solid, not realizing that it should have an air hole on each side, near the top. Our old outhouse had a diamond-shaped hole in each side wall, made by notching adjacent boards. We had never seen an outhouse with crescent holes, but that was the way they were pictured in the "Li'l Abner" comic strip, and Daddy thought it would be a great joke to cut them in the new toilet. By drawing arcs along the edges of two buckets of unequal diameters, Daddy outlined a cunning crescent on each side of the outhouse. He did not have any power tools at that time, so drilled pilot holes with his brace and bit, and then cut out the crescents with a keyhole handsaw.

There were two usual accessories in every outhouse, aside from toilet paper (and, in this case, corncobs). A bucket of lime sat in the corner with a dipper or can to dip up lime and sprinkle it down the hole to help assuage odor. And there was always an old edition of the Sears, Roebuck, & Co. catalog to provide emergency paper if the roll ran out—and also furnish some moderately entertaining reading material.

What swank to have two outhouses! Some farms were so poor they had no outhouse at all, their residents merely going out into the woods as the animals do. How dismal! Imagine having to be more careful where you step as the years go by. This epitomizes the expression, "Poor people have poor ways."

In North America the word "outhouse" is understood to refer to what is technically a pit latrine. In British English "outhouse" has no connotation of a toilet, but refers to any detached structure or outbuilding. There are many terms for an outdoor privy that are used in various countries and situations. Some of them are kybo, biffy, bog, dunny, long drop, and thunderbox.

Every country church and schoolhouse had outhouses in those days before rural electrification. There were usually two, one for gents and another for ladies. A favorite Halloween stunt of local hooligans was to tip over outhouses—usually at schools and churches, but occasionally those of private homes.

One of my earliest memories is of using that old oak outhouse. I am sure I was potty trained with a little graniteware potty at first. Then probably the summer when I was three years old I was transferred from potty to privy. In my mind I see Mama leading me down the hill and establishing my bottom over the hole. She told me, "I'll leave the door open, and when you're finished, you yell for me, and I'll come and wipe you." She was as good as her word. She would say, "Bend over!" and then apply the paper.

One of my great frights occurred in the outhouse a bit later, after I was in the self-wiping mode and had no hope of being rescued by Mama. My older sister Shirley had a fantastic phobia of spiders of every size and shape. Of course, she transferred this terror to her younger siblings, making all of us antipathetic to arachnids. One day I bounded merrily into the toilet, finished my mission, then glanced at the floor between where I sat and the door. On the floor sat a terrible tarantula, tremendous in size. My short life flashed before me, as I was certain my end was near. I huddled in horror for some time, fearing the beast would leap upon me and consume me. However I could not spend the rest of the day in the toilet, awaiting the departure or attack of the tarantula. Luckily I had left the door open. I very s-l-o-w-l-y stood and pulled up my trousers, then with a long jump that Carl Lewis might have envied, I leapt over the startled spider and raced up the hill to tell Mama.

Every family has humorous tales in its history, and a few of the Meadows stories have to do with outhouses.

The earliest involves my Uncle Albert, who was born in December 1908, and even as a toddler, tried to do what he thought was right. In 1911, my grandparents made the annual trip for supplies, the small family going from Bull Creek in Taney County by wagon and team to Springfield, Missouri. When the two-year-old Albert needed to relieve himself, his mother took him into a store, to the first real bathroom he had encountered. She stood him in front of the appropriate fixture, and told him to go. Little Albert refused. He kept pointing at the glistening white toilet bowl and saying, "Dish!" He knew it would be wrong to sully a piece of china, and his mother had to take him out back to find a traditional outhouse.

After Grandpa died, Daddy moved the fancy, whitewashed toilet with crescents to a new location behind our main house. Then we abandoned the old barn-wood toilet down the hill, which now stood idle unless an overflow of company forced its occasional use.

My eldest sister Anne and her family happened to come home for a visit at the same time that my Aunt Louise and her little boy Nathan were visiting my parents. My mischievous cousin Nathan noticed when Anne went out to the painted privy in due course. He had also noticed that the outhouse had a turn-button lock on the outside. While Anne was inside he gleefully sprinted out and quietly turned the lock. Anne shouted and banged on the door, but no one heard her for at least a half hour. Hell hath no fury like a woman locked in an outhouse. She stormed straight to the house, captured Nathan and marched him to the outhouse where she locked him in. Half an hour later she went and released him with strict admonitions that if he ever did that again, he would be sentenced to a full hour. He never did it again.

Eventually in 1961, Daddy partitioned off a corner of the upstairs and built the first bathroom ever to grace the old farmhouse. Shortly thereafter Anne and Harold and their brood of children came for a visit. The minute the visitors arrived in the house Little Roy proclaimed, "I need to pee." Thankful for the new bathroom, Anne took her son upstairs to the commode, but he said, "No! I want to use the dirty bathroom." He refused to go until she led him out to the toilet one last time.

Anne and Harold and their large family fairly monopolized the new bathroom, with some overflow to the white outhouse. When Daddy needed to go and found the bathroom occupied and a line waiting, he simply went down the hill to the old barn-wood toilet. That old outhouse had not been used in several years, and the contents were now dried into compost. A board had even fallen off down low at the back. As soon as Daddy got seated, his beagle ran around back and under the seat where the board was missing. It reached up and gave Daddy an affection lick on the bottom. Daddy claimed that he had a knot on his head from jumping so high he hit his head on the roof.

"Outhouse" is an old and respected family in the Cassville, Missouri, area where we live. Kevin Outhouse had an automobile repair service in Cassville, and one day I was in the office waiting for my car to be done. I chatted with Kevin's wife, Karen. I said, "I guess the kids get teased in school about the name Outhouse."

Karen said, "Oh yes, but other kids soon get used to the name. I tell my children that Outhouse is an honorable old name, and probably more respectable than the names of the kids teasing them, so just to grin and be proud of their name."

I left home for college in 1961 and lived in homes with modern conveniences. Judy and I were married in 1966 and lived in Columbia and Kansas City, Missouri, and later in Jonesboro, Arkansas. Everywhere we lived we had indoor facilities with hot and cold running water, and I was comfortable in the assurance that I would never be subjected to outhouses again.

Our dream had always been to move back to the area in southwest Missouri where I grew up. In 1983, I quit my job at Arkansas State University, and we bought a mail-order business and a dilapidated farm in the Ozarks. The farm was not only dilapidated but also outdated, as it did not have running water in the house! Suddenly we were back to the days of the barn-wood oak two-seater. The first thing I did was make neat wooden lids for the two holes and install a decent toilet-paper holder.

Is there anything good one can say about an outdoor privy? Certainly there is peace and quiet sitting out there remote from the house. There is not even the sound of flushing. One communes with nature on the way to and from, and this means keeping in touch with the weather. You know if it is raining or snowing, if it 100° or ten degrees below zero. You know if there is a cold wind from the north. Winters are the worst time for outhouse goers, especially when they are ill with the flu or some other malady. We even bought a chamber pot for Judy to use in the stilly watches of the night. If one of us males had to go "number one," at night we simply stepped outside and watered the grass. For "number two," I would light a lantern and hand it to the rover. Decades later our son Aaron reminisced, "There's nothing so peaceful as an outhouse and a kerosene lantern on a cold winter night."

Our youngest sons, Aaron and Alex, were six years old the spring we moved to the farm, and they quickly adapted to primitive living. By fall, when they went to school, they were used to the outhouse. In fact, they were so accustomed to the outhouse that they did not feel at ease using the bathrooms at school! During the four years or so before we added a bathroom to our house, Aaron and Alex refused to use the school bathrooms. When the afternoon school bus stopped at our place to let the boys off, Aaron and Alex would race down our driveway and out back to the toilet. They always left the door open, and we could look out there and see the two little boys sitting side by side on the two seats.

Our outhouse had a nice concrete reservoir, and periodically we would have a septic company come and pump it out. It was strange and somehow amusing that while they were pumping out the outhouse, buzzards always circled overhead. That lime did not quite do its reputed trick of minimizing odor.

After Judy and I added an addition with a bathroom, and our outhouse had sat idle for a few years, a neighbor asked if she could take some of the boards from it to make barn-wood crafts. Of course we assented, and she later gave us a wall hanging of three oak-leaf shapes cut from the old toilet. It now graces the least of the three bathrooms in the modern brick home we built in 2008.

In some societies, human waste has not been considered waste, but a valuable commodity. We own a book entitled *Poopoo Make Prant Glow* by Harvey Ward, copyright 1970, which tells of the use of human waste for fertilizer in China. It has been put to the same use in other oriental countries. I read of a trial in ancient Japan to decide whether the prized human waste belonged to the land owner or the renter. The judge's surprising decision was that the renter owned his own urine, but the property owner owned the solid waste. Perhaps giving each some ownership was the judge's attempt to force the two parties to work together in harmony, since both products had some value in that society.

Human waste was even more precious for the manufacture of gunpowder. Urine and manure of any kind can be mixed and fermented in tanks for several months, filtered through wood ashes, and evaporated in large trays to leave a residue of potassium nitrite or saltpeter, a vital component of gunpowder. During England's heyday the demand for gunpowder was huge. England ruled the seas with its large fleet of warships and also owned and controlled possessions around the globe.

In London and other large cities all the outhouses had trays or drawers that were pulled out from the back of the little building. The outhouse owners paid monthly fees to night-soil collectors to keep the drawers empty. When the collector had a full wagon, he received another emolument when he sold his load to the gunpowder manufacturers.

I have wondered if the advent of modern plumbing caused a shortage of gunpowder and brought down the power and glory of the British Empire. While British subjects sat in outhouses, the sun never set on the British Empire.

Our First Turkey

Life was simple in the Ozarks in the 1940s and 1950s, and we did not have things that we take for granted now. We saw pictures of Swiss cheese with holes in it, but the only cheese my family knew then was Velveta—at first in a wooden box and later cardboard. We saw pictures of beavers and their dams, but never dreamed we could see these creatures in person. Now there are beavers and dams in some Ozarks streams. There were no such things as ballpoint pens yet. Mama had a fountain pen, but most people used pencils. Many times as a boy I have heard my dad buying or selling a calf or pig, and someone would say, "Does anybody have an indelible pencil?"

Those were pencils that wrote in purple and were safe to use for writing a check. If someone tried to erase the writing, it merely smeared. I always wondered why indelible pencils had erasers.

In spite of the many deficiencies in those days, I grew up in a happy family. There was always laughter and singing and contentment. Looking back, I am amazed to realize that we were very poor—but at the time we children didn't know it. One person who knew our family told me, "You weren't poor! The only thing you didn't have was money." I am amazed that my father, working on that rocky farm, could feed his wife and six children and send all six kids to college.

My family never had turkey for Thanksgiving in those early days. In fact, nobody we knew did. All the wild turkeys in Missouri had been killed out early in the century, and the mass turkey operations were years in the future. I do not know if they had turkeys in the grocery store, but if they did, we couldn't afford them. We saw pictures on the cover of *Saturday Evening Post* of a family gathered around a baked turkey, but that was no different to us than seeing pictures of the new young queen of England in her gilded carriage or Aladdin with his magic lamp. It was a fantasy world we would never participate in.

So Mama would fix a roast from a home-grown beef or pork or kill a couple of chickens for our Thanksgiving meal, and we were all happy to have it. Then one year, as Thanksgiving approached, Daddy came to the decision that he was going to risk a dollar on the turkey shoot. Of course they didn't shoot turkeys at the turkey shoot; they shot at targets, and the best shot got the turkey. Daddy put a gun in our 1950 Chevrolet and took off on the morning of the turkey shoot.

Daddy always kept a .22 rifle, as good as he could afford, since he shot wild rabbits and squirrels to help feed the family in those days. The fanciest one he had was a Remington semi-automatic with traditional, or "open," sights. I do not know if he had that nice gun at the time of the famous turkey shoot, but whatever gun he owned, he did not take it. My oldest brother Roger had a heavy old Mossberg .22 rifle with both traditional sights and a peep sight. It was actually inappropriate for a young man, as it was so heavy, but Daddy no doubt got it at a bargain price or in a trade. Roger was extremely surprised when Daddy asked to borrow his Mossberg for the turkey shoot.

In the afternoon, Daddy drove into our driveway and got out of the car, all smiles. He called the family out, and we gathered around the car. Daddy dramatically opened the trunk to reveal a huge turkey! Using the peep sight, he had hit the bull's-eye exactly in the center! I am not talking about a frozen turkey or a dressed turkey in the trunk of the car. It was a real live, dark grey turkey, feathers and all, with its feet tied together.

Daddy kept the turkey in a pen and fed it for a few days till Thanksgiving, then chopped off its head; and he and Mama scalded it, plucked it, and dressed it, with all of us kids rowed up watching the whole show. Mama said it was a terrible job to pluck it, because of all the black pinfeathers, but that she didn't mind one bit, since we finally had a turkey for Thanksgiving.

So on Thanksgiving Day, we were just like the family on the cover of *Saturday Evening Post*. We were excited, happy, and thankful as Mama handed us our plates with real turkey on them. We all watched Daddy expectantly as he took his very first taste of turkey. He chewed it in the left side of his mouth and then in the right side. He shut his eyes and, wallowed it around with his tongue, and savored it. Finally he opened his eyes and announced, ". . . I like chicken better!"

Forget Us Our Debts

Judy and I suffered almost no bad debts during the years that we owned the M. L. Shipley Company from 1983 to 1991. We sent orders to every state in the union and some foreign countries. We extended credit to everyone without question. An unknown voice on the telephone would say, "Can you send me an order of clock parts and include a bill?" We would say, "Sure." Out of the thousands of transactions we conducted, there were only two debts we could not collect. Greg Monster of California wrote us a bad check for $15. Gerald Vernier in Oklahoma ordered about $110 worth of clock parts and never would pay for them. And then there was Bill Thomas.

Even on the telephone, Bill Thomas sounded bluff and important. I was later to learn that he was only *self*-important. In 1987, when he telephoned for the first time, Bill said, "I own the largest clock repair operation in Wichita, Kansas, and I would like to establish an account with you. I will expect to place several hundred dollars in orders each month, and I'd like to get started right now. We need some clock glass and parts pretty desperately, and I'd like you to send them out with an invoice today if possible."

This sounded good to me. It was our most poverty-stricken period. I was trying to build up our little business. Judy was unable to find a full-time professional job, and we had three school-age sons to provide for. I said, "I'll be glad to. What do you need?"

Bill ordered $150 worth of items, and I filled the order with joy, knowing how much we needed the money. A few days later Bill called again. He said, "The order arrived in fine condition, and I'm very happy with the quality of the merchandise. I'm putting a check in the mail today for this first order, but we are in a desperate pinch for a few more parts. I wonder if you could do me a favor and send them out too. I'll mail you another check the day I receive the package."

I was beginning to feel a little hesitant, but I did not wish to anger this wonderful new customer, who was going to provide us with a great source of income. So I agreed. Bill ordered ninety dollars worth of parts, which brought his total debt up to $240.

I optimistically opened the mailbox for a few days, expecting to see a fat check from Thomas. No check arrived. I thought that he might have decided to wait for the second order and send the whole $240 in one check. But the days rolled by, and no check of any size arrived from Bill Thomas.

After waiting a couple of weeks, I phoned Thomas to say I had not received payment for the orders. He acted surprised and embarrassed that he had neglected this trifle. "Oh my goodness!" he said. "Did I forget to send out that check? Well don't worry. I'll get it in the mail immediately."

He didn't. Over the next few months, I occasionally telephoned Bill Thomas or mailed him a dun. The duns were ignored, and the phone calls were treated with the same feigned surprise that he had forgotten to mail my insignificant check. Eventually I ceased wasting my postage and long distance telephone expense on him.

About a year after I sent the orders, Tom Atteberry telephoned me one Sunday. I had told this good friend and his octogenarian foster mother, Gretchen, about the Bill Thomas fiasco. Tom told me on the phone, "Granny Gretchen and I have to go to Wichita on Wednesday. She has some business out there, and I need to see Bill Thomas about some wooden clock movements he has for sale. If I spend more than $240, I'll deduct your debt, and write him the check for the remainder, and get your money for you. But why don't you come over Tuesday night and go with us? We'll get up about 4:00 a.m. and head for Wichita. We can give Bill Thomas a little surprise."

"I'll do it!" I said.

We arrived in Wichita before 9:00 a.m. on a rainy Wednesday. We easily found "The Clock Doc," Thomas's shop, right downtown. He was just flipping his sign to "OPEN." I was quicker on my feet than the arthritic Tom and the nearly ninety Gretchen, and I went bounding into the store first, to surprise Bill Thomas. I entered the showroom and held out my hand to the flabby, fiftyish man behind the counter. I said, "Hello, I'm Mark Meadows."

It was one of the few times in my life that I have seen a true double take. Bill started to turn towards my friends, who were entering the door, as he said, "I'm Bill Tho . . ." then snapped his head back towards me, "Did you say MARK MEADOWS?"

As I made the introductions, Bill seemed nervous, but didn't say anything about the debt he owed me. The establishment consisted of about five rooms, and Bill conducted us on a tour with a pompous and proprietary air. There was a showroom, a room with shelves of clocks waiting to be repaired, and a room holding inventory of clocks for sale. The largest room was the workroom, which contained the usual equipage of a clock shop. There were lathes, bushing presses, buffing wheels, a drill press, and other tools. There were cabinets and shelves with spare clock parts.

On one shelf I saw a few clock glasses that Judy and I had printed in our little factory at home, and which I had trustingly sent in the infamous orders. The workroom included workbenches to accommodate five clock repairers, but only two of the benches were occupied by men working on clocks. One man was an elderly, grey clockmaker and the other a callow neophyte, who I supposed was learning the trade. Bill did not introduce us to either man, but treated them as just two more pieces of the furniture. We were later to learn the young man's name.

As we looked through the shop, we saw a number of beautiful and marvelous clocks. I admired an English grandfather clock movement from *circa* 1840. There was no case, just the movement and dial. The dial was iron, and painted with five charming scenes of seascapes with castles and lighthouses in the four corners and arch. It had elaborate, hand-made and engraved brass hands.

Eventually Bill Thomas led us three visitors to his office off the workroom, where he leaned his bulky body importantly backward in a desk chair, with his outsized feet on his desk, and began to negotiate with Tom over the antique wooden movements he had for sale. Bill could see through the open door into the workroom behind us. One time he interrupted the conversation to yell, "Mervin! What are you doing at my bench?"

I turned to see the gawky young man standing by a workbench. He replied meekly, "I just needed to use your staking tool for a minute."

Bill said brusquely, "You use your own tools, and keep away from MY bench!"

Tom and Bill conversed a few more minutes, and then Bill asked us, "Would you like some coffee?"

Gretchen replied, "Yes, I'd like a cup."

I said, "If it's no trouble, I'd be glad for a cup."

Tom said, "No, thank you. I don't care for any."

Bill, who apparently wanted a cup for himself, bellowed, "MERVIN! Three coffees!"

We went on with our conversation, and about twenty minutes later, Mervin came in, dripping wet, carrying four Styrofoam cups of coffee.

Bill roared, "Mervin! Can't you understand plain English? I said THREE cups of coffee, and you got FOUR."

Tom came to the rescue, saying, "I was wishing I had asked for a cup, so I'm glad he got an extra."

I asked how Mervin got wet, and we learned that he had had to walk through the pouring rain to a McDonald's two blocks away to purchase the coffee—probably out of his own pocket money. I said, "I'm sorry we asked for coffee, if it meant Mervin had to go all that way in the rain."

Bill said, "No problem! Don't worry about it."

Tom and Bill went on talking about the wooden movements, until Tom accidentally upset his coffee, spilling it on the linoleum floor. He apologized, "Oh, I'm so sorry!"

Bill said, "Don't give it a second thought." He roared, "MERVIN! Paper towels!"

The myrmidon shuffled in with a roll of paper towels and groveled on hands and knees, mopping up the spill, then quietly stole away.

As Tom and Bill concluded their business, Bill seemed to get more and more uneasy, knowing that soon he would have to come to some sort of settlement with me. Finally he said awkwardly, "Mark, I seem to remember that I owe you a little money, don't I?"

"Yes," I said, "you owe me $240."

Bill said, "I'm a little bit short of capital at the moment. My son has had some financial problems, and I've had to bail him out. I noticed you admiring that English grandfather movement and dial. Would you be willing to accept that in settlement of the debt?"

I said, "Let Tom and me go in and look at it and discuss it."

We did so, and Tom said that he felt the movement and dial would be worth close to $500. He also volunteered to build a case for it, if I took it. We went back into Bill's office, and I said, "I'll take it!"

This conclusion relieved Bill of his nervousness, and he was his proud, self-important self once more.

A year after our expedition, Slater Jones telephoned from Wichita to place an order. I said, "We used to have a customer in Wichita named Bill Thomas. Did you ever hear of him?"

Slater said, "Did I ever hear of him! I've heard too much about him! He's given black eyes to all of us clock repairmen in Wichita. He packed up and left in the middle of the night. He moved out east somewhere and took several customers' clocks with him. Some of his customers went to the police. There are warrants out in Kansas for Bill Thomas."

A few years after that, Tom learned that Bill Thomas was going strong in Connecticut. He was even capitalizing on his name, by advertising himself as the descendant of the renowned early American clockmaker Seth Thomas. In answer to Shakespeare's famous question, "What's in a name?" we would have to answer, "Not much!" in comparing Seth Thomas and Bill Thomas.

In spite of his good intentions, Tom never did make the case he promised. He finally was beginning to work on it shortly before he died in June, 2001. I thought that one of these days, when I got caught up, I might make a case. In the meantime, the dial and movement were pleasant reminders of that long ago trip to Wichita, of Tom, of Gretchen, of Bill Thomas, and of course, of Mervin.

Another Chapter . . .

Ten years after Tom's death, I realized that I would never get around to making a case for the movement and dial. An appropriate case is a rather complex undertaking, and I knew I was not up to the task. A friend named David Lindow manufactures reproduction antique clock movements of various types, and he recommended the case maker William "Bill" Towne, who lived in New York State.

Bill Towne pointed out that the choice of case style was very limited, inasmuch as our dial is so large that most styles would look top-heavy if tailored to our dial. We chose the style Bill recommended in solid cherry.

In the meantime, I emailed pictures of our dial and movement to John Robey in England—a renowned expert on English tall case clocks. Neither dial nor movement have a maker's name, but John knew all about them. He said that the dial was made in Birmingham, England, about 1840. The movement was made at this same period in the Harlow factory of Ashbourne—just about two miles from where John Robey lived.

The Harlows of Ashbourne made thousands of good quality movements, which were mounted to dials and sold throughout the British Isles, as well as shipped to America to be cased there. Our clock was finished and running on September 26, 2011. It is a joyous addition to our home, and I never ever think of Bill Thomas when I look at it.

Spittoon & Gazing Ball

If you're like most people, you wonder what spittoons have to do with gazing balls. I am here to tell you. When Judy and I were married in 1966, we were still students at the University of Missouri. We each made $85 a month at student jobs. Our apartment cost $85 a month, so we had to live on love . . . and the other $85. Our main entertainment was going in our 1954 Chevrolet Bel Air to the Tuesday night auction at the Fair Grounds. We came home with all sorts of treasures, which we got for a quarter or a dollar. We bought several treadle sewing machines for one dollar each and gave them to friends and relatives. One time we bought a huge wicker baby buggy for six dollars, and it was FULL of good stuff. Later, when we were expecting Chris, our first son, we fixed up that buggy, had the wheels re-rubbered and all the fixtures re-chromed. After our kids no longer needed it, we sold it for two hundred and fifty dollars.

One thing we bought for a dollar was a beautiful spittoon, made of china or crockery, a shiny, rich green on the outside and snow white on the inside. It was made by Hall, that company famous for making teapots and china for hotels and restaurants. The spittoon was not something we needed, but as Keats says, "A thing of beauty is a joy forever." This thing of beauty was not fated to be a joy forever, however. After it had given us joy for only a few months, I dropped a small anvil on the beautiful spittoon, and it disintegrated into a pile of broken pottery—a sad surprise, as I am a careful person who rarely breaks anything. The cuspidor had been cursed! Judy, always looking on the bright side, said, "Oh well! That makes all the ones that are left more valuable."

Many years later, after Columbia, after Kansas City, after Jonesboro, when we were living in the old house in southwest Missouri, we went to the annual Foxtrotter Convention at Ava, Missouri, and there on one of the rummage sale tables was the exact duplicate of our beloved, green Hall spittoon! Judy was right; it was priced at fifteen dollars. Happily, the owner came down in price when I waved a green sawbuck in front of him.

While we still lived in that old house, our friends, Jess and Peggy Kessinger, gave us a gift of a beautiful blue, glass gazing ball on an iron Mediterranean style stand. We put this treasure in our guest bedroom, the only decent room in the old house. However, when grandchildren began to populate the premises, we were afraid they would tip over the stand and break the gazing ball. You can't trust kids to be careful.

So for our last few years in the old house, the gazing ball rested on the green spittoon on the dresser in the guest room. Incidentally, a spittoon makes the best imaginable base for a gazing ball. Of course, you do have to lift the ball up every time you want to spit.

After we built our new house in 2008, I set the spittoon on the floor next to the grandfather clock. I told Judy, "Won't you be horrified the first time somebody comes in the house and spits tobacco juice into that spittoon?" Ever pragmatic, she said, "I don't think that's likely to happen!"

Finally in our new house, things became as they should be with the empty green spittoon sitting on the floor next to the grandfather clock. Actually it was not empty, as we put a stuffed elephant in it to deter spitters. We placed the beautiful blue gazing ball on its handsome, black iron stand in the place of prominence it deserved. It stood elevated on the landing of the stairs, where everyone in the kitchen and family room area could admire it and see the distorted blue world reflected in its mirror surface.

Indeed we did enjoy the gazing ball for a few months as we ate meals or moved about in the room, and especially every time we climbed the stairs. It gave Judy a bit of anxiety, as I ran up and down the stairs, as she feared I would fall down the stairs and break the gazing ball.

When some of our kids and grandkids planned a visit, I told Judy, "I am greatly worried that when grandkids swarm into the house, they will knock over that gazing ball and break it, so I'm going to put it in a safe place. You know, you can't trust kids to be careful."

When I picked up the gazing ball, it reminded me of a greased pig, wriggling and leaping about. If I had been a farmer or juggler, I might have saved it, but it jumped right out of my hands, falling to the oak floor and smashing into a thousand pieces, thus removing all worry that the grandchildren would break it. Was this some lingering remnant of the curse of the cuspidor?

We looked in stores and garden centers now and then for a couple of years, trying to find a replacement for our gazing ball, but those balls were priced so high, the cheapest being fifty dollars, that we gave up. Then one Christmas season, Walmart had a display of glass gazing balls for only fifteen dollars. They did not have blue, so we bought red. Once again we could happily display our gazing ball now on its stand in the family room.

When the grandchildren came, I knew to put on rubber gloves that would not slip before moving the red gazing ball to rest in the comely green cuspidor on a high chest of drawers—out of reach to both children and spitters.

This plan worked great for a few years. In 2019, son Aaron and his wife Karen and their four kids surprised us with a visit. As the grandchildren surged into the house, the first thing nine-year-old Zephyr saw was the red gazing ball. She rushed to it with expressions of amazement and adoration. She noticed it was dusty and asked for a dust cloth, polishing it while I held my breath. When her back was turned I whisked the gazing ball into another room to hide on the spittoon. You know, you just can't trust kids to be careful.

After the family left, I put the red gazing ball back on its stand. As I turned, I bumped an elephant figurine on a nearby chest. It fell on the gazing ball and broke it into a thousand shards.

In July 2021, Aaron told us that he and his family were coming to visit us. Judy told me, "Remember how Zephyr admired the gazing ball? I'm going to order a blue one."

I said, "You'd better get an unbreakable stainless steel one. Because, you know, you just can't trust kids to be careful."

Dinosaurs & Stuff

Our twenty-fifth wedding anniversary went nearly unnoticed, as our energies were directed towards other family matters. By the time our thirtieth anniversary arrived on June 6, 1996, Judy and I were just a couple again. Our three tall sons were in college, and Judy and I had been coaxed into becoming square dancers. The numerous dancers we met became like family to us, and we decided to throw them a party by sponsoring a free thirtieth anniversary square dance.

I struggled to come up with a quatrain to write in Judy's anniversary card, but then four more lines came to me, and four more. I had a real poem! I decided to read it at the anniversary party. I would not tell Judy anything about my verse except the title, "Dinosaurs & Stuff." I could tell she was somewhat fretful about the poem. She later confessed that she feared it might paint us in embarrassing terms as being dinosaurs. She also confessed that she should have known better.

Judy completed other preparations. She made a red and black satin square dance outfit, with a matching shirt for me. She ordered two large, decorated cakes. Judy also signed the two of us up for a country-dance class, which taught two-step and waltz. Neither of us had danced a step in our lives until our recent experiences in square dancing, which does not require any particular footwork or dancing skill. Judy wanted us to be able to dance to the song "Anniversary Waltz" at our celebration.

When the time came, we made a complete flop of the "Anniversary Waltz," but this dance class was the start of years of fun in more classes and many wonderful evenings together doing two-step, waltz, and swing.

The big evening arrived and became one of our cherished memories. About one hundred guests attended and enjoyed the square dancing, refreshments, and music. I know they also enjoyed watching Judy and me brutalize the "Anniversary Waltz."

Finally it was time for my shining moment, and it surpassed my hopes. Judy and I stood together in front of the throng. I took the microphone and made a speech, thanking everyone, and especially Judy. I included several jokes to soften up the crowd. Then I read my poem. After the first verse, there was a ripple of laughter. By the time I finished the third verse, many people had been moved to tears. Afterward several ladies gave us emotional congratulations, and a few husbands asked me what I would charge to write customized poems they could read to their wives!

Here is the poem I wrote for Judy:

Dinosaurs and Stuff

About a million years ago, while rocks were still brand new,
God planned a perfect mate for me, and I think that was you.
It took a thousand eons, and dinosaurs and stuff,
But now I've finally got you, and what a sweet cream puff!

We met a few decades ago, and I thought you were fine;
My hopes and wishes all came true, when you said you'd be mine.
We've ridden horses, raised some kids, and cooked a meal or two,
And that old love I felt for you is still as good as new.

In love we walked together from youth to middle age,
And years stretch out ahead of us like an unwritten page.
Let's live those years together, until the very end;
In heaven there's no marriage, but I'll be your best friend.

Kicking Glass

Through many years of repairing clocks and owning a clock glass company, I have heard of several different methods of breaking glass. I cannot tell them all, but will mention a few.

A man named Jerry Ennis telephoned my clock shop to say that his daughter had broken the glass in the old kitchen clock. Jerry said, "It had a painted gold picture on the glass. I don't suppose there's any place you can get one of those, is there?"

I said, "Bring the clock and some of the pieces of broken glass, so I can see the pattern. I may even have it in stock. We used to be the main producers of painted clock glass in the United States, and I still have lots of glass in the back room."

When Jerry arrived with an old oak Ingraham clock and a box of glass pieces, I saw that the glass was what we used to list in our catalog as "Number 17." Sure enough, I still had four of them, and Jerry commented, "My wife will be amazed that we could get the same pattern locally."

I said, "If you lived in any other locale, you couldn't have!"

As I cut and installed the glass, I asked Jerry, "How did your daughter break this glass, anyhow?"

Jerry said, "Oh, it was really my fault. I was moving the clock from the bedroom into the front room, when the telephone rang. I set the clock down on the floor while I ran and answered the phone, and about then our eleven-year-old daughter came hurrying through the house. She didn't see the clock, and gave it a good kick."

"My goodness!" I said. "That's one way to break a clock glass!"

"Yes," said Jerry. "And she has to miss a couple of weeks of soccer practice. She had to get ten stitches in her foot."

A few years before that, someone left a Welch kitchen clock at the jewelry store in Cassville for me to pick up for repair. The case was in pieces and the glass broken. Some of the walnut pieces were fractured, and others were completely missing. Moreover, some of the wooden parts were badly charred. I consulted Ed Pace & LeMaster, a shop in Springfield that repairs and refinishes antique furniture, about making the missing walnut parts and restoring the case. I had the correct gold-printed Welch glass in stock, and of course, I would repair the movement. I telephoned the clock's owner and gave him a staggering estimate on the total cost of repair, including having the furniture shop make missing walnut case parts. The estimate was about three times what the clock was worth. He said brusquely "I don't care what it costs. Just fix it!"

Eventually the clock was finished. When I phoned the house this time, the wife answered. I said, "Your clock is all done. It looks simply beautiful and works perfectly."

"Oh, thank you! I'm so glad," she said.

I said, "I can't help but wonder how that clock got in such a fix, all broken up and charred."

She said, "Oh . . . uh . . . it fell off of the mantel into the fire."

Of course I knew that was not true. A mantelpiece is a very stable location, and the clock would not fall; it would have to be pushed. Furthermore, if the clock did fall, it would not fall with enough force to do that much damage, nor could it hurl itself down and jump backward into the fireplace. I believe that the clock was the victim of domestic conflict, one partner saying, "Here's what I think of you!" and heaving the other spouse's cherished clock into the fireplace.

I admit that I have broken my share of glass. Any person handling tens of thousands of pieces of glass over many years is bound to break a few. I have dropped them, cut too-tight fits for clock doors and broken the glasses installing them. I have broken them while packing them for shipment, and broken them with heat when soldering them into brass bezels. I have even broken several glasses when cutting them to odd shapes or using a dull glass cutter. I used only Fletcher glass cutters and bought them six dozen at a time. The Fletcher cutter is the best, but even it eventually gets dull.

There are many interesting ways to break glass, but probably the most dramatic methods are Al's and Barney's.

My friend Edmund Hershey, an archery hunter, told me about a visit to his friend Al, who enjoyed deer hunting with high-powered rifles. They sat in easy chairs in the basement family room, and Al would bring a couple of rifles at a time from his collection in the nearby gun safe to show Edmund. He told Edmund about each gun and let him examine it. When Al came to a certain brand of lever-action rifle, Edmund commented, "Somebody told me that the action on that brand of rifle tends to jam. Have you had that problem?"

Al said, "Heck no! It works like a dream every time. Watch this!"

Edmund watched. Al worked the lever, which operated smoothly and crisply. Al aimlessly aimed the gun at the antique Welch kitchen clock ticking peacefully on the mantel, and pulled the trigger. The clock absolutely exploded into a thousand fragments. In the deafening silence, both men stared in wordless wonder at the empty mantel. Finally the shooter said, "Oops! I thought I unloaded that gun. I've got to get these guns back in the safe, or my wife may use one of them on me. I'm glad she doesn't know the combination. That was her grandmother's clock."

An elderly electrician named Bill used to come from Rogers, Arkansas, every few months to buy clock parts and clock glasses from our company. During one such visit I was cutting Bill a clock glass to his pattern, when my dull cutter caused me to break the glass. "Drat!" I exclaimed. "I guess that was MY glass. Now I'll get out a new cutter and cut one for you."

Bill said, "Don't feel too bad about breaking one little glass. Let me tell you about my friend Barney."

One of the big banks was opening a drive-up branch in the parking lot of a shopping mall in Rogers. Bill was on the site doing the wiring, and Barney was one of the carpenters. Those drive-up facilities also have a small lobby, for walk-in customers. Inside the little bank there is a one-inch thick sheet of bulletproof glass between the customers and the tellers, and they have to hand checks and money through a little slot under the bulletproof glass.

Bill's friend Barney overheard the supervisor talking on the telephone about ordering the bulletproof glass for the building, and he thought ALL the glass in the bank was bulletproof glass. When the outer walls of the bank were complete, the whole front of the little building was a huge sheet of glass about twelve feet tall. One day a friend of Barney's stopped by to consult him about something, and the carpenter said, "Let me show you around."

Barney had his hammer in his hand, and as he showed his friend around, he pointed with his hammer to interesting features.

They ended the tour outside the front of the bank. Barney said to his friend, "Can you believe that this whole bank is made with bulletproof glass?"

To demonstrate the invulnerability of the bulletproof glass, he swung his hammer up over his head and hit the glass. That whole wall simply shattered in a colossal cascade of glimmering shards around their feet.

"I wonder if that really is bulletproof glass after all," mused the skeptical carpenter.

Keys Please!

An elderly person asked the doctor how to know whether
he had Alzheimer's Disease or just aging memory. The
doctor said, "If you forget where you put your keys,
that's normal geriatric memory. If you forget what your
keys are for, that's Alzheimer's."

I opine that the keys to a few earthly doors have given me
more trouble than the more crucial keys to the kingdom of
heaven give to Saint Peter.

I have several sets of keys for various purposes. My most
useful set contains four keys, those to the house, barn, and both
doors of the shop. I always kept that set in my left hand trouser
pocket. I attached a green plastic tab to the ring with the keys
and called this set "my green keys."

I was quite happy with my green keys for a few years. Then
one year during mowing season our neighbor Bob Reed, former
John Deere shop foreman, came to help me make some sort of
repair or adjustment on our John Deere zero-turn mower. Bob
needed a tool, and I went to my shop to fetch it. I used my green
keys to open the back door of the shop, and that was the last time
I saw my green keys!

The next time I reached into my pocket for the green keys,
the pocket was empty! Judy and I searched everywhere for the
keys. We knew they might be hiding, green keys in green grass,

so we searched carefully in the grass around the back door of the shop and also in the spot where Bob worked on the mower. No green keys!

When I relax or take a nap in a certain recliner, the contents of my pocket tend to slip out and fall through the chair to the floor below. Several times I have forgotten to remove the keys before reclining, so had to tip up the chair and retrieve them from underneath. But the elusive green keys were not under the recliner this time.

The next time we were in Springfield, I went to the famous Jay Key, and using keys from other sets had duplicates made of the four keys that had been my green keys. I put them on a ring with a blue tag and called them (You guessed it!) "my blue keys."

Life was once again good as I had my blue keys in my left pocket.

As I continued to mow each week during that summer, I would go into the barn and retrieve the mower key from a nail in a dark corner of the barn. Towards the end of the mowing season, I forgot to leave my hearing aids in the house so turned on the barn light to find a safe place to put them.

This time the mower key was visible in the bright light, and there on the nail behind the mower key were my green keys! When I got the tool for Bob I must have put the keys where they belonged in my left pocket. Then I put the mower key in the same pocket, and when I hung up the mower key, I absent-mindedly hung the green keys with it.

"Oh good!" exclaimed Judy, "Now I'll take the green keys, and I can have my very own set."

Life progressed happily for a time. Judy reveled in having her green keys, and I was sufficiently pleased to have my blue keys.

Then in July 2021, disaster struck! My blue keys vanished! We searched everywhere that we could conceive them to be. The first place we looked was under the recliner. In fact I jarred it about and looked under it several times. I looked in the pockets of all the pants I had worn recently. I searched in the shoes and boots in the bottom of my closet in case the keys fell from a pocket when I hung up pants. Everywhere both of us looked there were no blue keys.

I told Judy, "I'll have to borrow your green keys till we go to Springfield and I can have another set made."

"We-l-l, all ri-i-i-ght!" she said, as if she was reluctant to lend me her keys! She surely didn't think I would lose them. She handed them to me, but I had to tug to free them from her fingers.

In only a few weeks, Judy had an appointment in Springfield on August 17. While she was at her appointment I rushed up to Jay Key and got two sets of duplicates of the green keys. I put one set on a ring with a red tab and began to call that set "my red keys." I gave the other new set to son Aaron, since he and his family had moved to Springfield, in case he might need access to one of our buildings. I wonder if he would lend me that set, if I need to borrow it.

Once again life was good for the next couple of weeks. Judy had her green keys and I had my red keys.

On the night of September 3, something unusual happened. I got ready for bed and started to put my hearing aids away. I had only one hearing aid! My right ear was totally devoid of hearing aids.

Both Judy and I felt somewhat panicked, as that set of hearing aids cost $3600, and the tiny grey hearing aid could hide anywhere and be impossible to spot. We knew it was in the house, as I had removed the hearing aids to listen to the news with my earphones before supper, and then put the hearing aids back in my ears afterward. We removed our shoes to avoid crushing the hearing aid under foot.

We tipped up the recliner, but there was no hearing aid under it. We crawled around looking on the floor near any place I had been. Judy had me tip the recliner over and she got our powerful Maglite flashlight to look up into the bottom of the chair.

She exclaimed, "I didn't find the hearing aid, but look what I did find!"

There in the glare of the light were my blue keys, clamped securely in the mechanism of the recliner! They were difficult to remove, and we had to work the lever several times to free them.

As I stood up to turn the chair upright, I felt something under my right foot, and it was my missing hearing aid! This certainly proves Shakespeare's point, "All's well that ends well." At least, I hope this is the end of endless searches for keys. Now we can devote more time to looking for my watch.

While Dad's Away

Whenever my old friend Willard Patton stopped by my shop to buy brass cleaner or clock parts, I encouraged him to tell me tales of his youth. He usually had time to sit awhile and oblige me. During one visit, he told me these two stories.

It was easy for the two boys, Willard and Herman Patton, to stay out of trouble while they were helping their father with the farm work. But strange things seemed to happen on the occasions when Dad left the boys at home while he went to town, and they invariably happened to Willard.

The Patton family did not own a motor vehicle in the 1920s and early 1930s. The boys' father Jim went to the store to fetch supplies on horseback or with the wagon and team. Their mother Mary generally preferred to stay home. Fortunately for Willard, his father did not go very often.

"Those two calves are big enough now to be on grass," said Jim Patton, as he readied himself for the trip to the store. "While I'm gone, you boys move them down to the pasture."

This seemed a simple enough charge. All the boys had to do was lead the two calves from their pen beside the barn, down past the spring, through the valley to the pasture gate, and release them into the field. The task was made easier by the nice, wide road down the hill, which was used frequently to take the horses to water at the spring.

Herman asked, "Can you handle that littlest calf?"

"I sure can," said Willard.

"All right," Herman said, "I'll give you the little one, and I'll take the big one."

Herman went into the pen and roped the small calf, handing the end of the lariat to Willard. Then he roped the big calf and opened the gate. Willard went out the gate first, gripping firmly to the end of his rope with both hands. Out came his calf and started down the wide road. What luck! It was going exactly where he wanted it to go—something a calf would never do, if it realized that was what its manager wished. There was only one problem. The calf was running at breakneck speed down the hill. When it used up the slack in the rope, it pulled Willard right over on his face. It never occurred to Willard to let go of the rope, in fact quite the opposite. He vowed that nothing on earth would make him turn loose, for fear his calf would get away, and they would never be able to catch it.

Down the hill galloped the calf with Willard bouncing along behind it, belly down. By the time the two reached the bottom of the hill, Willard did not have a single button on his shirt front, and his hands were skinned up. The calf, which had been so mighty on the downhill slope, found that it could not pull Willard's dead weight on the level. As Willard lay painfully holding onto the rope, the calf kept leaping and lunging, trying either to move Willard an inch at a time towards the pasture or to jerk his arms out of their sockets. When Willard achingly turned his head to look back up the hill, he saw that Herman was having trouble holding his calf too—not because he lacked the strength to deal with it, but because he was laughing so hard!

Luckily, another time when Jim Patton went to the store, he gave the boys a much safer assignment: "While I'm gone, you boys can go work on stripping that sorghum cane, if you want to."

"When he said 'if you want to,'" Willard told me, "he was simply being polite. He meant, 'Do it!'"

Jim Patton always raised sorghum cane, which he made up into sorghum in the fall, both to use and to sell. In fact, he had a larger sorghum mill and evaporator than was usually found on a farm. The only larger one around was in the town of Butterfield, Missouri. Several neighbors brought the sorghum cane they raised to Willard's father to process into sorghum. Money was not plentiful, and they usually paid for the service with a share of the sorghum. The Pattons normally gained about two barrels of sorghum in this manner, and sold it out, a pail at a time, during the winter.

The average farmer who did have a sorghum mill had a small one and an eight-foot "set-off" evaporator, which two men could lift off the fire when the sorghum was ready. Jim Patton had a Number 12 sorghum mill and a sixteen-foot evaporator. The Number 12 mill weighed 556 pounds and required a heavy work horse or a team of lighter horses to operate. Operating at full capacity with good cane this mill would produce from forty to fifty-five gallons of juice per hour.

"The sixteen-foot evaporator was so big," Willard told me, "that the Number 12 press couldn't keep ahead of it. So Dad and his neighbor cut two feet off the end of it. They cut it, formed tabs, bent them up and soldered them, so it looked just like before. That fourteen foot evaporator and the Number 12 mill were a perfect match."

In modern times, hand labor is so expensive that the sorghum manufacturers do not strip the leaves from sorghum cane. They drive combine harvesters through sorghum cane fields to cut and grind up the whole plants, then run the chopped plants up a conveyer belt into a powerful mill to get the sap. Thus they get "green tasting" sap from the leaves and also get a share of the cinch bugs that usually inhabit the crotch of the leaves. Those bugs are removed when the leaves are stripped. Old timers assert that modern sorghum is not very good.

Herman and Willard formed a plan for a pleasant treat to enjoy while they worked on stripping the cane. Jim Patton smoked a pipe, and he grew some of his own tobacco. In fact, his latest harvest was hanging in the buggy shed drying at the very moment when he said, "You boys can work on stripping that sorghum cane."

"As soon as he's gone," said Herman, "we'll get us a leaf of that tobacco, then we can smoke while we strip the cane."

This sounded good to Willard. They had to hang around in the house for a time, until their mother stepped out of the kitchen, so they could grab a few matches from the matchbox holder on the wall. Then away they went to the buggy shed, where they picked out a nice leaf of long green tobacco. They did not have a pipe, so they took some newspaper with which to roll cigarettes.

The minute they reached the cane field, their first thought was not to get to work on stripping, but to get busy manufacturing their cigarettes. Willard got his rolled first, lit a match, and touched it to the end of the newspaper cigarette.

"I must have had mine rolled too loose," Willard confided in me. "When I touched that match to it, it caught on fire and flared up and burnt the end of my nose. Herman took more time on his and got it packed tighter or got it wetter. When he tried to light his, it didn't flare up, but it wouldn't burn at all."

"Shucks! This tobacco's too green!" Herman declared, when his cigarette would not burn.

Willard replied, "Well, I'm not going to be robbed of my tobacco! I'm going to chew some of it."

Both boys stuffed big wads of tobacco leaf into their mouths and started chewing. As Willard had to keep his head tilted to look up at the cane, in order to strip it and top it, he could not keep the tobacco juice from running down his throat. The longer he worked, the sicker he got. The canes started to sway, not from the breeze, but from waves of nausea. Willard began to look as green as a young stalk of cane and finally ran to the side of the field and threw up everything but his socks. Ever after that day, for years to come, the very sight and smell of a leaf of tobacco made Willard start turning green. Naturally, Herman was able to enjoy his tobacco with no ill effects.

Always one to look on the bright side, Willard told me, "At least, that nausea took my mind off that painful blister on my burnt nose."

Hereditary Sedentary

Judy and I are stay-at-homes, only traveling a few hundred miles once or twice a year to visit siblings or descendents. Our friends Gary & Linda love to travel. Gary showed me a United States map generated by Google with red tags for 359 cities that he and Linda have visited in the past two and one half years! Such a map strikes horror to my heart and gives me nightmares.

Think of all the things that can go wrong on road trips. Cars can have mechanical failures. In 1974 Judy and I dangerously drove from Jonesboro, Arkansas, to Champagne, Illinois, in our 1965 Oldsmobile 98 to visit my brother Denis and his wife Jeanne. In Cairo, Illinois, our water pump conked out! Luckily I could buy a new one and install it in the city park. But even if the car runs perfectly one can have an accident, get a traffic ticket, or get hopelessly lost. There are also the possibilities of running out of gas or finding no lodging. Why take such risks?

Our stationary lifestyle was good for our three sons growing up. Judy and I never went anywhere. That says it all. We were at home every night and weekend, unless a school function required our presence.

I inherited my lifestyle from my mother. My parents and we six children were at home on the farm almost always. We went twelve miles to Aurora, Missouri, now and then and forty miles to Springfield once a year. A couple of times we even went to Kansas City or into Kansas to visit relatives, but Mama put the fear in us kids when we set foot off the place. Daddy would never ask directions, so always got off the track, and when he did, Mama bemoaned our fate and made it clear we might never find our home again. Fear is contagious, and we kids felt it.

Mama's greatest deterrent to the future travel plans of her children was THE ANNOUNCEMENT. The announcement was always worded the same and expressed with the same certainty, yet it always surprised us children. With unerring timing, when we were too far from home to turn back, but not near enough our destination to hope of reaching it in a failing auto, Mama would announce, "I smell rubber burning!" Those words struck horror to our hearts. We sniffed and looked for smoke. We faulted our father for driving placidly on. We expected any moment to be engulfed in flames, and vowed when we grew up never, never to make unnecessary trips.

> *On long trips and even returning,*
> *Mom always would smell rubber burning.*
> *"I don't trust a car*
> *To go very far,"*
> *She said, for a horse and rig yearning.*

Hankering for a Haynes

I visited Maxine Hailey's home on business several times through the years. The tall, elegant old lady was stiff and formal, saying as little as necessary, and never smiling. The last time I visited Maxine before her death was in July 1998, when she was past ninety. I was surprised at the sudden change in her demeanor. Maxine had read an early version of a little article called "Hereditary Sedentary," which I wrote about my mother, and this tale had touched a tender spot in her heart. Maxine became mirthful and chatty as she talked about the article. "Sit down there on the divan and let me tell you about my family," she ordered.

When Maxine Hailey's grandfather died in 1917, he left a large estate to his three children, one of whom was Maxine's father. In the intervening months between the death and the execution of the will, the offspring and their spouses conspired fervently to decide how they would spend their portions. Maxine explained, "They had to negotiate until they agreed upon their main purchases. They had vowed that each of them would get the same things, so that none of them would upstage the others."

The heirs received their bequests in 1918. "When they got the money they began spending it as if born to the task," Maxine declared.

Each of the three children bought a swanky 1919 Haynes seven-passenger automobile. Each bought a brand new player piano, a signal status symbol of the day. All three improved their living accommodations. Maxine's parents built a beautiful mansion in the country, south of the rural town of Cassville, Missouri. They furnished it with fancy furniture shipped in from the famous old factories in the Carolinas. At this point in her story, Maxine got to her feet, retrieved a faded photograph from a mahogany secretary, and showed it to me. There in black and white were Maxine's parents sitting on the verandah of a three-story Victorian house with many gables.

Maxine's family had little need of the lavish limousine, as they rarely traveled any farther than Cassville, which was six miles away. "By the time I was married," said Maxine, "the farthest I had been from home was Miami, Oklahoma, and that's less than a hundred miles away!"

Maxine's mother was the roadblock to family travel. She worried incessantly about going far from home. She feared that the car would break down. She dreaded accidents, storms, and a hundred other things. She suspected that strangers would steal the children. "Who would have wanted us?" Maxine scoffed.

One time the family went to Springfield to select the player piano. On another occasion, they went to Joplin to search for fancy bathroom fixtures, and true to her mother's fears, her father ran into a boy on a bicycle. Her mother had hysterics. Neither the boy nor the bicycle was hurt, but Maxine's father bought the youth a new bicycle as a consolation for being hit.

Maxine's father was a terrible driver. Hitting the boy on the bicycle was only one example of his wanton driving. He often panicked and forgot how to stop the Haynes, thus running over, through, and into various things. Maxine said, "I can see him yet, clutching the wheel with white knuckles and yelling, 'Whoa! Whoa!' as the car went right on."

The family garaged their Haynes in the barn, and three times her father drove right through and took out the back wall of the barn. Soon the family learned that Maxine's ten-year-old brother, Gus, was a more proficient driver than his father. Gus was assigned the duty of family chauffeur, there being no driving license requirements in those days. Maxine's mother did not drive at all, but pulled her son from his farm tasks to drive her into Cassville when she needed to shop. Unlike most boys, Gus did not like to drive, but preferred helping in the fields with the hired men and their sons. When he and his mother returned from town, Gus parked the touring car in the driveway and went racing off to the field to join his friends, leaving his mother to carry in her purchases.

On one occasion, his mother called after him, "Gus! Come back and put the car away! It looks like rain."

But Gus was away and gone, leaving the car vulnerable with its top down. Sure enough, a short while later rain began to fall. The mother's anxiety about the car getting wet overcame her natural timidity, and she said to herself, "Well I know I can drive enough to move that car into the barn."

She got behind the wheel of the Haynes, started the motor, and drove into the barn. She crashed through the often-repaired back wall and drove right out into the field, scattering the workers who were coming in from the rain, and also proving that she was the equal of her husband in driving skill.

The sizable fortunes received in 1918 were gone by 1920, and the three heirs were once again penniless. Indeed all three of the once well-to-do couples struggled for money their whole lives and died poor.

Maxine concluded, "I know some people think that my brother and I are as tight as the bark on a tree, but we saw what happens to people who throw their money away on such things as fancy automobiles and player pianos. Neither of us has ever gone into debt or squandered money. Neither of us has had a great fortune, but both of us have lived more comfortably than our parents did."

The profligate waste of a great inheritance was a powerful lesson to Maxine and her brother. The old saying proved true: "If you cannot do anything else useful, you can serve as a bad example."

A Counterfeit Bag Lady

I had a number of clock repair customers, all of about the same vintage, named Maxine. It was obviously a popular name in a certain long-ago era.

In 1906, two best friends in Chicago were pregnant, though neither would have used that taboo word. All well-mannered people at that time would have said they were "in a delicate condition" or "eating for two."

One of the young ladies was almost certain that she was going to have a baby girl, and she planned to name the infant her favorite name: Maxine. She kept the name a secret and did not tell even her best friend. Just a few days before she delivered, her best friend gave birth to a baby girl and named the baby Maxine! The poor lass was heart-broken that she could not give her favorite name to her baby, but she was not daunted for long. She named her baby the same thing but spelled it Maxyne so that there would be no confusion between the two little girls.

Maxyne, my customer and friend, was born on November 27, 1906. Maxyne had a fascinating life. I wish I would have found out more details and written them down. I know that after she graduated from high school, she got a job in a Chicago jewelry store. She knew that she would have to get to work on time and would need an alarm clock. Luckily, the jewelry store sold clocks, and Maxyne chose a 30-hour oak Gilbert kitchen clock with time, strike, and alarm. The model was "Puck." The clock cost $2.50, but Maxyne's employer let her pay for it over time at 50¢ per month.

Maxyne met Oral F. Larkin and the two were married on June 25, 1926. Oral had been in the First World War, and after armistice he stayed in France for some months playing taps on the bugle several times a day as bodies of American soldiers were interred in their final resting places. Maxyne told me that for the rest of his life, whenever Oral heard taps, tears would stream down his face.

In the 1930s, both Oral and Maxyne got jobs at radio station WOC in Davenport, Iowa. Maxyne told me, "There was the nicest young man who worked there. He was so cordial and would do anything to help someone. His name was Dutch Reagan." Of course that was Ronald "Dutch" Reagan, who much later became our president.

From that time until I met Oral and Maxyne, there is a gap of many decades during which their activities are totally unknown to me. I met the two in the 1980s, when I repaired that little Gilbert clock.

Maxyne told me that they moved to Cassville when Oral retired, because of the Cassville Golf Course, which was well-known as a great course. Oral would now have time to play golf all he wished, and he did enjoy the course for several years. At the time I met them, Oral was in a wheelchair having had a stroke. I do not remember him ever saying a word to me on the occasions I was in their home. Oral was born June 2, 1897, and died on July 15, 1987.

One time while I knew her, Maxyne got infected gums and went to see a dentist. She received abominable treatment. When Maxyne dressed up to go out, she put on fancy clothes in a style one might have seen in the 1940s, and put on too much rouge as elderly ladies used to do. The result was that she looked not unlike a bag lady one might see wearing outdated attire and pushing a shopping cart full of old clothes and aluminum cans.

The dental assistant took Maxyne back to an examining room and put her in a chair. The dentist popped into the room briefly and said, "You'll have to go out front and pay for this visit in advance before I examine you." Little did he know that Maxyne could probably have bought him five times over and had enough change left to purchase a Lincoln Continental.

Maxyne went out and paid, then came back to the room. The dental assistant took some X-rays. The dentist stepped in again. He did not examine Maxyne, but looked at the X-rays and told Maxyne that she needed an enormous amount of dental work. He outlined all the procedures they would do, the great number of visits this would require, and the great expense. Maxyne made an appointment for her next visit.

By the time Maxyne got home, she was so infuriated at her cavalier treatment that she decided never to go back and not even to call them and cancel the appointment. She asked herself, "What would Daddy tell me to do?"

Her late father was a physician. She said, "Daddy would tell me to rinse my mouth several times a day with hydrogen peroxide." Maxyne did exactly as Daddy would have told her, and within a week all her problems were cleared up, and she never had any more infections or tooth problems the rest of her life.

Shortly before Maxyne died, my friend Darrell Ledenham visited her in her home. He worked at that time for the Missouri Division of Aging, and so got to visit elderly people to see if they had needs. Darrell found Maxyne disgusted by her infirmities, especially her failing eyesight. She said, "I've been trying to balance my checkbook, and my eyesight is so bad that I can't even do that."

In her disgust she hurled the checkbook across the room to Darrell. She said "Just look at that mess!"

Darrell looked at it and said with a chuckle, "Yes, I guess you're right. This says that you have $347,429 in your checking account!"

Maxyne said, "Oh, that's good! I guess I did it right after all."

She told Darrell that she had no family and not much to live for. She went on to say that she had left her estate to the College of the Ozarks. Darrell asked, "Did you go to school there?"

Maxyne said, "No, Oral and I drove through that campus once. We saw the chapel's stained glass windows from the outside and we both just loved them. I have always remembered the joy they gave us."

After Maxyne died on September 29, 1995, her lawyer, Senator Emory Melton, called me to say that Maxyne had indeed left her entire estate to the Ralph Foster Museum at College of the Ozarks—with one exception. She left her little Gilbert clock to me, and I could pick it up at his office next time I was in Cassville.

Linda Barton Riled

Linda Barton did not suffer fools gladly. I stopped by Barton's Service Center in Aurora, Missouri, on March 20, 2009, to check on our car. While standing and chatting with Blackie Barton, I heard Linda Barton royally telling off someone on the phone.

One of Bartons' employees had paid off a bill months before, and this collection agency kept calling the shop month after month demanding payment for the already paid account. The day before, Linda had sent them a FAX of the final receipt marked PAID, proving that the account was settled; and they promised never to call again. Then the very next day, while I was present, they did—and received just the earful they deserved.

Listening to Linda reaming them out, I commented to Blackie, "Man! I wouldn't want Linda mad at me!"

He said, "You're a wise man there. Linda is a terror when she gets mad."

Blackie told me a funny story. A few days previous, Linda was riding in a car driven by a girlfriend of hers. They had been to a meeting in another town and were on the way back home when the car conked out a few miles from Aurora. Of course Linda, in the shotgun seat, called Blackie to come with the tow truck. In a few minutes a van pulled in behind them, and a man got out, came to the driver's window, and gave Linda's friend his card. He said, "I'm a mechanic, and I fix cars at people's homes or wherever they are. Do you want me to fix your car?"

"No, thank you!" said Linda's friend. "We called Blackie Barton, and he's on the way."

The man said, "Oh, you shouldn't have called him. Blackie Barton is a big gyp and doesn't even know what he's doing."

Before the words had even died out of the air, Linda boiled out of her door and rushed around the car to confront the man and give him a piece of her mind. Trying to defend himself, he said, "Wait a minute, Lady! I know Blackie Barton."

Linda shouted, "You don't know him as well as I do. I sleep with him every night. I'm Blackie Barton's WIFE."

The mechanic said, "Oh! . . . Oh! . . . I meant Blackie PERIMAN! Blackie PERIMAN—NOT Blackie Barton!—Periman! Periman! PERIMAN!"

Such quick thinking probably saved his life.

Gretchen's Grit

Ross and Gretchen McKinley were well-known farmers and merchants in the vicinity of Wheaton and Rocky Comfort, Missouri. For many years, they owned and operated the Wheaton Locker Plant. When we met her, Gretchen was in her eighties, and Ross had been dead for a year or so. She became a close friend to Judy and me and was "Granny Gretch" to our sons.

Gretchen enjoyed mystifying people by telling them that she was not born in the United States of America. After a suitable period of tantalizing, Gretchen would reveal, "I was born in Oklahoma Territory before it became a state."

Sure enough her birth certificate revealed that she was born Gretchen Valentine on December 7, 1904, in "Oklahoma I. T.," meaning "Indian Territory." Her birth certificate was paper, not chiseled on a stone tablet, as some wags claimed.

Like all elderly people, Gretchen had a wealth of charming and interesting stories to tell. Three of my favorites had to do with Gretchen driving or riding on one conveyance or another. The earliest of these took place when Gretchen was a small child living on the family farm near Hot Springs, Arkansas.

Among other livestock, Mr. & Mrs. Valentine had a herd of goats on their hilly farm, and the old billy goat had his bluff in on little Gretchen—or "Peggy," as her parents called her. Whenever he spied her playing in the pasture, he would lower his head and come charging across the field straight for her. Gretchen would run for her life.

By the time she was ten years old, she was spunky enough that she was no longer willing to put up with this outrage. When the big, old goat came rushing at Gretchen, head down, she stepped aside, grabbed his horns and swung onto his back. Gretchen rode the goat until he was ready to drop. From then on, it was the goat who tried to avoid Gretchen, and if she wanted a ride, she had to lie in ambush and grab the goat. Gretchen knew that her parents would frown upon her secret life as a goat-back cowgirl, so never told them about her rides. A couple of times her mother said, "Good gracious, Peggy! You need a bath. You smell like a goat," Gretchen looked innocent and laughed inwardly.

One time Gretchen came a cropper. She was probably getting too big for goat riding the day they were cantering along and the goat tripped, throwing Gretchen onto a rock pile. When her parents asked her how she got skinned up, Gretchen said, "I tripped." She never rode the goat again.

When Gretchen was fifteen, her cousin Jim came to visit on his Indian motorcycle with sidecar. Gretchen felt she must ride that motorcycle and talked her cousin into allowing it. After some brief instructions from Jim, Gretchen straddled the Indian and headed down the driveway. The Valentines had a long driveway, and right across the graveled country road from their driveway was the swanky home of Mr. and Mrs. Upjohn. The Upjohn property had a white picket fence along the road.

Gretchen roared down the driveway on the motorcycle and turned left. She was going too fast for the turn and leaned so hard to the left that she lifted the sidecar off the ground. As Gretchen straightened the motorcycle, the sidecar came down on top of the picket fence and took off every picket as she headed down the road. Mr. Upjohn came running out of the house and stood in the road yelling and shaking his fist, as Gretchen disappeared in a cloud of dust. She was not attempting a getaway, but simply could not remember how to stop the machine. When Gretchen reappeared in a few minutes, Mr. Upjohn was waiting for her, and by now she knew how to stop. Mr. Upjohn told Gretchen how she would spend the next day. Gretchen had to nail all 121 pickets back in place and give them a fresh coat of paint.

In the spring of 1923, when Gretchen was eighteen, her parents sold their property at Hot Springs and prepared to move to Missouri. At just that time, an elderly neighbor came to ask a favor. Elihu Snaggs had become a widower a few months before, and he told the Valentines, "I don't have any folks here, so I've sold my place, and bought me a brand new Model T Ford. I aim to move to Minnesota where my cousins live, but I ain't up to drivin' that fur by myself at my age. If Gretchen will drive me, I'll buy her a bus ticket back home and pay her twenty dollars to boot."

Gretchen, who was always eager for adventure, talked her parents into allowing her this trip. A few days later, Mr. Snaggs drove to their home in a shiny black Model T touring car laden with the personal property he had kept to start his new life in Minnesota. As Gretchen tossed her bag into the back and climbed into the driver's seat, her mother said, "Remember, we'll be leaving in three or four days for Missouri, so get your bus ticket for as close to Rocky Comfort, Missouri, as you can."

Gretchen and Mr. Snaggs headed northeast for Little Rock, then on towards Springfield, Missouri, and points north. There were no paved highways between Arkansas and Minnesota in those days, and they averaged less than twenty miles per hour. The elderly gent and the young lady stayed in hotels a couple of nights, but most of the time they camped along the road. They ate mostly foods they prepared, such as bacon and eggs, fried on a campfire, for breakfast and usually had bread or crackers with cheese, bologna, or sardines for lunch. A few times they dined in cafés. Many eateries had blue-plate specials which cost from five to twenty cents. Mr. Snaggs was careful with his money.

After about a week, the pair reached their destination, New Ulm, Minnesota. As Gretchen drove into the town, Mr. Snaggs quickly spotted a hotel and told Gretchen to stop there. He said, "Bring your grip, and we'll get you a room for the night, and I'll go on to my cousin's house. I'll pick you up in the morning and take you to the bus station, and you can be on your way back home."

The next morning, Gretchen checked out of the hotel and sat on the porch with her little suitcase, waiting for Mr. Snaggs. She waited and waited and waited. By noon she was sure that Mr. Snaggs had deserted her. She left word with the desk clerk and walked around the town looking for some trace of him. No one had ever heard of any family by the name of Snaggs, and Gretchen did not actually know the name of his cousins.

Gretchen had no money, so found a job as waitress in a café. She took a room at a boarding house and wrote to her parents at "General Delivery, Rocky Comfort, Missouri," to tell them that she had decided to stay in Minnesota awhile. In time she might ask her parents to send money for a bus ticket, but she hated to admit to them that she had been scammed. In addition, Gretchen did not wish to leave town without settling with Mr. Snaggs. Month followed month without a trace of the old man.

After Gretchen had been living in New Ulm for over three months, she went out behind the café one day to dump some garbage. Looking down the block behind the store buildings, her view only slightly obstructed by the scaffoldings of back staircases, she saw Mr. Snaggs drive up behind the bank, get out of his flivver, leaving the engine running, and go quickly inside. Gretchen opened the screen door to snatch her purse. She sprinted down the alley to the Model T, jumped into the driver's seat and drove to her boarding house. She too left the motor running while she rushed inside to her room and grabbed what belongings she could. In five minutes she was driving out of town and heading south. Gretchen had driven five miles before she noticed that she was still wearing her café apron.

As thrifty as she was, Gretchen's meager hoard of cash began to run out before she reached her destination. The Model T had an immaculate new spare tire, and Gretchen sold it for gas money to complete her trip.

In only four days, Gretchen drove into the village of Rocky Comfort, Missouri, and asked directions to her parents' new home. She sold the Model T for fifty dollars. I asked Gretchen, "Why didn't you keep the Model T?"

She replied, "I didn't want to have to give it back to Mr. Snaggs if he came looking for it."

"Wasn't it worth more than fifty dollars?" I asked.

"Oh, yes, quite a bit more," she said, "but I was worried that Mr. Snaggs would come and demand the car back, and if he did, I didn't want to give him any more than fifty dollars."

Gretchen need not have worried, as she never heard of Mr. Snaggs again. She sometimes speculated that a man with Mr. Snaggs's moral code eventually would wind up in a place with a climate considerably warmer than that of Minnesota.

Grocery Story

Most of my growing-up years were during the 1950s—the drought years when many farmers lost their property. My father had to take a job as an over-the-road trucker delivering Studebakers and other brands of cars to the west coast. We lived on a farm and went to town once a week to buy groceries. Since my father was gone most of the time, usually just Mama and I went into Aurora, Missouri, each Saturday morning. Sometimes my younger brother Denis went along, but he preferred to stay home and sleep in. After 1954 Mama had to lug along baby John.

There were two grocery stores in Aurora, the B&T Market, a privately established store, and the IGA, part of a chain. Mama would look in *The Aurora Advertiser*, the local newspaper, and make two lists based upon what each store had on sale that week and the items she had accumulated on the grocery list posted in her kitchen. Mama knew the supermarkets so well that she always wrote her final shopping lists in the order in which she would come to them in each store.

Before we left home, Mama wrote out a check to the B&T for $25, which in those days was ample for our shopping needs for the week. We always went first to the B&T, as we knew the owners, Messrs. Beck, Thurman, and Journagan, and they were very friendly. Mama paid with her check and received her change. She had the carry-out boy put the groceries in the trunk.

Next we headed for the IGA and got their sale items and whatever else was on that particular list. Mama paid cash out of the change from the B&T. She did not want either store to know that she shopped at the other store, so she had the IGA carry-out boy put the groceries in the back seat. After he went back in the store, we moved the IGA groceries into the trunk to snuggle up with the B&T groceries.

After a stop at the Ben Franklin dime store for sundries, we were done and headed home. Sometimes while Mama was shopping I would visit second-hand stores on Madison Avenue, which is Aurora's main street. Even then I liked to buy junky little bargains. When I saw our car in front of the Ben Franklin Store, I would head over there and meet Mama for the trip home.

In the IGA and on the street, we sometimes saw an old lady that we called the "Axe-Handle Lady." I say "old," but she was probably only in her sixties. She was what we would now call a bag lady—poorly dressed with unkempt grey hair. We called her the Axe-Handle Lady because she used an axe handle for a cane.

Occasionally I would spring for a small jar of stuffed olives, which cost eleven cents in those days. After we left the store I would eat every one after offering some to Mama, an offer that was never accepted. Another favorite cheap treat of mine was a small ten-cent can of Frank's Kraut Juice—a treat I could not enjoy until we got home so I could use the can opener.

One time when I was debating between olives and kraut juice, which were both in the pickle aisle, the Axe-Handle Lady came right up beside me to select a jar of dill pickles. I said, "I love olives and pickles."

The old lady said, "I always keep pickles. I like them, and I also keep the juice, and when I have a scratchy throat I drink the pickle juice. It helps to cut the phlegm," — which she pronounced "fleem."

One day I got a blessing as I saw an interesting vignette and was glad I was in the IGA at that particular moment. I was shopping with Mama that day, and we chose some fresh vegetables in the produce department. It is not part of my story, but I will mention that carrots in those days were sold in bundles with the feathery green tops still attached.

When Mama and I were in the produce department I saw a walking cane hanging on one of the display cases. It was not a fancy cane by any means—just a very common cane. A bit later when I was exploring around the store I saw the Axe-Handle Lady approach Mr. Wilson, the manager, walking with her axe handle but holding the errant cane in her other hand. She asked the manager, "Do you think this walking stick belongs to anybody?"

Mr. Wilson said, "Lady, that cane's been hanging back there for several days. I'm sure if anybody wanted it they would have come back for it. You take it and welcome, and you'll be doing us a favor to get it out of our way."

Ever after that the Axe-Handle Lady was sporting that cane as she walked the streets of Aurora.

The Axe-Handle Lady lived in a detached garage in Northtown—which is the wrong side of the tracks in Aurora. That dilapidated old garage was a hovel and hardly fit for anybody to live in. Years later, after I had moved away to college and gotten married, the Axe-Handle Lady's horrible home burned to the ground! Luckily she was unhurt. I hope she salvaged her cane, but there she was homeless, penniless, and now much older than when I knew her. The local lumber companies donated materials, and the men of Aurora volunteered their labor and built her a very sweet little house on the location of her former hovel. I am sure the Axe-Handle Lady must be long gone now, but I never knew her real name, so I will never know the end of her story.

Goose Walk

I thought of *The Wonderful Adventures of Nils* on my walk the first day of November, 2002. Selma Lagerlöf, who won the Nobel Prize for Literature in 1909, wrote the Nils book in 1906. It is one of the most charming children's books in any language. It tells about a schoolboy who miraculously shrinks in size one day in the farmyard. As the wild geese fly over, the domestic goose begins flapping its wings. Nils, not realizing he is now tiny in size, rushes to hold the goose and prevent its loss, but instead he is carried away to have adventures as he travels with the wild geese all over Sweden. This book and its sequel were commissioned by the Swedish government as a tool for teaching Swedish geography in the schools. Both volumes are still in print more than a century after first publication.

As usual, I drove south from home one mile and parked near an unpaved county road. I walked westward a mile, then back east to my vehicle. On my drive to the parking spot, I saw one V of geese fly over.

The temperature was only thirty-four degrees Fahrenheit, a keen north wind was blowing, and the sky was overcast. I was dressed warmly in a coat and felt hat, as I headed out briskly with my inevitable anti-dog walking stick.

The fall colors remained beautiful, with shades ranging from bright, fire-engine red and brilliant, florescent orange through pale and bright yellows to rusts and browns. Sprinkled here and there were the pale greens of some sheltered trees and the dark green of cedars. The browns were beginning to predominate, and soon our fall colors would be gone for another year.

A half-mile down the road, I heard the honking of geese, and looked up to see the biggest flock of geese I have ever seen. It must have numbered in the thousands. As the first hundreds of geese flew southward above my head, the huge flock of oncoming geese faded into nothingness northward, where they blended into the grey sky. And when the last of those geese arrived above me, the forerunners were lost in the greyness to the south. There was a break now and then, between one V and the next, so this may have been several large flocks flying together temporarily to form one huge conglomerate.

After another quarter mile, I heard goose calls once again, and saw a modest flock heading southeast. A little later, I saw two more flocks going in the same direction.

On the walk back towards my Suburban, I heard geese twice, calling from the south, but could not see them. They had already passed over, leaving our lowering skies for brighter ones in the south.

I walked by a farmyard with domestic geese, and the four adult domestic birds were running in their pen, flapping their wings. I had never seen them do this as I passed by on previous days. I assume that the numerous flocks flying overhead and calling to them had stirred their passions. The tame geese still had the instinct to follow the flock, though their bodies were too heavy to allow flight. There was no miniature schoolboy in the gooselot, but perhaps there was in me. The sight touched me in an unexpected way. The agitation of these earthbound birds seemed to embody the strange melancholy that accompanies autumn—a longing for adventures that can only be imagined—sights forever hidden, and a life that will never be.

Wound Too Tight? I Think Not!

When a clock will not run, about ninety percent of people think it is wound too tight! Innumerable times I have heard customers say, "I don't think there is anything wrong with this clock. I just wound it too tight."

Early in 1999, a lady named Mary Jo Raymond from Fayette, Missouri, some 275 miles north of our home, left a clock with friends in the nearby town of Aurora for me to pick up. It was a beautiful Ansonia iron mantel clock, nicely embellished with decorations, including a stylized urn on top. In the 1940s her father said he was tired of winding the clock and had a jeweler replace the excellent large Ansonia movement with an electric time-only Telechron fit-up. Mary Jo wanted the clock restored to original condition. I warned her that might take from now till forever to find the correct movement and gong, and she said, "No problem!"

The semicircular ghost of the gong base was visible on the floor of the clock, and I found the exact replacement very quickly in the gong box of my old friend Horace Foster. After searching several months, I acquired a beat-up, iron Ansonia case containing the exact movement I needed—an excellent movement, not damaged nor butchered by clock tinkers. I cleaned, bushed, and repaired the movement and tested the clock in my shop. On a trip to Columbia in 2000, we drove the extra thirty miles to Fayette and delivered the clock in person.

I established the clock on an upright piano and told Mary Jo all about the clock, how to wind it and how to run it. I suppose I gave her a sheet of directions, as that would be normal. I warned her that the floor of her house was rather shaky, and someone walking heavily across the room might stop the clock. Mary Jo assured me that her husband and son were even then starting the process in the basement of shoring up the floors and installing sturdy pillars.

Time passed and the earth turned.

About a year later, I got a phone call from Mary Jo. She said, "I'm afraid I must have wound that clock too tight, as it won't run."

"I'm really surprised to hear that!" I told her. "Once I've gone through a clock like that, made repairs, and even come to the house and set it up, I would never expect to hear of it again."

"Well, it won't run," she said, "and I'm sure it's my fault for winding it too tight."

I replied, "I don't think that could be the problem, as I wind all my clocks all the way to the top. Have you moved the clock to a new location, or is it just where I put it?"

"It hasn't been moved a bit since you set it up."

"Is the floor still shaky?"

"No, my husband and son have finished their work, and the floor is like bedrock."

I asked her about any other possibilities I could think of, but no problems became apparent. I was certain, in my heart, that there was nothing wrong with the clock, but I lacked the intuition or inventiveness to ask the right questions to get a clue as to why the clock did not run. I asked, "How long has the clock failed to run?"

Mary Jo said, "Oh, it hasn't run for months! It ran down while we were on vacation, but when I wound it, I could not get it to go."

She told me that she and her husband were going to Oklahoma and would come by my shop and drop off the clock. I said that I could very likely see what the trouble was when she got here, and that at any event she could pick up the clock on the way back from Oklahoma. I warned her to remove the pendulum before moving the clock, and then concluded, "There can't be anything much the matter with the clock after I have overhauled it and tested it out thoroughly."

One morning Mary Jo and her husband arrived, and I met them in the driveway, so that I could carry in the cumbersome clock. Mary Jo's husband sat heavily in the driver's seat, but Mary Jo got out and announced, "We didn't bring the clock!"

I asked in wonder, "Oh! Well, why not?"

Mary Jo replied, "You told me to take off the pendulum before I moved the clock. When I reached around and opened the back door to get the pendulum, I accidentally nudged it, and it started swinging, and the clock is running like a top. I didn't know you had to START the clock again if you let it run down. I thought if you wound it up, it would start itself!"

Her husband piped up, "I guess I should have thought to tell her that, when she said the clock wouldn't run. I just thought EVERYBODY knew you had to start the pendulum."

For someone well-versed in a particular field, it is sometimes difficult to ratchet the mind down low enough to delve the minds of absolute novices. This was one more lesson to me not to assume that the customer knows anything at all about clocks. I learned that I was dealing with a quintessential babe in the woods in the person of Mary Jo.

Later in the day, I saw old Danny Grant, who lives a mile north of us. He asked me through his prodigious white beard, "Did those people find you this morning?"

"Yes," said I, "but how did you know about them?"

Danny said, "They came from the north, driving towards your house, but they turned into my drive and honked their horn. I was out back, feeding the animals, but before I could get to them, out they backed and drove back north, the way they had come from. I went back to the animals again. Then here they came again, from the north, and turned in my drive and honked.

116

Either I was quicker or they were slower, but this time I caught them and sent them on south to you."

I told Danny, "I gave that woman very careful, simple, and explicit directions to our house over the phone and even had her write them down."

I went on to tell Danny the whole story, and he exclaimed bushily, "Why! A pendulum is like a plumb bob; it's just going to hang there unless you give it a swing! Everybody ought to know that."

Before the Raymonds left me, I had said to Mary Jo, "I'm sorry that you had to drive twenty miles out of your way to tell me this. Perhaps you could have phoned me."

She said, "I forgot to call you before we left home yesterday. I almost tried to phone you from our motel in Aurora, but I just knew I wouldn't be able to figure out how to work the motel telephone."

"I expect you made the right decision, simply to come in person," I assured her.

The Purple Pooch

The late Benton Baker lived twenty-five miles north of us, but his farm was twelve miles south of us, so he drove by our house almost daily. When Judy hung out a sign "Eggs for Sale," Benton began stopping once a week to buy farm fresh eggs.

Benton was a lively old man with an interesting past. He told us engaging and remarkable stories and facts about his life and old time happenings in these Ozark hills. We became good friends through the egg years.

One time Benton pulled in the driveway, and I came out of my shop to go in the house and get his eggs. Benton got out of his Ford pickup, leaving the motor running, and slammed the door, saying, "Well, shut my mouth! I just locked myself out of my pickup."

I said, "I'll go in and phone your wife, and she can bring a key."

Benton said, "My wife's not home. Give me a hammer."

I got a claw hammer from my shop, and Benton lustily smashed the triangular glass "wing" next to the pickup window, reached in, and opened the door.

One summer day around 1998, after he had been to his farm, Benton stopped and told Judy and me that he had gone to his sister-in-law's house and gotten her dog. The lady had Alzheimer's Disease and was headed for a nursing home. Benton said, "This dog came to her house as a stray. I speculate that it got run over and its leg broken, so the owner didn't want it anymore and dumped it."

Benton reached in his pickup, took out a purple, three-legged rag mop of a dog, and handed it to Judy. He said, "I don't know anybody else to give this dog to. You'll like him. He's a smart, high-powered dog, and well-trained."

While we stood with our mouths open, Benton climbed into his pickup and sped away, leaving us holding the dog. My whole life I swore that no animal would ever live within the walls of our house except mice, and even they would be unwelcome. But Tony, as I named him, was so small, smart, engaging, and well-trained . . . and, he had only three legs. Actually he had four, but one front leg had been broken and not set, so was curled up and useless. He had to be a house dog.

It was summertime, and Tony had so much thick, curly, purple hair that we had him trimmed. The dog groomer said that Tony was a purebred miniature poodle, and she gave him a puppy cut—short all over. Then he actually looked like a poodle. Judy claimed that Tony was grey, but he always looked purple to me. Besides, who wants a grey dog, but who would not want a purple one?

Even on three legs, Tony was frisky, agile, and fun to play with. His tail was a metronome that never stopped. Every evening as I sat in my easy chair and read, Tony sat squeezed in beside me. I had a short-lived job at that time driving a van and making deliveries for Flex Fleet, and I sometimes took Tony with me on the route. He enjoyed the ride and was company for me. He was never a smidgeon of trouble. Tony had been a woman's dog, and yet he seemed very fond of me.

I have always been allergic to animal dander. Poodles don't shed, and Tony had short hair, but after only a few weeks, it became obvious that we could not keep Tony in the house. My nose tickled and stopped up in his presence. He was a sweet little three-legged dog, and we would not make him live outside.

We did not know anyone who wanted a little house dog, so I wrote a newspaper advertisement: "Miniature purple poodle.

Friendly, well-trained, three-legged, house dog. Free to a good home."

Next day on my Flex Fleet route, I stopped at the *Aurora Advertiser* to put in my advertisement. The lady at the desk read my notice and said, "Our kids have been pestering us to death to get them a dog. Would it be possible for me to see this dog?"

I said, "Certainly! He's right out here in my van."

I brought Tony in, and the lady fell in love with him immediately. She said, "I'd love to have him. Would you let me take him home? And if my husband objects, I'll call you, and we can still put the ad in."

I agreed, and left Tony in the newspaper office. The lady never phoned me, so I assumed that all was well. However, just to be sure, I stopped in at the newspaper office about three months later when I happened to be passing by. I asked the lady, "How did it work out with Tony?"

She told me, "When I took Tony home, the kids were crazy about him. He is so good with children—playful and sweet natured. But when my husband came home from work he laid down the law. He said, 'That dog can be in the house when I'm not here, but when I'm here he has to be in the back yard, and he has to sleep outside.'"

"I guess that would be all right," I said, "if you have a nice back porch."

She said, "Let me tell the rest of the story. The children would always be playing with Tony when Ed got home from work, and Tony does like to play with the children, but it soon became clear that he really loves Ed. The kids would be playing with Tony, when Ed would come home. The kids would get interested in something else, and next thing I knew, I would peek into the living room, and there was Ed reading the newspaper with Tony snuggled up beside him. Before long Ed would forget to remind us to put Tony outside at night. Now, every day when Ed comes home and opens the door, Tony races across the room and actually jumps up into Ed's arms. He has a little bed on the floor on Ed's side of our bed, and Tony never leaves the house except to go to the bathroom or on family outings or outings with just Ed."

Tony got a happy home, and I saved the price of a newspaper advertisement.

The Baffling Builder

In the fall of 2012, Judy and I hit a big eight-point buck deer, doing over $6,000 in damage to our Suburban and dealing a death blow to the buck. After that time we suffered from "deerophobia," the fear of hitting another deer. Finally on October 23, 2013, we stopped at A&R Sales in Washburn, Missouri, to have a sturdy chrome deer guard installed on the front of our Suburban.

It took the men in the shop over three hours to install the deer guard on this pesky vehicle. During those three hours, Judy and I conversed between customers with Wes Roller, the owner of the business. I told Wes many interesting tales, and he reciprocated double. At one point Wes said, "If you want to hear it, I'll tell you a very strange tale. Looking back, I have trouble believing it myself, but I have to, since I lived it."

For several years Wes and his wife attended a church named Rock Spring Church. He said, "At some point, we just felt led to leave that church and start a new church. There was no argument or disagreement—just a feeling that we needed to move on and start a new church. Two other couples joined us in this mission. We were all in the fifty-year age range, and had no experience at starting a new church, but everything we did seemed blessed."

They began meeting in homes around Washburn, but soon the opportunity opened for renting a building. The church acquired a very good pastor, and the church thrived. The original six had promised the Lord, "If our church ever reaches a congregation of 160 and has everything paid for, we'll start another church."

They thought this a very unlikely prospect, but in a few years they had paid for the building and the land that it stood on, and they had a congregation of 180. The original group began looking for another building to start a new church, and they found it at Seligman. This was the old New Salem Church, built in 1861, and now sitting vacant. The Confederate soldiers had used the new church building as headquarters for a time, as they built barricades to impede the Union force marching from the Battle of Wilson's Creek at Springfield, Missouri, to engage in battle at Pea Ridge, Arkansas.

The old church building was still sturdy, but the foundation had disintegrated. Wes took several builders to look at the edifice and make estimates on putting a new foundation under it. No one would take the job. It was that sort of piddling job that takes lots of time and usually has unforeseen problems. Nobody would take it on.

In the meantime, Wes and his wife and *compadres* still attended the "180 congregation" church, which had an active food pantry for the needy. One day, the welfare office in Cassville phoned Wes to say there was a man who needed some food and especially needed some men's toiletry items. Up till this time no donations or shipments for the church's pantry had included any men's toiletry items, but that very week they had received a supply of these materials for the first time. So Wes said, "Send him on down."

The man arrived in a beat-up old car with a dog in the seat beside him. When he emerged, Wes noticed that he looked exactly like Charles Manson, but without the swastika on his forehead. Wes supplied him with some food and toiletries. Then the man asked him, "Is there any kind of work a man can get around here?"

Wes asked, "Can you do carpentry work?"

123

The Manson-like man answered, "I've done building work all my life."

Wes drove the man down to Seligman and showed him the church and outlined what needed to be done. The man said, "I can do that, if you'll let me live in the church while I work. I don't have any place else to stay."

Wes knew that the man rolled his own cigarettes, and said, "You can stay in the church, if you will agree not to smoke or drink alcohol inside the building. And I can afford to pay you $300 per week."

This deal was agreeable to both parties. It was Friday afternoon, and the man was to begin on Monday morning. Wes hauled a house jack, cement mixer, and other tools down on Saturday and arranged to have cement, lumber, and other items delivered at the old church building.

Tuesday morning Wes drove down and took some food plus a big sack of dog food. He found that in only one day of work the carpenter had dug the trench all the way around the church for the concrete footing. He had used a hand saw to cut some timber and make blocks. He had the church jacked up and resting on blocks. He said, "I need water to mix this cement." Wes was in the volunteer fire department and had several barrels hauled down and filled from the tanker truck.

Wednesday, Wes found that the carpenter was ready to begin pouring cement, having carefully removed the lower clapboards and scabbed on new studs where the old ones were rotted at the bottom.

Every day, Wes went down and found the carpenter making more progress. Each day he took more food and ice for the ice chest. On Saturday, Wes went down and told the carpenter that he was there to pay for the first week's work. The carpenter said, "No, not yet."

The work went on day by day, with Wes visiting and bringing food and seeing progress. The next Saturday, he drove down planning to pay the carpenter $600 for his two week's work. When he arrived, the carpenter was in one of the barrels taking a bath. As Wes arrived, he jumped out of the barrel, as naked as the day he was born.

Wes drove on up to the church to see that the carpenter was virtually finished. He might spend two or three more days with some finishing touches, but for practical purposes he had completed the job. The naked carpenter approached, and Wes told him, "I've come to pay you for your two weeks' work."

The carpenter said, "No, not yet. But I have to tell you that I'm going to need $3,000 a day for the rest of the work on this building."

Wes said, "Three thousand dollars a day! Where would I get that kind of money? I'm here to pay you what we agreed on, but I don't have any such money as $3,000 a day."

The carpenter ran into the church and came back out, still stark naked, carrying a huge knife with a blade a foot long. Wes got on the other side of his pickup, and as the carpenter came around the pickup, Wes moved to keep on the opposite side. They went around about four or five times, before Wes noticed a 2" x 2" board about four feet long on the ground. He picked it up, stepped away from the pickup, and said, "Don't you come near me with that knife, or I'll hit you."

The carpenter, knife upraised, slowly approached Wes, and when he was close enough, Wes brought down his board, cracking the carpenter on the top of the head. The latter dropped his knife and fell to the ground, but soon jumped up, picked up the knife, and ran into the church house. Wes stayed by his pickup, wondering what this crazy carpenter would do next.

After a time, the carpenter came out of the church, fully dressed, carrying his stuff, with his dog behind him. He got in the old car and drove away. Wes went in the church to find that the carpenter had taken only what he came with. All Wes's tools were there. The cooler full of food was there. The sack mostly full of dog food was there. He had taken nothing he did not bring with him.

Wes told me, "I never saw the man again. I wanted to pay him, but when I called the welfare office that had sent him, nobody remembered him or recognized his name. I know the lady quite well, who called me about toiletry items, and I asked to speak with her, but she claimed she had never phoned me! I know she was not purposely lying, so I don't know what to think."

In this way the old church was shored up and repaired at no cost for labor. Wes concluded, "We had been praying for help with that old building. I would have thought this was an angel that God sent to help us, except for that crazy behavior at the last. Surely there are not insane angels. If there were, God would cure them!"

The new congregation thrived and grew, and a young preacher was happy to take this church as his first ministry. The church seemed blessed, in spite of this outlandish beginning.

Chess Pie—Checkmate?

I have been checkmated many times while playing the game of chess. Years ago a chess expert tempted me to play a game, and he checkmated me in three moves. Once I was almost checkmated while making chess pies.

The Jenkins Fire Department had two fundraisers each year, a fall fish fry and a spring chili supper. That chili supper had a strange methodology. The volunteers who worked the phones elicited donated pots of chili from innumerable cooks, and on the night of the event, all the donations were stirred together into one huge pot. Judy and I did not attend these fundraising suppers, but we heard that the final blend was probably better than any of the donations. The total was greater than the sum of its parts.

When the volunteer called me, I always promised two pies for the pie auction. Our neighbor Pat always bought my pies, so I asked her what kind she wanted and then made them. She usually chose one pecan pie and one of another flavor, freezing both for a future holiday or expected visit. The pies brought ten to fifteen dollars apiece. One particular time Pat told me that she would not be having family visits soon, so she was not going to buy my pies that time. I decided to make two of those easiest pies of all, chess pies. There are only seven ingredients, which you whomp together, pour into unbaked pie shells, and stick in the oven. The cornmeal in the batter rises to the top and forms a beautiful golden crust over the top of the pie. So easy! And everybody loves chess pie.

I had some leftover pork roast, so decided to make a huge amount of pastry dough, use part of it for the two chess pies, and then make a pork pot pie for supper. We lived in a ramshackle, dilapidated house at that time, and our old electric cooking range matched the house. It was on its last legs, with only three burners working, and the oven door that stood slightly ajar unless we put a chair against it.

Each chess pie contains a half cup of real butter, so my opening gambit was to put two sticks of frozen butter in a bowl to microwave at a low setting. In the meantime I made my gigantic recipe of pie dough and began to mix up the chess pie filling. On a good day I can have two chess pies in the oven in a half hour, including making the pastry and batter, but this was not a good day. I was interrupted by four or five lengthy phone calls, plus a friend who came to the back door to discuss something. I felt like a pawn in the hands of talkative people. It took most of the morning to get my pies in the oven in between these interruptions. What a relief I felt, when I finally shoved the pies into the oven and propped the door shut with a chair! I was frazzled and ready to kick back and relax, after what felt like a whole morning of combat cooking.

Chess pies bake nearly an hour at a low temperature. After mine had been in the oven for a half hour, I leapt to my feet, rushed to the microwave, and yanked open the door. The melted butter was sitting in there, looking smug and innocent in its ceramic bowl. I slammed the microwave, hurled the chair aside, and wrenched open the oven door.

The pies looked beautiful with the butter-colored cornmeal crust covering them. I jerked them from their warm home and put them on the table next to the batter bowl in which I had mixed up their filling. After carefully dipping all the hot filling, lovely cornmeal crust and all, back into the batter bowl, I dumped in the melted butter, and beat it all together with the electric mixer. Back in the pie shells, and back in the oven, the pies baked another forty-five minutes until a toothpick came out clean when dipped in their middles. The pies looked all right, but they did not have a crust on top. The rich golden cornmeal crust had become absorbed by the pie filling. The pies looked and smelled good, but I donated them anonymously.

Years ago, I made several pies for a fundraiser that Judy was conducting for the junior class at Verona School, for which she was sponsor. I wanted my pies to stand out from all the other donated pies, so I wrote a little poem and put a copy on each of my pies.

Yummy Pies

I make my homemade pies from scratch,
The crust and filling, every batch.
Nobody asks if they are good;
By now that's simply understood.
Eat them hot or eat them cold;
They're fine both ways—or so I'm told!
~ Crusty Pieman

Previously I always put the poem on my pies for the Jenkins Fire Department, but that year I left off the poem and hoped nobody knew who made them.

After that hectic morning when the chess pies almost checkmated me, I looked forward to the tranquility of making my peaceful pork pie in the evening. It required peeling and chopping vegetables, and making gravy, but my pastry was in the refrigerator, ready to roll, and I did not have to follow a recipe for this dish. I was watching the evening news, cooking the big pot of vegetable and pork filling, and rolling out dough, when the phone rang. It was the income tax lady with a list of questions to ask me. She called right at the time when they were about to draw a winner on the local news for a book contest I had entered, so I had to un-mute the television for a minute before answering the rest of her questions. Somebody named David won the book. Finally I got shed of the income tax lady, got my crust rolled out, lined a 9" x 13" cake pan, dumped in the filling, and covered it with a top crust. Ready to bake! When I opened the oven to insert my pork pie, the door fell off on the floor! How would I bake this colossal pie with no oven door? We have all heard of the heat manifested by the hinges of Hades, but my oven door hinges were plenty hot too. After some intricate manipulation with potholders, I was able to hook the door tenuously in place, and with the help of a chair-prop, got the pie baked. Wow! It was delicious, and we both would have liked two pieces, had we not been trying to lose weight.

I had been checked, but not checkmated. My pies were neither stale nor stalemated. Whether those chess pies were any good, we will never know. We do know that the buyers will never imagine the trouble and turmoil through which they came into being. Nor will they ever know who made them. At least we hope not. Shhhhh!

Mark's Chess Pie

4 eggs	1½ cups sugar
2 tbsp. Cornmeal	2 tbsp. vinegar
1 tsp. vanilla	

⅓ cup cream or evaporated milk
½ cup melted butter

Beat eggs. Beat in sugar and meal, and then beat in other ingredients. Pour into unbaked 9" pie shell. Bake at 325° for 45-55 minutes, until toothpick inserted comes out clean.

Note: In place of the evaporated milk and 2 tablespoons vinegar, I have used 1/3 cup plain whole-milk yogurt and only 1 tablespoon vinegar. This saves opening a can of evaporated milk for 1/3 cup—if you have plain whole-milk yogurt on hand.

Old Ironsides, the Recurrent Clock

There was a beguiling antique store in the 1950s on West College Street in Springfield, Missouri. My father and I visited it a number of times. The large emporium was crammed with dressers, chests of drawers, bedsteads, chairs, dining sets, and every other kind of household gear you can imagine. None of that interested Daddy and me. We had eyes only for the antique clocks, and there was a plethora of them.

The store had mantel clocks, wall clocks, and grandfather clocks in numerous designs, and the great thing was that they were priced dirt cheap even for the 1950s. There was one huge light blond maple grandfather clock that impressed me, but I will not mention it, since we did not buy it. We did buy several clocks. If we had been smart we would have bought them all, as it would have been a wise investment.

My father bought a Seth Thomas Globe, which is a long-drop-octagon clock, for twelve dollars. It was eventually passed down to one of his granddaughters. Daddy also bought a Sessions two-train Westminster chime clock, likewise for twelve dollars. I soon told him that two-train chime clocks are gimmicky, so he traded the chime clock to Odis Bowling, who malapropishly called it "a charm clock."

My sister Shirley bought an oak grandfather clock case with a beautiful silvered dial engraved with Dutch scenes. At my suggestion, she bought a fine, Jauch triple-chime movement,

131

which I installed in the case for her. She rewarded me by buying me the book *Practical Clock Repairing* by Donald de Carle.

I was a teenager in the College Street Antiques days and very interested in clocks, so I bought two clocks. One was a walnut Seth Thomas "Hudson" 30-day clock, a large, square office or gallery clock. I was dying to have this clock because it had a seconds hand. I paid ten dollars for it. Someone had painted the case and part of the glass a dark green color, apparently using a broom for a paintbrush. The dial was damaged by someone trying to wash it. I refinished the solid walnut case and years later had the dial repainted. When Judy and I built our new house in 2008, this clock became a permanent adornment on one wall of the master bedroom.

I also bought a New Haven "Fortuna," a black-enameled iron mantel clock, with a torn paper dial and open escapement. I wanted this clock because of that visible "Brocot" escapement. I gave six dollars and fifty cents for the clock.

I cleaned the movement of the New Haven, and it ran perfectly. I installed a new bright white paper dial and put up a shelf in the dining room of my parents' house. I used cuckoo chains to shore up the shelf for supporting the weighty iron clock. My parents loved the clock with its loud, resonant strike, and they dubbed it "Old Ironsides." When I left for college in 1961 the clock was still ticking on its shelf.

Old Ironsides happily counted the minutes and announced the hours in the dining room for about fifteen years. In 1969 Daddy decided to remodel the house by ripping out the south end of the house and extending the domicile southward. He made a family room, hallway, bathroom, and utility room. Daddy demolished the very wall that was home to Old Ironsides for so long. He carefully removed the faithful old clock and stored it in an upstairs bedroom.

In 1983, Judy and I bought a mail order business and moved ourselves and our boys from Jonesboro, Arkansas, to a farm in Missouri. Eventually, I moved my remaining possessions from my parents' home the twelve miles to our farm. This included

Old Ironsides, which I set up in my shop to begin again telling the time and sounding the hours.

In the meantime, now that she lived on a farm, Judy could indulge her lifelong desire to dabble in horses and ponies. She wished to have enough equines to mount the whole family— herself, me, and the three boys. Somehow during her buying and bartering of horses, she acquired a cranky Welch pony named Champ. He was just the right size for a cart horse, so fed Judy's immutable desire for a pony cart.

Not far away in Butterfield, Missouri, there lived an incompetent cobbler and clock tinker named Elmo Oakenstaff. When he was not ruining shoes, boots, clocks, and saddles, he was trading and trafficking in all sorts of oddments. About 1986, he acquired a fine red pony cart and full set of harness, for which he asked $300. We were not long on cash, but Elmo said he would trade the cart and harness for a couple of clocks. This spelled doom for Old Ironsides! I traded Old Ironsides and a Kundo electronic clock for the cart and harness. It was actually a whale of a deal for us, as the two clocks had nowhere near the value of the cart and harness.

As a side note, I might mention that those Kundo electronic clocks with their glass dome and swinging shiny pendulum are good trading fodder. When we lived in Jonesboro, Lonnie Clark, our neighbor, tried to trade me a refrigerator for that same clock.

Since this is the story of Old Ironsides, the happy clock, I will not mention our unhappy rides in the pony cart. I will not tell with what joy Judy and I drove the pony and cart down the lane and back and across the highway and down the gravel road and home again. I will not even impart how Champ suddenly had enough of this nonsense and went racing about our farm uncontrollably with us bouncing, shouting, and pulling on ineffectual reins behind him until he finally dumped us out. Do not ask me to recount how we tried one more cart ride, and Champ ran into the woods with us, tipping us over into a brush pile!

We will merely say that, after we took a couple of pony cart rides, we decided to sell the cart and harness. Judy found a buyer at Washburn Prairie who paid her three hundred and fifty dollars for the rig. We did quite well financially in the pony cart escapade, but it brought about our last goodbye to Old Ironsides.

About twenty years after we said *au revoir* to Old Ironsides, I was burrowing about in Two Sisters Flea Market in Cassville, Missouri. My eyes started from my head at the sight of an exact duplicate of Old Ironsides! It was priced thirty dollars. I left the flea market cogitating on whether or not I should invest this sum in Old Ironsides II. By the time I reached home, I had concluded that I would be a fool not to.

I phoned Sandy, the proprietor and one sister of Two Sisters Flea Market, and told her to slap my name on that clock in Booth 45. Next time I was in Cassville I went to plunk down my thirty dollars, but Sandy told me, "That booth belongs to Rosemary Krause, and she said that since it was you that wanted it, you can have it for fifteen collars."

Incidentally, "Krause" means "ruffle" in German, but I do not know if that is what caused Rosemary to be so generous. As it turns out, the original price of the clock in the New Haven catalog of 1890 was $14.50—pretty close to what I paid 116 years later, thanks to the kindness of Rosemary.

Old Ironsides II loafed about in my clock shop unrepaired for a number of years. In 2017, I decided to cut way back on repair work for others and devote my skills to some of our own clocks, one of them being Old Ironsides II.

I dismantled the New Haven movement, cleaned and repaired it. I installed bushings where needed, and made new pallets for the visible escapement. I even made what I thought was a clever improvement that they should have done at the factory.

Every time Judy came in my shop and saw Old Ironsides II, she would say, "You ought to clean this case."

I thought, "What an outlandish suggestion! It's a black iron case, so how can she tell it even needs cleaning?"

Finally I decided to try to clean it just so I could say I did, not that I thought it was dirty. I began spraying Simple Green on the case and wiping it with paper towels. Oh, my heavenly days! When I would spray the Simple Green on the vertical surface and see it dribbling down, it was a river of brown which colored my paper towels as I wiped! I wish I would have known to clean the case before I installed the movement and dial, as I could have done a better job. I know exactly what caused this coating of brown, as I have seen it time and again on the glasses of clocks that lived in the homes of smokers. Old Ironsides II must have been in a home where six people smoked two packs a day for forty years to get this coated.

I moved the heavy clock to an honored place in our house. It ran beautifully with a strike as loud and vibrant as that of Old Ironsides I. Everyone who sees the clock is fascinated by the visible escapement, as the pallets jump back and forth allowing the teeth of the escape wheel to click past, one at a time. With the case cleaned and waxed and the movement renovated, Old Ironsides II became indistinguishable from the original I had bought sixty years before.

I was reminded of Joel 2:25 where God says, "I will restore the years that the locust has eaten."

Maybe the years are not quite restored; my beard is now white. But at least Old Ironsides is restored to us. It is almost as if we never took a pony cart ride.

A Good Plot is Hard to Find

Wayne Jesseph and L. E. May were married to sisters, Clorene and Thelma, respectively. When the two couples retired, they built homes across the highway from us. They became our beloved neighbors for many years.

Saturday, May 3, 2014, when Clorene went to her mailbox, she spied me sitting on the porch reading and adorned with a neck brace after recent spinal surgery. She came over to visit. Clorene called herself "your nosy neighbor." She liked to keep up with what we were doing, and also learn from us any neighborhood news.

In the course of the conversation, I asked how long ago Thelma died. I think Clorene said seven years. Thelma is buried out in Kansas. Her kids wanted to have their mother buried here in Missouri, but L. E. said, "We already have plots out in Kansas, and I don't want to waste them."

Somehow, this got us talking about cemetery plots, and Clorene told me that she bought plots for her and her late husband Wayne in Muncie Chapel Cemetery near Wheaton, Missouri, where her parents are buried.

Clorene said that the sexton gave her such funny looks when she went over to pick out their plots. He told her that in each section of the cemetery, the plots are sold in order till a section is taken up. The plot shopper can choose his section, but not the exact plots he wishes.

First the sexton showed Clorene plots at the front of the cemetery. She said, "No, no, no! This won't do! This is too close to the highway, and I can never sleep well with all that traffic going by."

The sexton rewarded this comment with a suspicious squint. Then he showed her plots in another section. She said, "No, I don't want to be here. This is too low. Why, it's practically a sink hole, and I can't swim."

Again the sexton looked at her quizzically. The third plots he showed her were under a big tree. He said, "This is a nice shady spot to be buried."

Clorene said, "I'm afraid not! That tree will send roots all around my coffin and grip it tight. I have claustrophobia, and that would make me very uncomfortable."

The old sexton said, "Lady, I want you to have plots you like, but by the time you're here, none of the things you're worried about will actually bother you."

Clorene finally told him that she would prefer to be in the section where her parents were buried, if there were plots available. There were, and she bought four. Then she noticed that her other sister and husband are buried right in the next row, as close as can be. She said, "I'll enjoy being so close to family."

"I'm sure they will feel the same way," said the sexton, admitting defeat.

Some Don't Wait

"Fish and visitors smell in three days."
~ Poor Richard's Almanack, 1736

We used to hear a lot about Hortense Gorsley, who lived a few miles north of us. Our friend Darlene was a neighbor of Hortense's. Darlene spent quite a bit of time trying to avoid Hortense, and still more time telling us about the occasions when she failed.

Hortense Gorsley in those days was in her early sixties, stout and square of build, with iron-grey hair and a ceaseless voice. If Darlene ever allowed her entry to her home, Hortense attached herself like a barnacle and was nearly impossible to extricate. Darlene felt sorry for her and tried to assist her in times of need, by telephoning neighbors, in an effort to enlist them to help Hortense. The effort usually failed, as no one who knew Hortense was willing to have contact with her. She was a person that not even a mother could love. Hortense lived with her aged mother, and they cordially hated each other. Darlene said, "They can't stand each other, because they're exactly alike."

Hortense was divorced from Garman Gorsley, a corpulent, unpleasant, and unattractive man, who lived five miles south of us. Many of the stories Darlene told us involved Hortense's constant fraternization with her former husband. Indeed we saw Hortense's rattletrap car coming and going past our house on the way to and from Garman's mobile home. Garman was verbally abusive to Hortense, but seemed to hold her in thrall. When Darlene scolded Hortense about these visits, she replied, "I don't believe in divorce, because of my religion, so I still consider myself married to Garman."

Hortense did not share information on a need-to-know basis, but on a need-to-tell system . . . and she needed to tell everything to everybody. Her injudicious prittle-prattle cost Hortence her job more than once. Having to hear the details of Hortence's indiscretions was one reason Darlene shrank from her company.

Darlene moved away from Hortense's neighborhood, became divorced herself, and later was remarried to a man named Kenny. Judy and I had not heard the name of Hortense Gorsley for ten years, when Darlene telephoned to tell us a new story about this auld acquaintance.

Just before 3:00, on a Monday afternoon in 2005, Darlene was in the bedroom, reading and waiting for Kenny to arrive home from work. She and Kenny had planned an amiable afternoon and evening. They would go to the bank, then to Walmart to get Kenny's prescription, and then to the grocery store to do a leisurely shopping. After they got back home, they would have supper and then saddle up two horses for a pleasant evening ride on the country roads near their home. So Darlene was happy when she heard a car door slam, and thought, "Ah! He's home!"

She went eagerly to the window and looked out. She had to grab the window frame for support, when she saw Hortense Gorsley fumbling with the little gate into the yard. Her first thought was, "Oh no! She'll ruin our evening together, and I just can't take it!" Her second thought was, "Oh no! The front door is unlocked!"

Not a person to let I dare not wait upon I would, Darlene raced down the hall, threw herself to the floor, and crawled commando fashion across the living room carpet below window level, to reach up and turn the lock. She scrabbled back across the floor and hid in the bathroom as she heard the first ominous knock on the door and rattling of the doorknob, as Hortense tried to gain entry. While Darlene quavered in the bathroom wondering how Hortense had found out where she lived now, Hortense kept up a barrage on the door, yelling, "Darlene! It's Hortense! Darlene! Are you home?"

The assault on the door continued for several minutes, and from time to time Darlene could even see a foreboding shadow on the living room floor, as Hortense peered into a window. At last Darlene heard the most horrifying sound of all. The front door opened, and Kenny called cheerfully, "Darlene, you have a visitor!"

Darlene went resignedly into the living room to join Hortense and Kenny, feeling the same way Professor James Moriarty might have felt when entering the parlor at 221B Baker Street, to find Sherlock Holmes and Dr. Watson waiting expectantly for him. Hortense proclaimed, "I brought the wedding present I got for you."

Kenny, Darlene, and Hortense sat around the kitchen table, and Hortense began telling them everything that had happened during the past ten years. Her hair was white now, but she was still robust, sturdy, and in good voice. After sitting and listening to Hortense's abrasive voice for an hour and a quarter, Darlene, who had fibromyalgia, was stiff and uncomfortable.

Kenny and Darlene were distressed not only because of the hard chairs, but also due to the rank odor attendant with Hortense. Sometimes when Hortense was not looking, they would glance at each other, raise their eyebrows, and silently mouth the letters, "B. O."

They learned from Hortense's perpetual prattle that the smell was not due exclusively to her lack of personal hygiene. Hortense described in rich detail her elderly pet dog that awaited her at home. This ancient canine was blind and toothless. He was confined to a box in Hortense's home. The prehistoric pooch had lost control of his bowels and bladder, so that his fur was encrusted with excrement. Doubtless he added a rich aroma to the environment of Hortense's home.

Darlene said, "I'm in pain from sitting so long on this hard chair. I just can't sit here any longer."

Darlene vainly hoped that Hortense would take the hint and leave, but Hortense said amiably, "Let's move to the living room where it's more comfortable."

Suiting action to word, she went and plopped down in a recliner. Darlene and Kenny did not know what to do, but follow her and lounge comfortably on couch and easy chair to listen to more of Hortense's endless updates. After sprawling in the recliner for a few minutes, Hortense exclaimed, "Oh! Oh! Oh! I'm getting a leg cramp!"

Darlene said, "Maybe if you stand up and walk around, the cramp will let up."

It took both Darlene and Kenny to heave the heavy Hortense out of the chair, and she hopped around the room, shaking the moorings of the house, and complaining vociferously. Eventually Hortense could no longer take the pain of standing, but fell to the floor, rolling about, writhing and screaming, "OH, I'M IN PAIN, I'M IN PAIN! OH ME! I CAN'T STAND THE PAIN!"

Darlene tried to get the old lady to go into the bathroom and take down her slacks and rub liniment on the cramp, but Hortense would do nothing but roll around in the floor screaming. Darlene got the heating pad, turned it to high, and tried to get Hortense to hold it on the cramp, but Hortense continued to scream and spin like the hand of a giant clock on the floor. Darlene tried to apply the heating pad, but as Hortense wallowed about, she kicked, so that attempting to minister to her was as dangerous as approaching a bad tempered mule. Darlene tried to massage the cramp, a task she found unpleasant, since Hortense was so smelly, but this proved impossible and dangerous, due to the kicking. Darlene afterward commented, "Her behavior reminded me of someone in labor without the benefit of Lamaze training."

Finally Darlene asked, "Do you need to go to the emergency room?" Hortense said that she did.

Darlene and Kenny managed to wrestle the combative old lady off the floor, out the door, and into their car. They drove her to the emergency room and sat with her, waiting to see a doctor. They waited with Hortense for two hours, and she still had not been admitted to an examining room. It was now after 7:00 p.m., and Darlene told Hortense, "I have hypoglycemia, and I'm getting sick from lack of food. I simply have to go get something to eat. And also, we need to go to Walmart to pick up Kenny's prescription."

"Oh, don't leave me! Don't leave me!" Hortense beseeched.

Darlene said, "We'll be back, but we have to go for awhile."

Hortense entreated, "Don't forget me!"—as if God, in His mercy, was likely to grant them any such boon.

When Kenny and Darlene returned at about 8:00 p.m., Hortense had been taken to an examining room, but had not yet seen a doctor. Darlene made a nurse promise to phone her when Hortense was ready to leave, and she and Kenny made their break for home.

Back home Kenny and Darlene discussed the problem of getting Hortense and her van back to her own home, should she be unable to drive. Kenny said, "Just wake me up, even if it's midnight, and I'll follow you in her van when you take her home."

Darlene said, "No, you won't! You're exhausted, and you have to get up at four o'clock a.m. to go to work."

So Kenny went to bed at 8:30. Darlene decided she could take Hortense home and let her find some neighbor to bring her to pick up her van the following day, if such was necessary.

The nurse called Darlene about 10:15, and said that Hortense was ready to leave, so Darlene drove back into town and fetched her. Hortense was able to drive, indeed was eager to get home to her old dog, so went on her merry way about 11:00, approximately eight hours after she had first graced Darlene's threshold.

Darlene concluded her story to me with, "So that was what Kenny and I did instead of the fun evening we had planned to spend together."

I said, "You left out the most important detail. What did Hortense get you for a wedding present?"

Darlene replied, "It's actually something quite cute. It's a wooden napkin holder with salt and pepper shakers that fit in slots. It even matches our cabinets. We paid dearly for it, but it is something we need. Kenny dropped our salt shaker and broke it a couple of days ago."

Needless to say, when Kenny broke the salt shaker, he had not thrown a pinch of salt over his left shoulder.

The Cuptomaniac

I enjoy buying mugs at flea markets. My wife Judy tries to quell this urge, since the mug section of our cabinet is stuffed to the brim. Periodically, as my luck at flea markets flourishes, I have to carry a load of the less desirable mugs out to what our sons used to call "the mug vault," a couple of shelves in my shop.

In the 1990s, Judy and I were members of a Christian Church in another city. We took our turns holding Wednesday night Bible study in our home once a month. I enjoyed setting out a display of my choicest mugs, for our guests to have coffee and snacks. Excitement ran high one week, as I had just purchased a pair of enchanting mugs decorated with antique bicycles. One mug had green bicycles, while the other featured red ones.

A few days after Bible study, as I fixed breakfast, I decided to serve Judy and myself our hot tea in that pair of bicycle mugs. I could find only the red one. I tried to remember whether I had carried the green one out to my shop with coffee or tea, as I sometimes did. In the following days, we searched my shop, the kitchen cabinets, the pantry, indeed, the entire premises for that mug. Judy even made the ridiculous suggestion that someone at the Bible study might have purloined it. We both had to laugh at this silly notion; no one would come to a Bible study and steal a cup!

Early the next Sunday at church, members began to gather for our monthly board meeting. As I settled myself at the table, our friend Melvin came in with a cup of coffee from home . . . and the coffee was in our green bicycle mug! "Melvin!" I exclaimed, "That's our mug! We've been looking everywhere for it."

He said casually, "Oh, is this yours? I wondered where I got it."

A minute later Judy came in and exclaimed, "Melvin! That's our mug! We've been looking everywhere for it."

Melvin, clearly offended, said, "I was going to drink my coffee from it, but if you're going to make a big deal over it, I'll use another cup and give it back to you right now."

"Good!" I said. "Do that!"

Later we learned that innocently stealing mugs was simply the way Melvin lived. His wife Barbie was harried by Melvin's cuptomania. Strange mugs constantly showed up at their house, and Barbie tried, often unsuccessfully, to find the rightful owners. Barbie herself could not keep a set of matching mugs. Her set gradually dwindled as Melvin carried away mugs of coffee and left them in unremembered locations.

The odd part about Melvin's affliction was his attitude. Melvin acted as if everyone else was dreadfully eccentric to worry about such a trifle as coffee mugs. As our boys used to say about certain slackers at school, "He just don't care!"

Melvin's behavior in all other areas was at variance with his devil-may-care outlook toward coffee mugs. He was scrupulously honest in every other aspect of his life. Melvin had a demanding and responsible job, in charge of the physical plant at a window factory. He was a deacon in the church and the chairman of the Church Maintenance Committee. He did a splendid job of organizing and supervising building projects and repairs at the church and in his factory job. He had a keen mind, filled to bursting with data, facts, timetables, and projects that he was coordinating. He simply seemed to feel that cups and mugs were beneath his notice.

Barbie told Judy and me that one day Melvin went to the break room at the factory to get a cup of coffee. He saw a mug on the shelf and thought, "Oh, there's a mug from Barbie's set. I must have brought that to work." He filled it with coffee and started back toward his office. As he passed through one area, a lady yelled, "Melvin! Where are you going with my coffee cup?"

He said lamely, "Oh, I thought it was my wife's."

The other employee said, "Well, it's not your wife's. Take it back right now and put it where you got it."

Barbie confided, "I *am* missing some mugs from my set, but I guess that wasn't one of them."

Barbie solemnly related details of surprise raids on their house by Melvin's mother, who periodically searched Barbie's cupboards and took back mugs that belonged to her. I bought four attractive mugs at a flea market and gave them to Barbie. She appreciated them, but said she wished she could get ones to fill out her set. She said, "Once this week, when I washed the dishes, I found I had lost another mug, but wound up with one mug and two bowls I had never seen before, and Melvin doesn't know where he got them."

This meant that we had to keep an eye on our bowls, as well as our mugs, at subsequent Bible studies.

On a later occasion when we arrived at church, we beheld a fancy stainless steel travel mug on the counter. Someone had stuck a note on it saying, "This is Melvin's."

Later an elder came to me with the mug, and asked, "Is this your mug."

"No," I said, "It had a note on it saying it was Melvin's."

The elder said, "I asked Melvin, and he said he had never seen it before!"

"Ask Barbie," I told him.

Later, I saw Melvin drinking from the stainless steel mug, and he even kept track of it for three or four weeks. This was Barbie's latest attempt to deal with Melvin's cuptomania. She thought that if she bought him an expensive mug, his pride of ownership would make him understand the value that others placed on their mugs. But the stainless mug eventually went the way of all mugs, since it was not handcuffed to Melvin's wrist.

I admit that even "misdemeanor" may be too dire a designation for Melvin's annoying behavior. Still, I got a certain satisfaction from fantasizing the police surrounding Melvin and arresting him, as he sipped from stolen plunder. My favorite part of the fantasy was Melvin being booked at headquarters and standing for mug shots.

Grandpa's Crosstie Business

My grandfather, Washington Irving Meadows, was born in 1875 and died in 1954, when I was ten years old. When anyone asked him his name, he always said, "They call me 'Wash.'"

Grandpa moved so-o-o-o slo-o-o-wly that he reminded my parents of the joke wherein the old man comes into the house and says, "I saw a snail on the roses.

His wife asks, "Did you kill it?

"No," he replies, "it got away."

Yet, Grandpa claimed that his nickname as a young man was "Lightning," because he was so quick at everything. At the end of his life, after Grandma was killed in a traffic accident, Grandpa lived with us. I spent hours sitting in the porch swing reading to him, as his eyesight was failing. When I came to a word I did not know, I would spell it to Grandpa, and he would pronounce it and tell me what it meant. There was never a single word that he did not know.

Among the interesting things Grandpa told me were two riddles, which he probably learned in the 1880s when he was a boy.

What is round and flat and brown as a fiddle
And has a little spot right dab in the middle?

As I was walking down the road,
I met a man with a heavy load.
He tipped his hat and drew his cane,
And in this riddle, I said his name.

Grandpa told me that his first money-making enterprise was cutting railroad ties in the late 1890s. The railroads were expanding, especially in the western United States, and every mile of track required 3,500 crossties. The Missouri and Arkansas Ozarks were prime suppliers of railroad ties. It was a poor agricultural region that had plenty of oak trees and many needy men who were glad to do the hard work of tie cutting to feed their families. In 1912, a few years after Grandpa's experience, the railroads bought 15,000,000 hand-hewed ties made in Missouri.

Grandpa mentioned in passing that his mustache was so long in his tie-making days that he could curl the tips around his ears! Young Wash would fell the trees and cut them into eight-foot lengths with a one-man crosscut saw. He would split them if necessary, with wedges and a mall, and then hew out the ties with a twelve-inch broadaxe weighing six or seven pounds.

Wash carried each tie on his shoulder up out of the hollow where he was working, sometimes a quarter of a mile or more, to the wagon road. Imagine his strength to be able to carry a green oak tie in that manner! Wooden ties are made in various sizes for different types of rail lines, but the smallest standard tie is six inches by eight inches by eight feet long. A green oak tie this size would weigh close to 200 pounds.

When Wash got a load, he would stack them on his wagon and drive some twenty miles from Bull Creek to the railroad at Ozark, Missouri, to sell them. This was about a forty-mile round trip in a wagon pulled by two horses over poor dirt roads. The pay at the time for all this hard labor and time consuming cartage was a nickel a tie!

The rule of thumb for horse-drawn transport is that each horse can pull about a ton. This means that Wash could carry twenty or twenty-one ties, depending upon whether he stacked two layers of ten or three layers of seven. At any rate, each load was worth about a dollar. At this time some laborers were glad to get work that paid fifty cents per day. A good tie cutter could cut up to twenty ties in a day, so this puts the operation in perspective.

The railroad men would look at the ties as they unloaded them, and would always reject three ties as not meeting their standards. Wash would take his money and his rejected ties and leave. When he got into the woods outside Ozark, he carried the three ties into the forest and put each one up across the limbs of a tree to keep it off the ground. When Wash came with his next load of ties, he would retrieve the three rejected ties and mix them into his load.

At the railroad, the tie buyers would examine the ties and reject three of them as usual, but not the same three they had rejected before. Wash would repeat the process each time of stowing the rejects in the woods and picking them up for the next load.

Grandpa laughed and told me, "And do you know what? When I decided to get into another line of work, and took my last load of ties to the railroad, they bought every tie! So I never cut a single tie that I did not get paid for."

Riddle answers: spot tick and Andrew — in case you didn't guess.

Greyhound Greyhairs

I never would willingly spend time in a bus terminal waiting room. The chairs are uncomfortable. The temperature is never just right. The décor and choice of colors are depressing. The room always smells of disinfectant and looks as if it needs another dose. People, who themselves might benefit from a treatment of disinfectant, tend to haunt these rooms. Some of the people in bus terminals are not waiting for a bus, but go there because they have no place to go. The food in bus terminal cafeterias is overpriced and unappetizing.

The minutes and hours drag by slowly, as the captive traveler reads a book, checks his watch, paces the floor, re-examines the bus schedules, checks to be sure which pocket contains his ticket, watches the other detainees (always an odd lot), gets a paper cup of woebegone coffee, tries once more to concentrate on his book, and begins again the cycle of trying to kill time which refuses to die.

Bus travel itself is not for the faint of heart. This mode of travel is tiring and uncomfortable. One cannot sleep peacefully and wake up refreshed on a bus. The tiny bathroom is jostling and smelly. The schedules for transferring to another bus always seem to work out with a breathtaking five minutes to make the connection or an endless seven-hour wait for the next bus. The average person arrives at his destination, disheveled and grateful to be off the bus and out of the terminal, and hopeful that he will never have to ride a bus again. But some people are exceptions.

Several years ago, Greyhound Bus Lines offered a "senior pass" at a reasonable price to elderly customers. This pass allowed the bearer to ride anywhere, anytime, on a Greyhound bus for thirty days. It was intended to allow Grandma and Grandpa to go anywhere in the country to visit children and grandchildren. They could stay for two or three weeks and still have time to come home on their thirty-day passes.

When my uncle and aunt, Lee and Esther, heard about the senior pass, they were ecstatic. Uncle Lee was in his eighties, and Aunt Esther was in her sixties. They bought the senior passes several times, but they did not use them as intended. They did not go to a destination and back again. They simply lived on busses for thirty days at a time. Someone at the station in Seattle might notice a rumpled, elderly couple boarding a bus. A week later, passersby in Fort Lauderdale might see the same couple changing busses. There were sightings of the couple in Texas, Maine, Idaho, and . . . well, you get the idea. In fact, only the size of the United States and the length of a month limited their travel itinerary.

Their relative anywhere in the country might receive an unexpected phone call, with the cheerful news, "We're right here in town at the bus station! Can you come down and pick us up?"

Sometimes, the relative did not receive this much notice, but answered the doorbell to find the smiling, travel-worn couple standing on the doorstep. Aunt Esther was an expert at negotiating a lift from local people disembarking from a bus. The visits never lasted longer than overnight, but gave Aunt Esther and Uncle Lee a chance to bathe and have some home-cooked food. They considered any time spent off the bus a waste of their tickets, so were eager to get back to the station and continue on their endless excursions.

Radio commentator, Paul Harvey, said, "Any self-made millionaire knows that he can't live like one." Uncle Lee and Aunt Esther had plenty of money, but did not believe in living high on the hog. They would never dine at the bus station cafeterias, as they considered the food too pricey. Rather, they would use the designated lunch stop to walk to a nearby greasy-spoon café or fast-food eatery in their search for inexpensive provender.

One time in Kansas, they had left the bus station to forage for food, and were on their way back, when they saw their bus leave the station and head out of town! They had their passes in their pockets, but their luggage, battered though it might be, was on the bus. They ran towards the station, not knowing what they would do. At the first intersection, there was a car waiting at a traffic signal. Uncle Lee and Aunt Esther ran to the car, snatched open the back door, and leapt inside. "Follow that bus!" ordered Aunt Esther to the startled man behind the wheel.

"Why . . . why, I can't follow that bus," protested the driver.

"Yes, you *can* follow it, and *you have to catch it*," urged Aunt Esther. "All our luggage is on that bus. Now GO! And be quick about it!"

The driver went and quickly. With Aunt Esther's encouragement, the gentleman proved born to the task of chasing busses. In no time he had run the bus to ground and pulled alongside honking his horn. Aunt Esther waved a handkerchief out the window and showed her face. The bus driver pulled over, and the couple parted from their newfound friend and boarded.

The unknown hero not only had the high adventure of chasing a bus at breakneck speeds, but received a monetary reward as well. Aunt Esther had left two dollars on the back seat of his car.

Inventors and innovators usually do not devise the perfect new technique or formula on the first try. Uncle Lee and Aunt Esther were no exception. Their system of buying two senior-citizen bus tickets was just the first, imperfect step towards their goal of limitless, cheap bus travel. They eventually invented an improved plan.

In the new plan, they bought only one thirty-day bus pass. They got it under Uncle Lee's name, since "Lee" can be either a man's or a woman's name. Aunt Esther took the ticket and headed for the wide-open spaces, leaving Uncle Lee to cool his heels at home. If any official questioned why her driver's license had one name and her bus ticket another, she merely claimed that she went by her middle name, which was "Lee." Aunt Esther was never short on bravado.

After Aunt Esther had stayed on the bus for fifteen days, traveling the width and breadth of the land, she would wind up on a pre-arranged date to change busses in Springfield, Missouri. Uncle Lee would drive to Springfield, suitcase in hand. Aunt Esther would step off of one bus, and hand Uncle Lee the ticket. He would board another bus and enjoy fifteen days on the road. Aunt Esther would drive the car home and spend fifteen days of peace and quiet devising her next adventure.

Possibly the most ingenious stratagem was the Hopscotch Plan. This game plan depended upon the fast and efficient mail service we had in those days. For example, Aunt Esther would take the solitary thirty-day bus ticket and ride to the home of some relative that would welcome her visit for a few days. When she reached that destination, she would mail the bus ticket back to Uncle Lee. He would travel to meet Aunt Esther. She would take the ticket and head for the home of another relative.

Uncle Lee and Aunt Esther embodied the saying that traveling leaves you speechless, but turns you into a storyteller. They were welcome visitors in every home, with their endless, interesting tales. No matter what problems they faced, they were never sad or depressed. Uncle Lee and Aunt Esther were happy, cheerful spirits who brought life and encouragement to every home they visited.

Uncle Lee would stay with Relative Number One and watch the mail for the bus ticket. He would join Aunt Esther at the home of Relative Number Two and give her the ticket. They would repeat this process, hopscotching across the United States, as long as the thirty-day ticket and supply of relatives held out. As expiration approached, one of the couple would head home to Marionville, Missouri, and mail the ticket back to the home of the last relative visited, in time for the other party to make it home.

Suddenly one day when Lee was about ninety, he felt terrible pain in his eyes. He had never had his eyes examined in his entire life. Aunt Esther rushed him to the local optometrist, who proclaimed that Uncle Lee had advanced glaucoma. Even with treatment, Uncle Lee's eyesight deteriorated rapidly, and soon he was almost blind, certainly too visually impaired for endless wanderings on a bus.

The fun ended and the perfected plan fell into disuse. There are bright stars in every field whose hope is unfulfilled. We think of Mozart, John Keats, Edgar Allan Poe, and others. We must add Uncle Lee and Aunt Esther to the list. They were sailing high, but were brought down at the zenith of their gallivanting zeal. Now the world must await another genius to create those breakthroughs in the travel industry, which were doubtless at the thresholds of their teeming minds.

Even after Uncle Lee departed this life, Aunt Esther retained her love of the open road. Age limited the length and frequency of her travels, but not their enjoyment. On one of her visits to her son Jerry and family, the bus arrived in his town of Portland, Oregon, at 2:00 a.m. She did not wish to phone Jerry before six o'clock, so she simply stayed on the bus and rode north to Seattle and back. She arrived back in Portland at 4:00 p.m., preferring to spend fourteen more hours on the bus over sitting in the terminal for four hours.

On another occasion, Aunt Esther's son Dale and his family were visiting Jerry in Portland, and their mother was also in attendance. With Dale and his wife and five children packed in the car, there was not room to offer Aunt Esther a lift part-way home. She probably preferred the bus anyhow. Miles down the road, as evening approached, Dale saw a Greyhound bus, driving in the left lane up ahead. He said, "Let's watch for Grandma as we pass that bus."

Sure enough! As they slowly came alongside the bus, Dale looked up to see his mother's face pressed close to the window.

She was the picture of pure happiness as she eagerly enjoyed every passing sight. Dale said, "It reminded me of that look of unadulterated bliss that you see on a dog's face as it leans its head forward out of a car window."

Aunt Esther spent her life enjoying each passing vista, and pressing ahead, high-hearted with a hunger for the new.

Serendipity Beside a Spring

The second week of the New Year 2008, Judy went for a ride on Rudy, her Missouri Foxtrotter. As she rode through a wooded hollow in the hills a mile east of our home, she passed a spring. She did a double take, when she spied a dead buck lying near the spring. The deer probably had been wounded by a hunter, and come to the spring for water before it died. All that was left of the carcass was the ribcage, neck, and head. It had been cleaned by coyotes and other varmints, but the head and antlers were intact. In describing her adventure, Judy said, "I hated to see that nice trophy go to waste."

Judy dismounted, and with the reins over one arm, she tried to dislodge the head from the dead animal. This proved to be a daunting task, and she finally turned the head around and around many times until it came free. She feared that the horse would shy from the antlered head, but Rudy accepted its proximity calmly.

Mounting the horse proved to be a problem. Judy tightened the girth and picked up her prize, but could not leap lightly to the English saddle while holding a deer head with its large rack. Rudy, who was trained to stand still as Judy mounted, chose this time to disobey. He would start forward each time she attempted to swing into the saddle, while trying to hold the deer's head, the reins, and grasp Rudy's mane for leverage.

Judy finally was able to mount, after several attempts, but the saddle slipped sideways, and the horse started forward. She was hanging on, leaning sideways, and trying to get her right foot in the stirrup, so she could jerk the saddle straight. Judy got the horse stopped, transferred the head temporarily to her left hand, used her right hand to put her foot in the stirrup. Now she could adjust the saddle by leaning on the stirrup, and was ready to ride home to show her treasure to me. The head was fairly heavy, but she braced one of it's antlers against her right thigh.

I was working at the computer when Judy's voice behind me said, "Look at this!"

My eyes started from my head when I turned to see a large rack of antlers with a partially-bare, attached skull staring at me with empty eye sockets.

Judy, being a librarian and purveyor of arcane knowledge, told Devin Hall, a Verona School student, about her escapade. He recommended that she display the deer skull as a European mount.

Judy soon found detailed directions on the Internet for "European mount," which is a style of displaying a trophy as a white skull with attached antlers. She asked me, "Will you buy me some sal soda next time you're in town?"

"Sure," I said.

This proved to be more difficult than I expected. Sal soda or sodium carbonate was once was found in every household. It is a caustic powder that was used for various cleaning purposes, including adding a bit to wash water to give laundry soap a boost in the days before detergents. I checked a couple of Walmart super stores, a pharmacy, and a hardware store. Not only did they not have sal soda, but not a single person except me had ever even heard of it! Finally, in a Price-Cutter Supermarket I found Arm & Hammer Washing Soda, which is, in fact, sal soda.

Following the directions from the Internet, Judy boiled the deer head in a solution of sal soda and water for three hours. This turned the brains to jelly and loosened the skin and soft tissue. She was then able to discard the lower jaw, clean the

158

brains from the cranial cavity, and remove skin and other tissue from the skull. The result was a clean, white skull with eight-point rack attached, ready to mount on a wall plaque in the European fashion. And she got her trophy without firing a shot!

Years later, we learned that Judy's methodology was not according to Hoyle. Legally, she should have reported the dead deer and received permission from the Missouri Department of Conservation before removing the head. So far, no game warden has knocked on our door, and we can only hope that the statute of limitations has run out.

A few days after Judy's picture with the story of her deer trophy appeared in the local newspaper, I was waiting my turn at the register in the supermarket. I started chatting with the middle-aged guy behind me in the line. He was buying some ground sirloin, and we talked about beef prices. Then he changed the subject to venison and deer hunting.

I said, "Say, did you see the article I sent to the newspaper last week about the lady who found the deer head?"

He said, "Oh yes! I read that. She boiled it up and cleaned it for a trophy. It had a nice rack. That was a neat story and a good picture of the girl with her deer head. Was that your DAUGHTER in the picture?"

I said, "Well, er, ah . . . actually, that was my WIFE."

"Oh, uh . . . Really?" He looked keenly at my snow white beard and said, "That was your wife? Your wife? . . . Really?"

"Scout's honor!" I said.

Biscuits & Gravy

Biscuits and gravy are so engrained in Ozarks life that it came as a surprise when a friend in Connecticut said, "What are biscuits and gravy? That's a meal they don't have around here. Please send me your recipe."

Dear me! How could I describe something as common as biscuits and gravy? Biscuits are little round cakes, usually about three inches across, made of soft, white-flour dough, raised by baking powder—almost like British scones, but with no sugar or fruit. The gravy is basically white sauce made from sausage drippings and containing sausage bits. I have read that this white gravy is called "sawmill gravy" in some southern localities. A few people have even found a way to mispronounce this humble meal, calling it "bixets and gravy."

Since pigs were imported from England to the Jamestown Colony in the early 1600s, almost any rural family could afford to raise a hog or two to butcher in the fall for economical meat. Our late neighbor, Nola Ash, recalled one facet of the butchering process in the days before household refrigeration, "We'd grind up some of the meat and make a lot of sausage. We made patties and fried up all that sausage and put it in crocks. You put the sausages in layers and pour hot, melted hog fat over each layer. That sausage will keep for months in that crock of cooled grease. When you get ready for breakfast, you just dig out however many patties you want and use a handful of grease to make gravy and biscuits."

Every country household had a milk cow, and flour was an essential staple in every home. Before baking powder was commercially available, cooks used clabber to raise their biscuits. A substitute baking powder also can be made out of baking soda and cream of tartar. Thus even the poorest families had the ingredients for biscuits and gravy, a cheap and hearty food, and that is what the poorest families had every morning for breakfast.

My parents moved their growing family to a farm near Leann, Missouri, in 1942. Southern rural communities in those days started the day fueled by biscuits and gravy. All the old residents around Leann had biscuits and gravy for breakfast as day followed night. One couple was having marital problems, and a neighbor said, "She won't even bake his biscuits for him." Translation: "She will not cook his breakfast."

Our neighbor, the late Mary Bennett, was the eldest daughter in an enormous family, mostly of big strapping boys. When she was a young lady in the 1930s, it was her job to make breakfast for the family. Mary told me, "I'd get up before everybody else and start a big pot of coffee to cooking. Then I'd make a batch of thirty-six big biscuits and a gallon of gravy. That was our breakfast every morning. If eggs were cheap, I'd fry us an egg apiece, but if they were worth anything, we had to sell them to make a little money."

In the days of my youth, people a notch or two up on the social scale scorned biscuits and gravy as "po' folk's food." No restaurant or café would demean its menu with biscuits and gravy. We never had biscuits and gravy at our house. I believe that my mother thought biscuits and gravy were simply too plebeian for her to serve. She and her mother were left desperately poor by the death of my grandfather, James Miller, in 1920. Mama was a little girl, and her mother made biscuits and gravy frequently, since they did not have funds for fancier food.

This left Mama feeling that if you could not afford anything good for breakfast, you made biscuits and gravy. In my day, Mama could always come up with something she considered better than that. So far as I know, she never made biscuits and gravy in her long life of cooking fabulous meals.

My father grew up in the rough hills of Taney County, Missouri, the true backwoods. His family went to shop in the city of Springfield once a year in a horse-drawn wagon. Daddy was one of nine children, and when the boys or their father could kill two or three wild rabbits, Grandma fried them for breakfast and made white gravy in the drippings to serve over biscuits.

When I was a boy, Daddy killed a couple of rabbits one night, shining their eyes in the light of his carbide lamp, and shooting them with his .22 rifle. The next day Mama was frying them for lunch—or what we called "dinner" in those days. Uncle Orville, my father's brother, happened by for an impromptu visit and said scornfully, "I can't imagine having breakfast food for dinner!"

This remark made my mother so angry that I fancied I actually could see steam issuing from her ears.

In the twenty-first century, our tax dollars provide free breakfasts and lunches for most of the school children in America, and much food is wasted. My father told me that when he and his siblings left the house to walk down the road to the Meadows School overlooking Bull Creek, they were carrying one cold biscuit apiece, which their mother supplied them for their lunches.

An elderly gent named Clyde Blades was our neighbor when I was young. One day, Clyde told us his boyhood memory of his grandfather eating biscuits and gravy. The most prominent feature on the face of Grandpa Blades was a gigantic mustache. This mustache was significantly similar in nature to that hybrid vegetable described by the great comedian Victor Borge: "My uncle was a great botanist. He invented a new vegetable. Yes, he actually crossed a potato with a sponge. It tasted terrible . . . but it sure held a lot of gravy!"

We do not know about the taste of Grandpa Blades's mustache, but we do know that it sure held a lot of gravy. At the conclusion of his repast, as the squeamish averted their eyes, the old man would press his right forefinger firmly against his upper lip, just below the nose, and slowly slide it downward, squeezing all the gravy from his mustache into his mouth for one last gulp.

White gravy was not restricted to breakfast use, and often a big bowl of it graced the supper table. When my grandfather, Washington Irving Meadows, was a young man he had to take a trip of several days. I forget whether this journey was for business or to visit relatives. His mother cooked up a big mess of corn dodgers, which are fairly hard cornmeal sticks akin to johnnycakes. Wash tied the sack of corn dodgers on his saddle with his bedroll and rode out one early morning. He stopped for lunch near a stream and crunched a corn dodger, washing it down with branch water.

As evening fell, Wash came upon a farm and stopped to ask if he could sleep in the barn. When Wash came in the house, the family was sitting down for the evening meal, and the lady invited him to, "Come and put your feet under this here table and have some supper."

Wash was a shy young man and did not wish to inflict himself on them, so said, "I don't want to use up your food, Ma'am, but I'd admire to wallop my dodger in some of that gravy."

When Judy and I were married in June 1966, we spent the second night of our honeymoon in Branson, Missouri. There were no country music shows, no 76 Strip, and not much population. It was simply a little Podunk of a town on Lake Taneycomo. The next morning we headed for Eureka Springs, Arkansas. Before we reached the Kimberling Bridge, we came upon a little country café and stopped for breakfast.

As we scanned the menu I exclaimed, "Well, I'll be! They have biscuits and gravy."

Judy said, "What are biscuits and gravy?" She had grown up in California, and never heard of this dish.

I said, "It's what some people used to eat for breakfast when I was a kid. We never had it, but the people around us did. Why don't we give it a try?"

We did, and both of us liked it. Apparently a lot of other people tried it and liked it too. In the twenty-first century, biscuits and gravy is on practically every breakfast menu in the Midwest and South. Even the franchises such as Denny's, Hardee's, and many others, sport biscuits and gravy on the menu. It is usually not as good as you would make at home, but still biscuits and gravy is probably the most popular breakfast dish among old and young, rich and poor. It is so familiar and well-liked that it is often referred to by its initials, "I'd like B and G and coffee."

There are even two schools of thought about the orientation of the biscuits on the plate. Before putting on the gravy, the diner breaks open his biscuit into two halves like a miniature hamburger bun. Should he put soft side up or crusty side up before inundating it in gravy? Each orientation has its aficionados. Should he break each half into bite-sized pieces or leave them whole? Do as you wish, and let's not argue about it!

It is often disappointing to order biscuits and gravy in a restaurant. Many restaurants use commercial biscuits rather than making their own. The gravy is often not good either. Some restaurants use canned gravy or powdered gravy mix. Some even add sugar to the gravy, thus ruining it for most people—though one time I saw a man in a restaurant pour honey all over his biscuits and gravy, and, worse yet, eat it. Whenever Judy has B&G in a restaurant, she always tells me, "It's all right, but not as good as you make." I'm glad I married her!

I must give one last word of warning. Always remember which side of the Atlantic you are on. In England, the word "biscuits" refers to cookies, and you do not want cookies and gravy!

The Dubious Debut

My wife Judy and I used to attend a church where music was especially lively. At Ozark Christian Church, we sang old hymns and modern praise choruses with spirit and verve. Debbie Berger planned the services and also played the piano. She was one of those phenomenal pianists who play at a fast tempo, throwing in all the extra notes and putting her instrument through its paces. Sometimes I have imagined that I saw the piano stand up straighter, determined to do its best, as she headed for her bench. Beside her, the estimable musician Terry Black wielded the organ for a melodious accompaniment to the piano.

Ozark Christian Church did not have a separate choir, as the congregation was the choir. Debbie's husband Bob was the worship director who waved his arms adroitly to bring out our best singing. Bob and Debbie were not afraid to try the most intricate rounds and techniques with the congregation. We rattled the rafters with rousing hymns or sang softly and sweetly, as Bob directed. We even did fancy songs wherein the men sang one set of words and the ladies another simultaneously. Our most common trick was for only the ladies to sing one verse and the gentlemen to sing the next.

On a certain Sunday, Bob Berger had to be absent, and his usual substitute also was out of town. Debbie asked the oldest Berger daughter, college-age Kristy, to lead the service in Bob's place. Debbie always prepared a detailed "order of worship"

165

sheet for all those involved in the service, so this would be a clear-cut task for Kristy.

After the congregation sang the first verse of a favorite old hymn, Kristy, following her order of worship sheet, proclaimed, "Women sing verse two!"

Beautiful, blended soprano voices floated heavenward with the heartbreakingly harmonious tones of:

Through days of toil when heart doth fail, God will take care of you;
When dangers fierce your path assail, God will take care of you.
God will take care of you, through every day, o'er all the way;
He will take care of you, God will take care of you.

Angels bent their eyes earthward to determine from whence on the planet came this rapturous resonance.

"Men sing verse three!" Kristy demanded.

That plan sounded good on paper, when Debbie wrote the church service earlier that week in the seclusion of her study. What she did not realize was that not only Bob Berger would be absent that Sunday, but Bob Black, Bob Brown, and Bob Brite were also absent. So were Tom, Dick, and Harry. In fact, by an improbably contrary coincidence, every man of the congregation was absent except THREE: Pastor Rick Hazlett, Bill Gorman, and me. Pastor Rick had been swigging a big cup of coffee before the service began, and he chose this hymn to absent himself to use the bathroom in the basement, in preparation for giving his sermon.

When Kristy said, "Men sing verse three," I started to raise my hymnal to give the song my best effort, but the book slipped in my hands and slammed shut. This meant that I had to shuffle among Judy's and my Bibles, Sunday school books, and other impedimenta on the pew to find my bulletin, search it to learn the hymn number, then paw through the pages to locate the hymn. While I did this, only one man, the throaty Bill Gorman, was left to obey Kristy's order.

Debbie's fingers danced on the keys optimistically, and Terry echoed enthusiastically on the organ. Bill, looking wide-eyed and horrified, sang softly: *"All you may need He will provide, God will take care of you."*

I do not intend to criticize Bill's singing voice. I doubt that either he or I would describe his own singing voice as "mellifluous." I could tell that Bill was attempting to sing barely loud enough to be certified as singing, but softly enough so that no one could hear him.

Bill plowed ahead manfully in a husky, hushed voice, *"Nothing you ask will be denied, God will take care of you."* The angels must have wondered what happened.

I finally found my bulletin, as the congregation strained to hear that still, small voice singing all alone.

"God will take care of you, through every day, o'er all the way," Bill warbled weakly. I found the hymn number listed in my bulletin and began to search through my hymnal. All eyes turned back to focus on the person from whom issued that small, still voice.

"He will take care of you, God will take care of you," Bill lilted lugubriously, and finally, just as I found my place, God did take care of Bill.

"Now *everybody* sing verse four!" Kristy announced.

After the service I mirthfully apologized to Bill for losing my place, just at the wrong time, so that he had to sing a solo.

"You bet I sang a solo," said honest Bill. "I sang so low nobody could hear me!"

Darrell and the Elderly Invaders

In 1993, my friend Darrell Ledenham got a job with the US Postal Service. He had to go to Springfield, Missouri, and stay in a hotel for three weeks to attend training sessions every day. One night after he had occupied his hotel room for two weeks, he changed into his pajamas and watched TV for a while. He turned down his bed and went into the bathroom.

While Darrell was in the bathroom he heard a noise from his room, but thought it was just the television. However, when Darrell emerged from the bathroom, he found an elderly couple sitting on his bed watching the television, with their suitcases and other trappings in the middle of the floor.

Darrell paused in his narrative to tell me, "You have to believe they were pretty dumb, to come into a room in which my suitcases were open and my stuff spread around, with the television going, and not to realize someone was occupying the room. But they marched right in and sat down and didn't even change the channel."

Darrell demanded, "What are you doing in my room!"

The oldsters said, "What are YOU doing in OUR room?"

Darrell said, "I've been occupying this room for two weeks and will be staying for another week, so you'll have to leave.

The couple refused to budge, saying, "This is our room! This is the room they assigned us and gave us a key for, and we're staying right here."

To grab the phone and call the front desk was, with Darrell, the work of a moment. The desk clerk said he would send someone to evict the old couple and stash them in a different room. In the meantime, Darrell noticed that the old people had a cart loaded to the brim with antique clocks, so asked what was going on. The man said, "We came to the hotel for the NAWCC regional convention."

Darrell said, "The NA-what convention?"

The old timer patiently explained about the National Association of Watch & Clock Collectors. He said, "There will be hundreds of clocks and tools for sale in the convention center tomorrow, but it is only open to NAWCC members."

Darrell was all ears, as he absorbed the details. Little clock dials danced in his eyes, as he loved antique clocks. The next day he went down to the convention hall and joined the NAWCC, so that he could go in and look at the clocks and tools. Darrell let his membership lapse after that one year and never joined again. Still, he bought several clocks, so the invasion of his room was actually serendipitous.

This frightful experience taught Darrell two things: (1) He learned that NAWCC stands for National Association of Watch & Clock Collectors. (2) He learned always to put the safety chain on the door when staying in a hotel room. This time it was an elderly couple. Next time it might be Mafia assassins with silencers on their weapons or Kichwa Indians with blow gun darts dipped in poisonous frog venom.

The Youth Within

When Lou Stapleton was ninety-seven years old, she had surgery to remove half her colon, which was infected with cancer. After the surgery, the doctor told her, "I have to ask you something. I was amazed during the operation to see your internal organs. All your organs appear to be those of a forty-year-old. Do you have any ideas that might explain this?"

Lou said, "I'm sorry, but I have no idea."

A few months later Lou was pondering this phenomenon. "I have forty-year-old organs. Wonder what I was doing when I was forty." And Lou remembered a strange incident that happened in the early 1940s, when she was about forty years of age.

Lou's friend Gladys Caruthers had poor vision and serious eye problems, including severely crossed eyes. She had a speech impediment too. She asked Lou to drive her to the Snyder Sanitarium at Glen Rose, Texas. Lou did not relish the drive, but took her friend. While they were there, Gladys urged Lou to have a treatment, too, so that she might get some personal benefit from the trip. Lou agreed to do so. Dr. Snyder usually gave patients two treatments several days apart, but since Lou did not wish to come back, she got two treatments in one day.

Lou told me that they were strange treatments. "They were called 'magnetic healing.' The patient had to wear light cotton clothing and lie on his or her back on a table. The doctor passed his hand above the patient's body, from head to feet, and then snapped his fingers! He never touched the patient, just moved his hand down over the body and always snapped his fingers at the end of a sweep," she said."

Lou continued, "I couldn't feel a thing or tell that he was doing anything, but I wasn't going to say so! There was a man patient there, who was very obnoxious in claiming that the doctor wasn't doing anything."

The gentleman said, "You're taking my money and not doing a thing!"

Dr. Snyder said, "You can't tell it, but I *am* doing something."

The patient said, "I think this is a scam. If you have the power to heal me, you must have the ability to prove it."

The doctor said, "All right, you get up and leave, and before you reach the end of that hallway, you will be struck with severe diarrhea."

The man said, "Oh piffle! Surely you can do better than that. I don't believe a word you're saying."

Dr. Snyder said, "Go ahead and leave."

The man did so, and before he reached the front door he became acutely ill, as the doctor had predicted.

The doctor said, "Now come back, and I'll reverse it."

Dr. Snyder did indeed cure Gladys's eyes. They were no longer crossed, and Gladys could see well for the first time in her life. He also helped her speech problem.

Since Lou's surgeon claimed that her organs were those of a forty-year-old, she could not help but wonder if she might actually have received some lasting benefit from that strange medical treatment. Lou said, "I wonder if you could find out anything about the Snyder Sanitarium on the Internet."

I could and did. The town of Glen Rose, Texas, had its genesis in 1849, when a trading post was established at a picturesque spot on the Paluxy River, just above its confluence with the Brazos River. By 1900, Glen Rose was a well-known recreation spot, thanks to the sulfur water wells and the natural beauty of the terrain.

Soon after 1900, George P. Snyder established the Snyder Drugless Health Sanitarium at Glen Rose. He was a charismatic and charming person, who touted himself as a "magnetic healer." Dr. Snyder's original complex of buildings included the main sanitarium, a kitchen and dining building, and a structure housing a water system with sulfur water from the flowing wells for patient baths. The sanitarium became so popular that Dr. Snyder built a hotel next door with rooms for his patients. He added a certain exotic interest by allowing his pet ostrich, Judy, to wander the grounds. Dr. Snyder's institute of health and pleasure became the largest contributor to Glen Rose's economy.

Dr. Snyder's charisma, charm, medical abilities, and insight into human nature allowed him to treat and cure thousands of patients over several decades, much to the consternation of the city's traditional doctors.

We scoff at ideas of supernatural healing, and from Lou's description, we surely would have to place Dr. Snyder's abilities in that category. If Dr. Snyder did have this miraculous ability, I would surmise that it died with him, and that it would have been impossible for him to train others to use the same technique.

Whether Dr. Snyder was the cause or not, Lou had the satisfaction for the rest of her life of knowing that her insides were fifty years younger than the rest of her!

Dancing Like Fools

In 1995, Judy and I met a couple named Tom and Pam at church. They passionately loved to square dance and were determined to introduce us to this activity. We submitted to the extent that we went one night to watch a square dance. It did not look like anything we wished to do, and we said so.

Pam and Tom were undeterred. When a new class started in September, Pam said, "The first lesson is free! You can't lose anything just going to one lesson."

She was so urgent in her arguments that we agreed to go to one lesson. The square dance lessons were surprisingly great fun. Caller Bob Loyd taught them with the help of experienced dancers he called angels. We loved Bob, and became good friends with him. Bob lived at Siloam Springs, Arkansas, and raised chickens for his main employment.

Square dancing was the springboard for us to take lessons in two-step and waltz. We enjoyed hundreds of dances over the next fifteen years.

But, back to the square dance lessons, we hit it off with Fred and Jean Whisenhunt, another couple in the class. Fred and I had many laughs over our good-natured insults about each other's dancing ability.

As the end of the classes approached, with a graduation ceremony scheduled, I wrote a poem to read on that occasion.

Fred and Mark Learn to Square Dance
or
Bob Loyd's *Nightmare*

If a fellow wants to learn to dance,
He shouldn't leave it to luck or chance.
If he wants to dance, and he isn't a fool,
He'll pay his dues and go to school.

Now Teacher Bob is Caller Bob,
And that's the same as Farmer Bob.
At night he calls for the local dance;
But by day he runs a chicken ranch.

About sundown, since he was a youth,
Bob steps inside of a telephone booth
And comes out slimmer and a little taller
And all dressed up like a square dance caller.

A new class started one bright September
With some students that Bob would always remember;
Two men who would tax his imagination
Licked their pencils and signed at the registration.

Why Fred and Mark want to do-sa-do
They just won't say, so we'll never know;
But both enrolled in Bob's dance classes,
And they took along their pretty lasses.

Nobody thought there was a chance
Bob could teach Fred Whisenhunt to dance;
But there's old Fred kickin' up his heel.
That's not square dance! It's Virginia reel!

Mark thought that he was full of grace
And would learn to dance at a very fast pace.
He thought that he would "knock 'em dead,"
But he's only a little bit better than Fred.

When Mark was dancing at Holiday Islan'
He saw some people pointin' and smilin.'
He thought his dancing needed correction
Till he saw they were looking in Fred's direction.

When menfolk do the jumps and jives
They need to rely on help from wives.
Judy would like to keep Mark straight,
But she always arrives a little too late.

Jean wants her Fred to be Fred Astaire,
But he slips in mistakes when she isn't there.
By using wives and angels as tools
Both men are out there dancing like fools.

How Bob taught this pair to cut the rug
Is a question that causes some to shrug;
A lot of teachers in a lot of places
Turned and ran at the sight of their faces.

There's a rumor down at Siloam Springs
Of a chicken flock that twirls and swings.
To get Fred and Mark to dancin' and kickin'
It took a teacher who could train a chicken!

Girls Don't Want to Be Stung

One of my great joys in years past was climbing the four old fire lookout towers near our home in southwest Missouri. Those four (in alphabetical order, since I am a librarian) were Jenkins Tower, Lohmer Tower, Piney Tower, and Sugar Camp Tower. The view from atop the old lookout towers is fabulous. From Lohmer Tower at Shell Knob, Missouri, one can see Inspiration Tower at Branson, forty miles away. Looking from all four towers in spring and summer, the undulant folds of tree-covered hills and ridges fall away to the south as far as the eye can see, changing gradually from the dark green of near foliage to lighter green and then grey green. One cannot quite distinguish the point at which the distant sage-colored hills change to blue, but they do, and then merge with the blue sky somewhere in Arkansas. In autumn, before the bright leaves fall, the same view is a Technicolor feast. Sadly, all the lookout towers that remain are now enshrouded in high fences with razor wire, so visitors can no longer experience this delight. Upkeep on the unused towers would have been prohibitive.

Piney Creek Wilderness is a section of the Mark Twain National Forest, and is the home of Piney Tower. One time when I climbed Piney Tower, a funny episode happened. It was funny to *me*, anyhow. As I descended the many stairs and landings, I saw a Forest Service king-cab pickup pull in. About a half dozen elderly men and women disembarked. They were Green Thumb

176

workers. The Green Thumb Program placed senior citizens in part-time jobs, where they helped out and received a small salary. Some worked in schools, some in other public organizations. These were hired by the Forest Service to go to various sites, raking, picking up trash, and generally tidying up. Just as I alighted from the bottom flight, the group from the Forest Service vehicle made straight for me and began ogling the ground under the tower.

I said, "What are you looking for?"

Elder No. 1 said, "We're looking for money."

Elder No. 2 said, "People go up in the tower and throw down coins."

The group continued to pore over the ground, while I slipped my hand into my pocket and grasped a $100 bill, which I happened to have on me. Presently, Elder No. 1 bent over and held up a metal disc, saying, "Here's a nickel!"

Then Elder No. 2 bent down, held up a coin, and said, "I found a penny!"

Elder No. 3 reached down, and straightened up, excitedly saying, "I found a QUARTER!"

I leaned over and stood up, waving my bill and exclaiming, "Look! I found a $100 bill!"

A row of wrinkled, frowning faces scrutinized me, as the silent senior citizens stood with slack jaws. Luckily they had left their rakes and shovels in the truck; otherwise, I might not have made it out with both my money and my life!

Judy and I love to ride our horses at Piney Creek Wilderness. On a beautiful September day in 2001, Judy and I took our horses Omar and Rudy in the trailer to the Piney South Trailhead to meet a friend. We went for a ride, with Jo Ann on Khadija, Judy on Rudy, and me on Omar. Jo Ann was a tentative and cautious rider, so Judy and I could not ride at our usual hasty and energetic pace, and for Jo Ann's sake, we avoided the rough, rugged trails we love.

It was pleasant, if pokey, riding on the woodland trails and chatting, but Omar, my big Arabian, was bursting with pent-up energy and hard for me to hold at the plodding pace. He and I normally rode swiftly. At one fork, I departed from the ladies and rode off on a big loop, alone on the bold horse, so that he could use up abundant energy doing his fast trot.

The ladies rode on to my relative's hunting cabin, then across on a lakeside trail to meet me at a pre-arranged spot. We had our lunch on the shore overlooking an arm of beautiful Table Rock Lake.

As we rode back toward the trailers, we turned aside from the trail to show Jo Ann a large sinkhole that always impressed us. It may be seventy-five feet across and thirty-five feet deep. We feel sure that it is the dome of a cave that has fallen in. Since the sinkhole remains dry, the rainwater must drain into a cave or fissure beneath. I always jokingly tried to get Judy to climb down to the bottom of it and jump up and down to see if it is solid, but she seemed reluctant.

This time, as we sat astride our mounts, looking down into the sinkhole, Rudy started jumping and leaping all around and it was hard for Judy to control him. Khadija was frightened by the commotion and almost leapt into the sinkhole with Jo Ann, but Jo was able to wheel the steed about and keep her from going over the edge. Omar and I were placid. Finally something stung Judy, and she said, "Let's get out of here quick!"

We all went loping back to the trail and away. Apparently we had disturbed a hole of yellow jackets. A couple of them even followed us far down the trail, and Judy had to dismount and swat them as they tried to sting Rudy.

Yellow jackets are members of the wasp family. They live in egg-shaped paper nests that look like hornets' nests, but are underground, usually in a disused animal den. In the late summer they become aggressive, as they are short on food, and are also at their peak of strength, sometimes having a nest population of 5,000. In the fall the males leave the nest and fan out, looking for other colonies. There they breed females, who will become queens the next spring. The whole hive dies out when winter comes, except for the bred females, who hibernate under pieces of bark or in some other protected spots and start a new hive in the spring.

All bees and wasps apparently feel aggressive towards dark colors, such as Judy's hair and horse. Both Jo Ann and I had white horses. I had the further protection of a white hat, white shirt, and white beard.

When we got back to our trailers, we counted six big welts on Rudy and three on Judy. When Jo Ann expressed relief that she and her horse had not gone to the bottom of the sinkhole, I said, "Well, at least we might have found out if there's really a cave beneath it."

The Puzzling Pizza

I made a delicious pepperoni pizza for supper one Sunday night in January 2019, with stir-fried spinach for a side dish. Down cellar we have vegetables and cheeses in one freezer and meats and breads in the other. I danced down the stairs and grabbed a bag of shredded mozzarella to use on the pizza.

I say "danced," because one time Jim Ronchetto, our brother-in-law, wanted to see our basement. He is a big man with bad knees. I went bounding down to the basement, and he laboriously crept down. After the tour, I went galloping up the stairs. When Jim finally made it back up to the ground floor he said, "I wish I could dance up and down those stairs the way you do."

But back to my story, I danced up the stairs with my mozzarella and put it aside to thaw a bit, as I did the rest of the pizza. The cheese goes on almost last—only black olives and fennel seeds going on top of the cheese. I thought this mozzarella was nicer than we usually get from Sam's, as it was in such even shreds, and they were not frozen together in clumps. I thought it must have come from the discount grocery. I put my beautiful pizza in the oven for twenty minutes at 425° as the recipe demands.

When I took my prepossessing pizza from the oven, Judy looked at it and exclaimed, "This pizza's not done! The cheese isn't even melted!"

We puzzled and pondered and speculated. Finally Judy took a shred of the unmelted cheese from the pizza and ate it. "This is not cheese!" she exclaimed. "This is shredded potatoes!"

"Heavenly days!" I shouted. "What will we do?"

Judy said, "There's only one thing we CAN do. We'll add mozzarella to the top, put it back in the oven, and have a potato pizza."

Judy went dancing downstairs to fetch up the mozzarella, came back in the kitchen and handed it to me. "This is another bag of shredded potatoes!" I exclaimed.

Judy said, "Oh my goodness! Well, pour the two bags of potatoes together, and write on the bag what they are! I'll take them down and try to find some actual mozzarella."

While Judy was in the basement, I pawed through the freezer bin of our refrigerator in the kitchen and found a bag of mozzarella. I yelled to Judy, and she danced back up the stairs. We covered the pizza with a mantle of cheese and put it back in the oven for ten minutes.

The pizza was so hearty that Judy and I could eat only half a piece each. I said, "This tastes like something one ought to have for breakfast."

Judy said, "Let's try that! It's almost, but not entirely, unlike pizza."

"We could put scrambled eggs on top of it," I suggested.

-o-o-o-o-o-o-o-o-o-o-o-

The tale of the potato pizza reminded us of another culinary bombshell many years before in Jonesboro, when Judy was the chief cook. We always have made our own noodles. Judy prepared tuna-noodle casserole for supper one day, using whole-wheat noodles that she had made. Judy and I and the three boys loved the delicious casserole, and some of us had seconds. After the meal, Judy began to clear up. When she looked at the kitchen counter, there sat two unopened cans of tuna! She had made tuna-noodle casserole with no tuna, and nobody noticed!

Microwave Time

In 1945, Percy Spencer, an employee of Raytheon, experimented with a microwave generator and was astonished when the chocolate candy bar in his pocket melted. This was the discovery of the heating ability of microwaves. Percy's colleagues did not believe him until he played some tricks on them. The first foods cooked on purpose with microwaves were popcorn and an egg—which exploded in the face of one of Percy's doubters. In 1947, Raytheon built the first commercially available microwave oven. It was almost six feet tall, weighed 750 pounds, and cost $5,000.

Judy and I had never heard of a microwave oven until about 1970 when Judy was in graduate school. A fellow student told her, "I'm going to get my parents a microwave oven for Christmas." Judy said, "What's a microwave oven?"

My brother Roger and his wife Wanda were more technologically advanced than the rest of the family. They were the first to buy that innovative device, a microwave oven. It was a big Amana Radarange brand unit with backbreaking heft. A few years later, Roger took a job in Wisconsin, and his family moved from North Carolina, taking their microwave with them.

Arriving at their new Wisconsin home in 1989, they found an identical Amana microwave already installed in a custom made cubbyhole in the kitchen cabinets. Next time they visited Missouri, Roger and Wanda brought their original microwave and gave it to Judy and me. We accepted the gift with good grace, but after they left, we looked at each other questioningly and agreed, "What on earth would we do with a microwave? That's certainly nothing we would ever use."

Judy said, "Just put it out in the clock shop. I don't think we want to take up room in our kitchen with it." I did so, and within a few days Judy and I would meet each other on the walkway between the shop and house, I carrying a freshly heated cup of coffee back to the house, and her bringing a dish of frozen vegetables to the shop to cook for our meal.

I bought a high-quality oak stand for our kitchen and carried the ponderous microwave in from the shop. After a couple of years we had to have the keypad replaced on the old Amana. An appliance repairman could actually repair those early microwaves. Later microwaves became cheap and disposable.

A few years later we added onto our house and had kitchen cabinets built, so we had a cubbyhole made for the microwave. I told the cabinetmaker, "I see that you made that cubbyhole just the right size for this exact microwave, but what about when it wears out and we get another one? Will this space be big enough?"

He said, "Believe me, you will never have another microwave as big as this one!" He was right.

I do not know how many microwave ovens we have owned through the years, buying a new one when the old one quit functioning. In the 1990s one of our college-aged sons wished for a microwave for his campus apartment. I bought a good used one at a flea market for thirty-five dollars. When he moved to a different apartment he set that microwave on the curb to load on the pickup. Distracted, he drove off and left it there, never to see it again, a bit of carelessness that was easily forgiven by those who know the hassle of moving.

During our long association with microwave ovens, one of our units developed a strange affliction. Like most microwaves, this one featured a digital clock. We would set the clock to the correct time, but over the next few hours, whenever a "1" appeared as part of the time, the clock would retain that digit. Over time the clock always wound up with the permanent reading of 11:11, eventually training us to forego setting the clock. To this day when Judy or I notice a clock reading eleven minutes past eleven, we comment, "Oh, it's microwave time!" And the other always knows exactly what time it is.

Train Coupler as Home Improvement Tool

My father owned a strange block of iron. It had a square hole through it and was bisected by odd grooves and channels. Two corners were dog-eared to form perfect hand holds for picking it up—something only the mighty would do, as it weighed one hundred and eleven pounds. Nobody knew where the big iron block came from or what its original purpose was. Somebody once told Daddy that it was a train coupler, so Daddy called it his train coupler, even though it almost certainly was not one.

Daddy used his train coupler as an anvil for straightening rods or bending metal straps to repair farm equipment. He rested the sickle bar for his mower across the train coupler for knocking out rivets and replacing broken sections. When he needed extra weight on a plow, on went the train coupler. We children used it as a handy place to crack black walnuts with a hammer. As we used the heavy block for these mundane purposes, none of us could imagine the exciting role it would one day play in a family adventure.

When rural electrification reached our rocky southwest Missouri farm in 1949, it did not make a dramatic difference in the life of our family. My parents scratched out only a meager income to feed and clothe the five children at home at that time. There was no possibility of piping water into the kitchen, let alone adding a bathroom. Our well was so weak that Mama had to save up hand-drawn water for three days, before she could wash clothes in the wringer Maytag, with its kick-start gasoline motor. The expense of deepening the well prohibited water in the house for several years. Daddy did pay a third-rate, shade-tree electrician to wire our house with war-surplus wire that was insulated with black, sticky tar paper. At least we got to blow out the kerosene lamps and marvel at the bright electric bulbs.

The Great Drought of the 1950s decimated farm incomes. In 1952 Daddy was forced to take a job delivering Studebaker cars for Dallas & Mavis Forwarding Company of South Bend, Indiana. He hauled cars intermittently for the next ten years. This outside income allowed him to hire a local well driller to deepen the well, which enabled him to pipe hot and cold running water to a free-standing, white enamel kitchen sink. What luxury! But we still had to use the outhouse for several more years before Daddy would undertake the home improvement project of adding a bathroom.

In the summer of 1961 Daddy decided to partition off a corner upstairs in our old farmhouse and install a bathroom. I had graduated from high school and would start college that fall. My two younger brothers still lived at home also, and we all got to help him. The first step would be installing a septic system. Always a great do-it-yourselfer, Daddy ordered plans from an advertisement in a farm magazine for how to make a concrete septic tank.

Daddy used pick and shovel to dig a neat rectangular hole in the back yard, with very little help from his sons. It was six feet wide and eight feet long, and was supposed to be six feet deep. Unfortunately, he hit solid limestone bedrock at four and one half feet! Daddy said, "There's nothing to do but drill into the rock and blast it out." He went into town and bought a supply of dynamite, caps, and fuse from the hardware store. There were no restrictions on buying dynamite in those days.

Our first attempt at drilling dynamite holes in the hard limestone was the old fashioned way. The drill was a four and one-half foot length of steel rod, wedge-shaped on the bottom end. As the oldest available son, I had to hold the drill as Daddy hit it with a sledge hammer. I had seen Daddy drive thousands of sharpened oak and cedar fence posts with a twelve-pound mall and never miss a lick, but when he asked me to hold that drill, I understood why the drill holder is called the "shaker." John Henry's words from the old song gave me small comfort: "Shaker, you'd better pray, for if ever I miss that piece of steel, tomorrow'll be your buryin' day." Daddy told me, "Don't be afraid! If you hold it steady, I promise I'll never miss." And he never did.

I held the drill, and Daddy pounded it with a mighty swing. Then I rotated it half a turn, and he pounded it again. After hammering most of a day, we drilled one hole down about a foot. To my overwhelming relief, Daddy announced, "This won't work. I'll have to go to town and hire somebody with a jackhammer."

The jackhammer man came a few days later, and the Ozark hills echoed for one day with the unheard-of noise of RAT-A-TAT-TAT-TAT-TAT-TAT." When the man took his equipment away, the bedrock sported row after row of neat holes about eighteen inches deep. The next morning the fun began.

The procedure was simple. Daddy put a cap with a five-minute fuse into the end of a stick of dynamite. He dropped another stick of dynamite in a hole first, then put his fused stick in on top of it, so both would go off together. He put the train coupler over the dynamite in order to hold the blast down in the hole so it would break the rock. Before he lit the fuse, he would say, "One of you boys go in and get Mama, so she can see the blast too." And one of us did.

Mama was an inveterate letter-writer, and one thing that made leaving home tolerable for her children was the weekly long letter from Mama. That morning, Mama was at the dining table rattling away on her portable Smith-Corona, typing a letter to someone. She would stop in mid-sentence and come out to watch the show.

The explosions were not great shows. Daddy would light the fuse and run over to where the rest of us waited at a safe distance. We stood in dreadful anticipation for what seemed like more than five minutes. Finally there was a loud BANG, and the train coupler, along with some assorted fragments of rock, would jump out onto the grass beside the hole. Mama would return to her typing, and Daddy and we boys would remove the debris from the excavation. Daddy would get another charge ready and send a boy in to get Mama.

When Daddy had the sixth charge ready to light, I happened to be the one who went in to retrieve Mama. She said, "I really want to get this letter in the mail, and I've been running in and out all morning to see those blasts. I think I'll just stay here this time."

I said, "Aw, why don't you come on out? It's more fun to have you watching too." So she did.

As we waited in anticipation, we had no way of knowing that this one time, Daddy had centered the mass of the train coupler over the hole with an exactitude that NASA would have envied. When the BANG came, we watched with wide eyes and open mouths as the 111-pound train coupler soared straight up, up, up, seventy-five feet into the air, then down, down, down right through the roof of our two-story farmhouse. Daddy stood frozen and speechless for a moment before we all raced towards the house.

The train coupler had come through the roof then through the attic, and brought down the ceiling in the dining room, damaged Mama's typewriter, and landed right on the chair where Mama had been sitting, smashing it to smithereens.

Daddy quietly carried the train coupler back outside to the blast site. He didn't say much, as he put away his dynamite and digging tools and got out his carpenter tools. He spent the next two weeks repairing the roof and ceiling. On one trip to Joplin for materials he took the typewriter and left it to be repaired. Mama finished her letter with her Parker 51 fountain pen.

When blasting time arrived again, Daddy not only made sure to place the train coupler purposely off center, but also covered the excavation with a row of thick cedar poles to help contain coupler and rocks. Mama came outside to watch every single blast. You can't be too careful when someone is playing with dynamite.

Eggs Have Bottoms Too

Square dances are reminiscent of church socials. Both have in common the zeal, the sense of fellowship, and the employment of delicious food as a lure. "Feed them and they will come," is an admonition one hears in connection with both functions, and a laden table is featured at every square dance. Some victuals are perennial favorites. Among desserts, pies take the prize, but the most cherished non-dessert viand is deviled eggs. If you hanker for either choice, it is well to be standing nonchalantly near the provender when the call is made, "The food table is open!"

At a Shell Knob, Missouri, dance sponsored by the Table Rockers club, my ears perked for joy at the food table announcement. I raced across the room to find that Dennis Smith, the canny caller for the visiting Arkansas club, must have been standing right by the table when the call was made. There he stood six feet from the table, his snowy beard leaping as he grazed from a bountiful plate. Between him and the table, four ladies progressed in line, their backs to Dennis, as they selected food. I stopped to chat with the amiable caller and noticed two puzzling shiny, white hemispheres on his plate. When I realized what they were, I decided to comment.

If you wish to make a remark to someone in a room filled with a din of music, loud talk, and laughter, you have two choices: Method One is to speak at the top of your voice, but

Method Two is to lean forward and speak quietly into the very ear of the person you are addressing.

I leaned close to Dennis and said softly, "In all these years I've seen hundreds of deviled eggs on people's plates, but this is the first time I ever saw any upside-down. They have cute little bottoms, don't they?"

Dennis chose Method One and bellowed in a thunderous voice, "THEY SHORE DO HAVE CUTE LITTLE BOTTOMS!"

All four ladies at the table turned, as puppets controlled by a single string, and all gave Dennis the exact same withering stare. That was when I realized that Dennis's beard must be prematurely white, as no one above the age of thirty could move as fast as Dennis did. I glanced from Dennis to the ladies, then back to a vacuum where Dennis had stood. Looking farther afield I saw him with his plate at the farthest possible corner of the hall. He appeared to be stuffing deviled eggs whole into his mouth.

Rallying Round the Rolling Pin

My mother was a great cook, able to provide one large and luscious meal after another, when all of her descendants descended upon my parents for a prolonged visit. In my callow youth, I did not realize what a great feat she was accomplishing or how tiring it must have been for her. She actually seemed to enjoy it. Now that Judy and I have clouds of descendants, I know how much planning and effort went into her meals, which were more elaborate than the ones we serve to our guests.

My first year in college at the University of Missouri-Columbia, I had a meal plan at a local boarding house, so was well fed. It was run by an elderly couple, who I now realize were much younger than I am at present. They owned a farm and raised their own beef, pork, and poultry, to the benefit of us college kids who ate at their boarding house.

Over those sumptuous meals, I developed a friendship with another boy, three years or so older than me, named Eldon Miller. We decided we would get an apartment together with a kitchenette and save money on our room and board. So from my sophomore year on, I did my own cooking.

Mama gathered up a box of spare pots and pans, a casserole dish, a skillet, some measuring spoons and cups, utensils, a few dishes, and other equipment she felt would be useful to me. Best of all, she bought me a brand new copy of *Betty Crocker's New Picture Cook Book*, copyright 1961. Even sixty years later this is widely recognized as the best general Betty Crocker cookbook ever produced, and used copies sell for $50 or more.

Mama told me, "I hear people all the time say that they can't cook." She handed me the cookbook. "That's nonsense!" she scoffed. "Anybody who can read can cook. All you have to do is find a recipe that looks good and follow the directions. You can cook just as well as anybody else, if you simply do what this book tells you."

Armed with my cookbook and cooking utensils, I negotiated with Eldon about the division of labor and expense for our meals. We were both agreeable for me to do the shopping and cooking. Eldon would pay half the grocery bills and would wash all the dishes and pots and pans.

This arrangement was satisfactory to both of us. Eldon put on weight and was constantly complimentary concerning my culinary skills. Skills? I had not actually developed any, but just followed the clear directions accompanying each recipe. However, as I kept on cooking and Eldon kept on eating, I am sure that my skill and dash did grow. Soon I was undaunted by any recipe in the book. Making Avery Island Devilled Shrimp became no more to me than falling off a log, and Hamburger Stroganoff was a piece of cake.

Eldon and I did imbibe in a few victuals that were not of my making. Some nights when we were studying late, our stomachs would begin to growl in protest of their emptiness. Then either Eldon or I would walk the four nocturnal blocks to Joe's Bar & Grill and bring back two fried egg sandwiches and two bottles of beer. I think the beer and sandwiches cost the same amount, fifteen cents. So this treat cost a total of sixty cents.

My junior year I continued to cook for myself and develop my handiness in the kitchen. Eldon had graduated, and my new roommate was a rather unconventional little chap named Brian Rude. Brian did not wish to keep the arrangement I had enjoyed with Eldon, so I continued to cook for myself and to wash my own dishes.

Brian lived mostly on white bread, eggs, and canned beans. He even chose the least appealing of beans, red kidney beans, as his main staple. Brian did not even heat his beans, but simply opened a can and began eating from it with a spoon, while chomping a slice of bread along with it. There was often an open can of beans in the refrigerator awaiting Brian's next meal.

I am happy to say that Brian did cook his eggs—fried or scrambled them. You have heard that expression, "The place was so clean that you could eat off the floor." Our apartment was not. However, one time I saw Brian preparing to cook some eggs. As he tried to break an egg into his hot skillet, his hand slipped, and the raw egg fell to the dirty floor, leaving Brian holding the shell. Brian took the spatula and scooped the egg from the filthy floor, adding it to the skillet with the other eggs he was cooking. I have often joked that it is a good idea to add some black pepper to whatever one is cooking, so if there is a speck in the food, no one will notice. Those were definitely eggs that called for black pepper!

On Brian's birthday I cooked a beautiful birthday cake for him. It was a chocolate cake with butterscotch icing, and spelled across the top in red kidney beans was the word BRIAN. Brian Rude consumed the cake with gusto and enjoyment, but did not even thank me for it, which I considered rude. I wondered if some ancestor had received the family surname in a similar situation.

It has nothing to do with cooking, but I must tell one more remarkable tale about Brian. Brian owned a little putt-putt motor scooter. His widowed mother lived in Neosho, Missouri, and on holidays Brian would go to visit her. The trip from Columbia to Neosho took him eight hours each way on his motor scooter, sometimes in inclement weather. Though one might question Brian's wisdom, his fortitude was never in doubt.

My last two years as an undergraduate I got to live rent-free in the huge, stone Missouri Methodist Church. The church had three bedrooms which the church board let at no charge to three college boys. This turned the church into an "occupied building," which qualified for cheaper insurance rates. It was like living in a castle. Aside from the gigantic sanctuary with its fortune in stained glass windows, the building had four floors with some quaint rooms on the floor above that were reachable by little almost hidden stairways. And there was the large room on the top floor full of air pumps and machinery that operated the mammoth pipe organ down below in the sanctuary.

We three "church meece," as we were called, had the run of the whole building and had only to go around before bedtime to be sure all the doors and windows were secure. The third floor, where our rooms were located, was also the floor for the Wesley Foundation, the Methodist youth ministry. There were meeting rooms and a kitchen, where we could prepare our meals, and also where volunteers cooked a Sunday supper for the meeting of Wesley Foundation.

One year, I volunteered to be Wesley Foundation Food Chairman. So I was in charge of those Sunday evening meals, figuring out the menus, securing required foods and ingredients, and supervising the four or five volunteers, who helped me cook for about thirty people. Somehow I also got roped into being in charge of the meals for a weekend Wesley retreat at Lake of the Ozarks. My volunteers and I had to supply all six meals for over 250 people during the weekend retreat. All these experiences furthered my cooking education.

At Wesley Foundation I met a lovely, intelligent girl who had enchanting eyes and looked good in sweaters. Unfortunately she was informally engaged to another boy. Fortunately he left for graduate school in the east. Later Judy had to call him and tell him she would not be coming east to join him after all. Judy and I had our first real date the last day of finals first semester and got married on the last day of finals second semester on June 6, 1966.

Judy's mother had majored in Home Economics and was a good cook, but she simply did all the cooking at home and did not train her children how to cook. When Judy and I were married, I was much more at home in the kitchen than she was.

Judy knew of my cooking prowess from her membership in Wesley Foundation. She wished to do the cooking in our new home, so was a bit defensive and sometimes resented my wise advice and proffered assistance in the kitchen. Judy may have burnt a meal or two, which is the right of all new brides, but she was always a quick study, and in no time she was my equal in cooking ability. Soon she fearlessly attacked even the most complicated recipes with pluck and verve. Of course I did tell her what Mama said about anyone who can read being able to cook. I'm sure that helped.

Over the next twenty-five or thirty years Judy did almost all the cooking for our home. She made all our bread. She made homemade noodles. Soufflés, spoon bread, pies—she attempted and succeeded at any food she wished to make. No recipe daunted or dismayed her.

In 1973, with the birth of Chris, our first son, Judy quit work to raise children, and three years later, two more sons, Aaron and Alex, entered the family. Judy continued to fill me and the three boys with delicious foods. I worked as a college librarian until 1983. At that time we bought The M. L. Shipley Company, manufacturers and purveyors of reproduction antique clock glasses and dials. I resigned my job as Head Catalog Librarian at Arkansas State University, and we moved to southwest Missouri, where I had been born and raised.

We spread our resources thin when we bought the clock parts company as well as an 85-acre wooded farm. The horrible old ramshackle house we moved to did not have running water. At first there was not even an adequate or safe well, so we had to haul all our drinking water from my parents' house twelve miles away. All hot water for bathing or washing dishes had to be heated on the stove.

Our drafty house was heated by a wood stove that did not extend much of its beneficence to the outer reaches, including the waterless, sinkless kitchen. Yet, Judy manfully—or maybe I should say "womanfully"—jumped out of bed in the cold winter predawn, stoked the fire, and prepared breakfast and school lunches in the cold kitchen, before awaking the four males. Life became much easier when we had a well drilled and built on a kitchen, bathroom, and laundry room, adding indoor plumbing! It became easier still twenty-five years later in 2008 when we built a new two-story brick house with central heating and air.

In 1991, our situation changed dramatically. We sold The M. L. Shipley Company. My ten years away from the library world were the exact ten years when computers came to dominate library work. In order to go back to work in libraries, I would have to retrain. Judy said, "Our boys are in college and I have a job that will support us, so why don't you simply repair clocks and stay at home."

That sounded good to me! So at age fifty I became semi-retired. Since I was at home each day, and Judy was away working as a school librarian, it became natural for me to start preparations for supper to help her along when she got home. Gradually this evolved into me doing almost all the cooking. I found that absence had made my heart grow fonder of cooking, and in fact, I loved to cook! Judy said, "After all these years of cooking, I admit that the only reason I like to cook is that I like to eat."

So the situation suited both of us. Since that change I did almost all the cooking. I was never a better cook than Judy, but a more flamboyant one and more apt to toot my own horn. Thus, even when Judy cooked some delicious viand, our visiting children were apt to say unknowingly, "This is really good, Dad!"

Dining

We may live without poetry, music, and art;
We may live without conscience, and live without heart;
We may live without friends; we may live without books;
But civilized man cannot live without cooks.

He may live without books,—what is knowledge but grieving?
He may live without hope,—what is hope but deceiving?
He may live without love,—what is passion but pining?
But where is the man that can live without dining?"

~Edward Robert Bulwer-Lytton,
1st earl of Lytton (1831–1891)

The Carven Head

One of my favorite customers was Carol McNeely, for whom I repaired several clocks. It was a pleasure to pick up or set up a clock at her house, as the charming Carol always had some funny stories to tell.

Carol told about Charmaine, her condescending cousin, visiting from New York City. Possibly, Charmaine did not realize that she had no call to feel superior to Carol. It is unlikely that she was more erudite than Carol or had been to as many places around the globe. Carol's house was replete with artifacts from Europe, the South Seas, and other places.

Charmaine made it obvious that she thought everyone in Missouri was a hayseed. Carol played along. One day when Charmaine obviously was bored, Carol remarked, "Let's sit on the front porch for awhile."

Charmaine said, "Sit on the front porch! What on earth for?"

"We enjoy sitting out there and getting some fresh air and seeing a car go by now and then. Some of the people know us and wave or honk. We enjoy simply sitting and watching the cars go by," Carol replied.

Charmaine said, "Good grief! Where we live in New York City, there's a constant stream of cars going by all day and all night in front of our house."

"Shucky darn!" exclaimed Carol, "Wouldn't we have a ball on your front porch!"

One time when I delivered a clock to Carol, we had a "lost purse" episode. My bill was $225, and Carol said, "I'll write you a check."

While I admired objets d'art and gewgaws, Carol searched the house for the purse, which contained her checkbook. She finally cried calf rope, as we say in the Ozarks, and said, "You go ahead and do your shopping and errands, and stop by before you go home. I'll keep up the search."

When I returned two hours later, Carol still had not found the purse. To my surprise, she plunked down three one-hundred-dollar bills, saying, "Mama always said to keep a little cash on hand."

I was taken aback, but looked in my billfold and amazingly had correct change for her!

During Carol's earlier search, as I admired her curios, I decided that my favorite was a beautifully carved wooden head that was aboriginal in appearance. I told Carol so and said, "Tell me the story of this head."

She laughed and said, "Talking about that head brings a vivid picture to my mind!"

Carol and her husband lived on a Pacific island for two or three years. The nearest town for shopping was on Guam, 700 miles away. One day, Carol was near the beach, when a very large and very dark man came in a canoe from another island. He approached Carol with this carving.

Carol told me, "He was totally naked except for a loincloth. Either the loincloth was too small or what it covered was too big. Maybe the loincloth was just a formality, but everything he had was plainly visible to everyone present. Put another way, his private parts were no more than semiprivate!"

When Carol asked the big fellow what she could do for him, he said, "Wife sick. Doctor want twenty dollar. I made this. Want twenty dollar."

Carol said, "This is a very nice carving. Don't you want more than twenty dollars for it? I'll give you forty dollars."

He said, "Want twenty dollar. Don't want no more. Want twenty dollar."

The man took the twenty-dollar bill and departed in his canoe. Carol told me, "My worry has always been, where would he carry that money as he paddled back to his island?"

A Risky Repair

Since time out of mind, a giant jeweler's regulator clock has hung on the wall of the jewelry store in Cassville, Missouri. It is that typical clock of its type, with gleaming white porcelain dial and shiny brass pendulum, both over a foot in diameter. The case is about six-feet tall, made of carved and embellished oak. The clock was made in the 1880s or 1890s. Through the decades, as one jewelry store would go out of business and another start up in a new location, the big clock would magically appear in the new store. Since Tomblin's Jewelry & Gifts opened in 1964, the clock has hung in that business. Everyone familiar with Cassville is familiar with the clock. I expect that even H. G. Wells saw it when he visited Cassville in 1910, to enjoy the therapeutic baths at nearby Mineral Springs.

One night in June 1986, a fire broke out on the north side of the town square and destroyed several buildings. When the fire chief realized that the fire would soon advance to the jewelry store in spite of the efforts of his crew, he sought out Chloe among the crowd of onlookers. Chloe and her sister Dana were co-owners of Tomblin's Jewelry and daughters of its founder. The chief told Chloe, "The fire will soon take your store, and there's not a thing we can do. We're willing to make one trip inside, if you can name one or two things you'd most like to save."

Tomblin's occupied a former bank building, and Chloe knew that the most valuable merchandise was safe inside the old walk-in bank vault, which was encased in foot-thick brick walls, impenetrable by the heat of the fire. She thought a moment and exclaimed, "The clock! The clock! Please save the big clock if you can."

One swing of a fire axe broke the lock on the front door. Several firemen rushed in and hauled the heavy clock down off the wall, carried it like a coffin out into the street, and laid it in the pickup bed of a friend of Chloe's.

During the following year or two, all the merchants, including Chloe, rebuilt their shops. Chloe had the big clock re-hung in its old place on the front wall of the bank vault, facing the street, so that passersby could see it through the store windows. Of course it would not run, after its rough removal during the fire, and Chloe asked me to repair it.

The most common jeweler's regulator is a French Comtoise clock with pinwheel escapement and sweep second hand. Chloe's clock looks exactly like one of these from the outside, but actually is quite different. Chloe's clock is German, rather than French or Swiss. It has deadbeat escapement, rather than pinwheel. The brass movement plates, though thicker than those in mass-produced clocks, do not approach the three-sixteenths inch thickness of the French regulators. The Comtoise regulators have a six-pound weight at the end of the weight cord, while Chloe's clock has a nine-pound weight, compounded by a pulley on the weight cord, so only four and one half pounds of weight drive that giant pendulum. The French clockmakers hung the pendulum on the front of the movement, but this clock has the pendulum on the back.

The center arbor in all of these jeweler's regulators bears the escape wheel inside the movement, and extends out the front of the dial to carry the sweep second hand. The huge pendulum swings an arc of only two or three inches, which gives it a lazy appearance. With each swing of the pendulum, the second hand leaps ahead one second. When I overhauled Chloe's clock, I discovered that there was excessive endplay in the center arbor. I could grasp the arbor with tweezers and jiggle it back and forth quite freely. Since I had to install a bushing at the rear end of this arbor anyhow, I used an extra thick bushing to extend inside the back plate and eliminate the unnecessary endplay.

When I placed the repaired movement on my test stand, I found that I had to cut oblong slots in the sides of the stand to accommodate the gentle swing of the large, lethargic pendulum. The clock ran perfectly on the stand, and I informed Chloe that I would return it to the store on a certain day. Chloe said, "Since that's such a famous clock around here, I talked to the newspaper editor about you repairing it. When you bring it in, I'm supposed to inform her, and she'll send over a reporter to interview you and take our picture with the repaired clock."

I said, "That will be just fine," as I thought of the great advertising this would be for my clock repair business.

I had to make several trips from my vehicle into the jewelry store to carry my tool case, the weight, pendulum, and, finally, the movement with attached dial. I began installing the clock in its case, and Chloe asked, "Is it all right if I call the newspaper now?"

"Certainly," I said confidently. "I'll have it going in five minutes."

A couple of minutes later, Chloe yelled to me from the back of the store to say, "She'll be here with the camera in ten or fifteen minutes."

By now I had the clock in the case, had hooked the weight on the pulley, and hung the huge pendulum in place on the stud at the rear of the movement. I wound the clock and gave the pendulum a gentle push. The clock refused to run! I was filled with horror, as I imagined headlines, "Local Clockmaker Fails in First Attempt to Repair Historic Clock" or "If At First You Don't Succeed; Meadows Will Make Second Attempt to Repair Tomblin Clock."

I frantically studied the clock, which for two weeks had been running with *joi d'vivre* in my shop. The heavy pendulum continued to swing from the momentum I had given it, but the delicate second hand remained as still as if painted on the dial. I manipulated various wheels and parts in the clock, while fixing my eyes on the second hand and hoping for a reaction. In a couple of minutes I discovered the problem, but what could I do about it?

When the clock had rested on a seatboard on my test stand in the shop, the front and back plates of the movement were "relaxed." However, the movement was mounted in the case in such a way that the weight of the twelve and one-half pound pendulum on the back of the movement put a pry on the back plate, flexing it inward. That was the reason the maker had allowed excessive endplay in the center arbor. When the movement was in the clock case, the leverage of the pendulum pressed the back plate inward, eliminating the endplay. This squeezed the center arbor between the two plates like a vise. I had eliminated that necessary excessive endplay with my extra-long bushing.

I imagined the reporter walking along the street towards the store with her camera, cheerfully greeting the townspeople she met, unaware of the great embarrassment she was about to cause me. I felt desperate. What could I do? I thought of a perilous possibility. If I tapped on the end of the center arbor where it protruded slightly through the hub of the second hand, could I move that rear bushing enough to provide some endplay? It did not seem likely, but I had to try it.

I opened my tool case and extracted a brass-headed hammer. Luckily, all three ladies on duty in the store that day were at the back, out of sight of the clock. I mounted the stepladder, looked fearfully at the priceless porcelain dial, said a quick prayer, took aim, and clouted the arbor a smart rap with the hammer. The irreplaceable dial rattled alarmingly, but the second hand began to pace deliberately around the dial with each slow swing of the pendulum. "Tick . . . tock . . . tick . . . tock . . . tick . . . tock . . . tick . . . tock . . . tick . . . tock."

The hand marked off ten seconds and then stopped dead. I climbed down and peeked around the corner to be sure the ladies were still safely in the back. I climbed up, took careful aim, and whacked it again. The dial gave an unnerving clatter, but the second hand began its march again. For over twenty years I saw the clock unhurriedly ticking off time almost every time I was in Cassville. Twenty-three years later, almost to the day, it stopped, and I brought it back to my shop for cleaning and lubrication—and to correct that lack of endplay in the center arbor.

Now and then I run across a copy of that old newspaper clipping. Under the headline, "Meadows Restores Well-Known Clock" is a picture of me standing with Chloe beside the giant clock. We both have cheerful smiles on our faces. Funny that no one ever noticed those crossed fingers on both of my hands.

Lavern in Peril

Our friend, Lavern Madison, was our farrier for many years. He was the same in animation and appearance at eighty as he was at fifty. People said, "I knew Lavern when I was a kid. I kept getting older, but he just stayed the same."

Lavern started shoeing horses when he was in his twenties, and continued shoeing them for the next sixty years. When he first started, he got six dollars per horse. He was working full time for the Missouri Department of Transportation, so he shod twelve horses every Saturday and made seventy-two dollars.

Lavern told me that he had two close calls while shoeing horses.

One time, Lavern was shoeing a stallion and holding its front foot between his legs as he trimmed it. All of a sudden the stallion reared up and knocked Lavern down on the ground. Then it reared again and tried to bring its front hooves down on Lavern to kill him. Lavern rolled, and WHAM, the hooves landed right beside him. The stallion reared again, and Lavern rolled again, and WHAM, they came beside him again. Rear and roll, rear and roll! It was rear and roll (not rock and roll) until Lavern finally rolled under his pickup.

On another occasion, a lady called Lavern to come and shoe a retired race horse she had bought. Once again, Lavern was working on the front foot, and the horse reared up and actually threw Lavern through the air. He landed, and the horse came after him, rearing to come down and kill him with the front feet. Lavern was too quick for the horse. He jumped up and ran under the rearing horse's front legs. Lavern gave the horse a mighty shove, and it toppled over backward!

Lavern finished shoeing the chastened horse and told the woman, "Don't ever call me again to shoe that horse. I'd as lief not be killed shoeing a horse, if I can avoid it."

Lavern had dozens of stories. One horse owner told him, "Nobody can shoe this horse's hind feet. Can you shoe them?"

Lavern said, "Yes, I can if you'll lift his tail up over his back and keep it pressed down there while I shoe." Lavern told me that he had the rear hooves shod in fifteen minutes and that he never had done that tail trick before or since.

"How on earth did you know that would work?" I asked.

He said, "That's the old trick I heard they used to use on bulls when they castrated them."

Lavern was still going strong at age eighty-six. He never stopped shoeing horses, and he was still winning buckles in rodeo competitions against men half his age and younger. In 2020, in a team penning competition, the mare he was riding reared and went over backward on top of Lavern, killing him. Lavern died young at age eighty-six, doing what he loved to do!

Herman Again

In October 2002, our son Chris sent me a CD-ROM of the *Complete Herman Collection*. The Herman cartoons, written by Jim Unger, ran from 1974 to 1994, and this CD contains every one. The collection reminded me of another Herman collection in another time and another place—1980 in Jonesboro, Arkansas, to be specific.

The hot summer of 1980 was one of record heat, with temperatures in Jonesboro, Arkansas, rising above 100° Fahrenheit for three weeks running. It was so blistering that Judy sometimes found our cats lying in the shade, panting and debilitated. She would grab up each one in turn and wet it down with chilly water from the garden hose to cool it off, a kind gesture that went unappreciated by the cats.

The hot summer of 1980, I had a tooth that was giving me fits. My dentist said that I required some sort of surgery to cut the nerve at the end of the tooth's root. I believe that it was called a "something-ectomy." My dentist sent me to Dr. Newby, a dental surgeon.

Dr. Newby was a green young man, fresh out of dental college. I do not know if I was his first patient, but I must have been among the first. I tell every medical provider that I am highly allergic to aspirin. Indeed, Dr. Newby's nurse wrote "ASPIRIN ALLERGY" in bold red letters on the front of the file folder she prepared for me.

As Judy drove me home from the surgery, she stopped at a drugstore to pick up Dr. Newby's prescription for pain pills. At home, I took the first pill and prepared to go to bed. However, I began to suffer anaphylactic shock, which indicated that the pain pills contained aspirin. Judy bundled our little boys, Chris, Aaron, and Alex, into the car with me, and drove to the emergency room, where a nurse consulted Dr. Newby at home, and then injected me with epinephrine. The epinephrine opened my breathing passages, but left me very shaky and ill. The nurse told us that Dr. Newby was calling the drug store and ordering a different pain prescription for me.

A few days later I returned to Dr. Newby for my follow-up visit. He held up my folder and said with a cheerful chuckle, "Look at that! It says 'ASPIRIN ALLERGY' in big red letters on your folder. Isn't it funny that I went ahead and prescribed it anyhow?"

I said, "It's not funny to me, since I had to go to the emergency room. In fact, I have the bill for the emergency room right here, and I expect you to pay it, since you caused it."

Dr. Newby said, "Oh, I don't think I could do that."

He left the examining room. When he came back a few minutes later, he said, "I was just joking about not paying the emergency room bill. Give it here, and I'll be happy to pay it."

Of course I knew that he had phoned his lawyer and been told, "Consider yourself lucky that you're getting off this easily. He has an iron-clad case for a malpractice suit. He can sue you from hell to breakfast, and any judge or jury would convict you."

But getting back to the day of the surgery, it was night by the time we waited the required time at the emergency room, then went to the pharmacy again, and finally got home. I went straight to bed. The next day I was quite feeble, from the anaphylactic shock and the epinephrine on top of the surgery. The day grew hotter, and so did the house. We finally realized that our air conditioning had broken down! The temperature was going to be over 100 degrees again that day. Our house, which was designed for central air conditioning, brought to mind the old expression about the hubs of Hades. I remembered someone saying, "It was 100° in the shade . . . and there WASN'T any shade!"

I got the small window air-conditioner from the window of our garage workshop and installed it in the window of the master bedroom. This provided an oasis of cool in a desert of heat. As I lay in a stupor of pain pills, Judy and the three boys would come into the bedroom and read or play in the coolness. Judy would go out into the sweltering house to cook or do some chores, then return to get cool. The air conditioning repairman came and went. He had to get a part from Memphis to fix our system, and that would take another day or two. In the meantime, we lived mostly in our bedroom island of cool in the house of heat.

Judy was anxious not only about my health, but also because her friend, Judy Schaefer, was due to arrive all the way from Michigan to visit us for a few days, bringing her little boy Matthew with her. Would our air conditioning be repaired in time? If our house was still as broiling as a blast furnace, would there be room for two more on the floor of our cool bedroom? When Judy Schaefer arrived, would I even be well enough to go meet her at the train station? These imponderables hung in the hot air as we went about our new life in the sweltering house with one cool room.

The air conditioning man came with the part from Memphis, and I did get well enough to go get Judy Schaefer and Matthew. The only thing I remember about her visit was going to pick her up at the train station. My Judy stayed home, since the train would arrive after 10:00 p.m., well past our boys' bedtime. I drove alone to the station at Marked Tree, Arkansas, about twenty-five miles away. Marked Tree is surrounded by amply irrigated rice fields, and the depot was just outside town where the tracks ran through those sultry, soggy fields. On that blistering night, the mosquitoes were so plentiful and vicious that Judy Shaefer and I could barely get her luggage and little boy stowed in the car and speed away without being eaten alive.

But getting back to my recuperation before the air conditioner was fixed, the second day after my operation, I felt well enough to get up and sit in the shade, outside the sweltering house. When the mailman came that day, he brought a package for me. Several weeks earlier, I had seen an advertisement for the first collection of Herman cartoons in book form. Judy had said, "Why don't you get it, since you enjoy Herman so much."

So my book arrived, just at the right time to cheer me up. Judy and I sat in the shade, and I began reading my new book and laughing and laughing and laughing. I cackled. I chortled. I guffawed. In fact, I laughed so hard and uncontrollably that I began to suffer pain and discomfort from all the laughter and had to lie down on the parched grass, trying to think unhappy thoughts to quell my mirth. My first exposure to a collection of Herman cartoons ended with this conversation:

Judy: "Give me that book!"

Mark: "But I want to read it."

Judy: "You're not going to read it now. You don't know what's good for you. All this laughing is making you sick, and I won't have it. Hand it over!"

Mark: "But . . . "

Judy: "Give me the book!"

Mark: "Yes, Dear."

Herman cartoons have remained favorites of mine, but they never again evoked in me the hilarity that they did on that hot day in 1980.

The Unforthcoming Carrier

As far back into my childhood as my memory extends, my parents subscribed to the *Joplin Globe*, a good conservative newspaper published in Joplin, Missouri. We children enjoyed the black and white comic strips in the daily paper—Alley Oop, Dick Tracy, Li'l Abner, Bringing Up Father, and many more. Since we lived far out in the country, the newspaper came by mail, each issue arriving the day after it was published. On Monday we got no paper. On Tuesdays we received the Monday paper and also the Sunday paper, which had the comic section we called "the colored funnies."

Even after Daddy died in 1990, Mama continued to subscribe to the *Joplin Globe*, which she read avidly. In 2004, when she was eighty-nine, Mama moved to an apartment in the Ozarks Methodist Manor at Marionville, Missouri. For some three years she had the luxury of a paper carrier who brought the *Joplin Globe* to her door on the very day it was published. After about three years, her carrier moved on to another job, and the newspaper office was unable to find anyone to do the piddling job of delivering the *Joplin Globe* in Marionville. Mama once again began receiving her paper by mail a day late.

Mama's newspaper carrier was rather odd. She often spoke to him, but he never said a word in reply. He was a big, heavy, young guy and walked with a strange, lumbering gait. Mama thought he was in his twenties, but he was probably in his thirties. Mama always underestimated ages. When I saw him and tried to talk to him, I got the impression that he was mentally challenged, and possibly unable to speak. Dianne, the housekeeper, told Mama that she too tried to talk with him, but he would not say a word. He kept his silent gaze downcast and never smiled.

When Mama got her bill for the next year of *Joplin Globe*, there was a place on the form that said, "Tip for Carrier." Mama decided it would be best to leave that blank and simply give the carrier a tip in person.

She put a $20 bill in an envelope and waited for the paper carrier. He came silently trudging along with her paper, and she said, "I just sent in my renewal for another year of the *Joplin Globe*, and here's something for you."

She handed him the envelope. He opened it on the spot and exclaimed, "Oh, thank you! Thank you!" He grabbed Mama and hugged her and kissed her. She was delighted as well as amused.

Always after that, the carrier was as mute as ever with every person he encountered—except one. Whenever he saw Mama, the paper carrier's face lighted with a grin, and he greeted her warmly. Kindness and generosity can have unexpected results.

The Tobacco War

Tobacco is a dirty weed. I like it.
It satisfies no normal need. I like it.
It makes you thin. It makes you lean.
It takes the hair right off your bean.
It's the worst darn stuff I've ever seen:
I like it.

Cornwall Products
(copied from an old wooden tobacco box)

My Uncle Lee and Aunt Esther had tastes for a wide variety of indulgences in the way of food and drink, but there was one luxury they never enjoyed: an after-dinner smoke. Aunt Esther was flamboyance and flame. Acquaintances marveled at her colorful behavior and changeability, sometimes not even noticing the more subdued Uncle Lee in the background. But Uncle Lee was steadiness and steel. He stuck to certain beliefs doggedly year after year. Uncle Lee was passionately opposed to all tobacco products. In fact, few remembered in later years, that when Lee married Esther, he married a young lady who was puffing pleasurably on cigarettes. That flame was quickly and quietly doused by the silent resolve of her new husband.

The cross that Uncle Lee had to bear most of his life was that his father Will was a lifelong cigarette smoker. By the time I was aware of this conflict, Uncle Lee was in his sixties, and his father was in his eighties. At that time Uncle Lee and Aunt Esther lived out of state, but every few months they would come to Missouri for a visit. Invariably, Uncle Lee would beard his father and make one more try at tempting the old fellow to give up his "coffin nails."

As a child, I overheard Uncle Lee ranting on the subject in our home, his agitation adding a Swedish rhythm to his clipped speech. He told my father, "Dad doesn't get out and around much anymore. He mostly sits there in his overstuffed rocking chair, rolling those damned cigarettes and smoking. The whole attic is full of Prince Albert and Velvet tobacco cans. And as soon as he gets the cigarette going good, he dozes off. I won't be surprised if he burns the house down, with him and Mom inside."

The tobacco argument was one, which Uncle Lee could never win, as his father simply agreed with everything he said. Lee said, "No telling how much damage you've done to your lungs with all your smoking."

Will replied, "Yes, by golly, I'd be better off if I never had started smoking."

"That cigarette smoke is bad for Mom, too," Lee continued.

Will agreed, "I bet you're right on that. It's bound to take a toll on her health."

"And you may burn the house down one of these days, if you don't stop falling asleep with a burning cigarette in your hand," argued Lee.

Will said, "Yes, probably will. I'd better try and stay awake."

Lee drove his point home, "What you should do is stop smoking right now."

"Yes, that would be the thing to do," said the old man, as he sprinkled Velvet tobacco into a cigarette paper.

It is emasculating and frustrating to argue with someone who agrees with everything you say, but continues blatantly to do what you both agree should not be done. Uncle Lee took the only action left open to him.

God had blessed old Will with the ability to grow a mustache of gigantic and startling dimensions, a mustache that most men could aspire to only in dreams. God intended for the mustache to be white, but tobacco dyed it yellow. Will was a slight man, but the magnificence of his huge mustache seemed to enlarge his stature, so that no one thought of him as smaller than other men.

When Uncle Lee lost the tobacco argument, actually lost it by winning it, he drew his barber scissors and attacked the monstrous mustache. While he snipped, he admonished his father, "You're bound to catch these whiskers on fire, so we're going to trim them down to a safe size."

With a snip, snip, snip, and a snicker-snack, he reduced the gargantuan growth to mere stubble. I think that there was more to the assault than reducing the fire hazard. I believe it also was a way for Uncle Lee to overcome the impotence he felt at his father always winning the argument by agreeing with him. With his colossal mustache removed, Will lost his impressive deportment and was transformed into simply a little old man with a cigarette.

Old Will had the last laugh, in that his whiskers grew with surprising rapidity. In no time at all he was living life again behind a fabulous façade . . . a yellow façade, but a fabulous one.

Uncle Lee worked himself into an ecstasy of annoyance as he told my father about his frustration in failing to get his father to give up cigarettes. My father always ended the discussion by declaring mirthfully, "Yes, I agree one hundred percent. Those cigarettes are going to kill him . . . *if he lives long enough!*"

Sure enough, Will did not live to see his one-hundredth year, but was snatched away at the age of ninety. It had to be that dirty weed!

A Bell for the Farm

Hear the tolling of the bells — iron bells!
What a world of solemn thought their monody compels!
~from Edgar Allen Poe "The Bells"

In 1983, I noticed an advertisement in a magazine for iron farm bells from a foundry in Georgia. The notice extolled the bells as all that one could ever wish to own for his farm and at a very reasonable cost. I think they were twenty-nine dollars plus shipping. I decided to order one, and told my father what I was going to do. He immediately said, "I always wanted a farm bell, so order me one too."

In those days the letters flew back and forth between my mother and all her children. Mama soon spread the word that Daddy and I were buying farm bells. Both my sister Shirley and brother Denis asked me to order a bell apiece for them. I wrote a check for the total amount and mailed in my order for four bells.

A few weeks later I got a phone call from the railway freight company that I had four boxes awaiting pickup. On my lunch hour I drove my Dodge van to the railway freight company and picked up the four boxes.

At the time when I ordered the four bells, I was Head Catalog Librarian at Arkansas State University. I had twelve or fifteen ladies working for me. Several were intrigued by the purchase of these bells and were eager to see what they looked like. So, for our afternoon coffee break, I invited any of the ladies who wished, to come down to the parking lot with me.

I opened the side door of the van and pulled over one of the four boxes at random, saying, "This one will be mine."

I opened the box. The bell was not assembled. The bell, upright, yoke, clapper, and crank were loose in the box. The clapper was not installed in the bell. I handed Susie Vick a big wrench and said, "I'll put my fist inside the bell and hold it up, then you whack it a good one."

When Susie hit it, the bell rang so loud and energetically that it almost vibrated my head off. If I were given to strong language, I might have exclaimed, "Hell's bells!"—an expletive I have heard many times from salty persons.

During a quick visit to Missouri, we dropped off the three unopened boxes at my parents' house. Back in Jonesboro, I soon got a letter from Mama. Daddy had opened first one box and then another, trying the bells. All three were DUDS! Daddy was quoted as saying, "These bells have as much ring as you'd get hitting an iron stove with a hammer."

Daddy went ahead and installed his bell on a pole just for looks. I do not know what my sister Shirley did with her bell. Knowing my brother Denis's aversion to junk, I think it likely that he sold the bad bell in a garage sale and gave it a glad farewell.

Our bell was kicking around in our barn for over twenty-five years after we moved to Missouri. When we built a new house in 2008, I set a pole in the yard, bolted the upright to it, and shakily carried the heavy bell up a ladder to hang it in place. Now our grandchildren love to ring the swell bell where we dwell.

I still ponder how uncanny it was that I inadvertently chose the one good bell in the lot by random selection.

The Bungled Belle Terre Break-In

My sister Anne met Harold Sorbet, a soldier boy, on the bus in 1953. He was going home to south Louisiana at the end of the Korean War. They wrote letters back and forth, and in a couple of years got married and presently settled in Louisiana. In a line-up of Cajuns, my sister would fit right in with the rest. Harold maintained, "When it comes to Louisiana cookin', I'll put her up against anybody." Those people in south Louisiana, including Harold, still speak French on the street and have a culture quite different from what we civilized Ozarkians have.

After my father died in 1990, Harold and Anne bought fourteen acres off the old family farm and built a vacation home here in the Ozarks. They actually rebuilt in the sturdy stone walls of a house that burned soon after they met. They called it Belle Terre. Harold and Anne had lived in south Louisiana for over fifty years when the Belle Terre burglary occurred.

I think it was in August 2007 that three miscreants broke into Belle Terre, and stole some items. They then messed the place up, turning over the sink unit and the water heater, breaking it loose from its pipes, and dumping out all the boxes and drawers in the house. Then they went down the road to a fancy large home, broke in and stole some things, but worst of all, they tore the place apart. They even broke the porcelain toilets and lavatories, doing tens of thousands of dollars worth of damage.

These were not the brilliant villains you read about in novels, who commit the almost-perfect crime. No Arsèn Lupin, A. J. Raffles, and Professor James Moriarty were they! They had more in common with Larry, Moe, and Curly. In less than a month, the Barry County sheriff's office ran them to ground and arrested them. Two men confessed, but the third, a young man named Gulbrandsen, proclaimed his innocence and demanded his legal rights in the courts system.

Johnny Cox, the Prosecuting Attorney of Barry County, Missouri, decided to try Gulbransen separately for the monumental crime of trashing the fancy big house and the lesser crime of pillaging Belle Terre. Gulbransen's first Belle Terre hearing was on the afternoon of March 27, 2008, at the new Municipal Courts Building.

Harold and Anne came from Louisiana to attend, and went to the Prosecuting Attorney's office after lunch on the appointed day. Johnny Cox went over lists of damaged and stolen items with Harold, who felt some items were assessed at too high a price. A metal outside door at Belle Terre had a slit driven through it by Harold's favorite tool, my father's double-bitted axe, which was stolen. Harold asked that a door be added to the list. Johnny Cox apologized that he had another commitment and would have to assign his assistant to handle the court appearance.

There were supposed to be two prime witnesses in the court room, Harold and someone else, but the other witness did not show up. The judge, a distinguished white-haired gentleman, said that they would normally postpone the hearing until the wayward witness could be corralled. But since Harold had come so far, he said, they would proceed as far as they could, and then continue the hearing to a future date.

The courtroom had several officials, including the two attorneys, bailiff, officers, and judge. The audience included a woman that Anne and Harold believed to be the mother of the defendant.

When it was Harold's turn to testify, the judge asked him a few friendly questions, such as where he lived in Louisiana. Then the Assistant Prosecuting Attorney held sway and led Harold through his notification of the crime and the identification of the list of lost and damaged items.

At last it was the turn of the defense attorney, a middle-aged man with a black mustache. He questioned Harold about various aspects of the crime. Anne and Harold thought he tried to trip Harold up a time or two, but the testimony was cut and dried. Eventually he asked Harold, "When was the latest time you visited the premises before the break-in?"

Harold said, "Ummm . . . er . . . now let me think about that . . . uh . . ."

Anne could see that, as she put it, "Harold's elevator was stuck in the basement." She knew that he could sit there all day hemming and hawing and would never be able to figure out when he was previously at Belle Terre. She knew that if she merely called out a date, he would know the date, but not the scenario. He would still be lost, should there be further questions.

Anne knew that there was one two-word phrase that would bring it all back to Harold: not only the date, but also why they were there, that they had their friend Clair with them, that certain family members met them at Belle Terre, and that others would meet them in Kansas City, and the group would proceed west to the Sorbet family reunion. Two words would bring all this memory flooding back to Harold's meandering mind. She called out the two words softly enough to avoid being intrusive but loud enough for Harold to hear.

Harold heard Anne's still, small voice, slapped his forehead with the heel of his palm in a Gallic gesture and loudly repeated Anne's clue, which had restored his memory, "Bastille Day! Of course . . . it was BASTILLE DAY!"

The courtroom erupted in laughter. The attorneys laughed. The officers laughed. The bailiff laughed. Even the defendant and his mother roared with laughter. The judge almost fell off his chair laughing. When the laughter subsided, and the defense attorney got control of himself, he said with a last giggle, "No further questions, Your Honor."

His Honor wiped his eyes with a handkerchief and turned to Harold, "Thank you for your testimony, Mr. Sorbet. You may be excused."

The judge smiled at Harold in such a friendly way that Harold reached across the railing and shook hands with him. Having started, he could not stop. He shook hands with both attorneys and anyone else he could get his hands on—even with the defendant.

"This hearing is continued until a future time and date to be specified hereafter," said the judge, and banged his gavel. Everyone exited the courtroom in a happier mood than they had entered it.

As Harold and Anne left, they heard a voice from the courtroom behind them explain, "They're from Louisiana, you know," with the same intonation as one explaining, "They're from Mars, you know."

Hammering a Blade

On that long list of dying or dead arts we surely would find "hammering saw blades." Ordinary nine-inch and ten-inch saw blades used in woodworking shops are so economical these days that many consider them disposable. We don't even have them sharpened, let alone "hammered." I did not know the art of hammering a saw blade existed until the 1970s, when we lived at Jonesboro, Arkansas.

While working on a woodworking project, I let my radial arm saw get away from me and climb up onto a wooden two-by-four that I was trying to cut. The blade was bent, so that it wobbled. Since it was my only sharp blade, I took some others in to be sharpened and mentioned what had happened. The man at the sharpening shop said, "Bring that blade in. I hammer blades, and I can fix it."

I did and he did, and the blade ran true as new. How did he know where to hammer and how hard? What kind of hammer did he use? I always regretted that I did not insist upon watching him perform this mysterious rite.

My old friend Willard Patton was a carpenter and builder, so one time I asked him if he ever saw anyone hammer a saw blade. Willard told me this story.

In the early 1940s, Willard and his brother Leamon bought all the red oak timber on 1200 acres of land. Leamon Patton owned a sawmill, and they set it up near the west end of the property.

They cut and sawed into lumber all the red oak above eight inches diameter. The forest ranger came and inspected their work as they progressed, and gave them kudos for the good job they were doing of thinning and preserving the timber on the land. As they worked through the timber, they pulled up the sawmill and moved it eastward twice, so they would reduce the distance of hauling logs. About the time they finished this tract, the market for oak lumber plummeted. This was caused by some of the insurance companies announcing that they no longer would insure new houses framed in green oak.

Willard told me that every now and then, in spite of all care, a sawyer would twist his blade, so that it would wobble. There were only a few people who knew how to hammer a blade. One was in Springfield, and there was another one or two here and there, but they possessed varying degrees of expertise. It was acknowledged that the best of all the saw hammerers was Old Man Tippet at Wyandotte, Oklahoma. One time when the blade on Leamon's mill lost its truth, he said to Willard, "I think we need to get Old Man Tippet to work on this blade. I'd like you to take it out there."

They threw the forty-two inch blade on the flatbed truck, and Leamon drove a spike nail into the wooden truck bed through the eye of the saw to keep the blade from sliding off. Willard climbed in the truck and lit a shuck for Wyandotte.

"When I drove into Wyandotte," Willard said, "all I found was a little dusty town about the size of Butterfield, Missouri, and I didn't see anything that looked like a saw shop. The only sign of life was a group of rough-looking Indians playing cards under a cherry tree. I didn't much like the look of those Indians!"

If this fear seems fanciful, looking back from the twenty-first century, we should remember three things: Willard's outing was only fifty years after the end of the Indian wars; Willard was just a callow boy under twenty years of age, without a man's wisdom; and Willard had hair at that time. He drove down the street, turned around, and came back, so that the Indians would be on the left side, and he could talk to them through the open window of his truck, without getting out. "Can you tell me how to find Mr. Tippet's saw shop?"

"Follow that road, top of the hill, on the right."

Willard followed the road to the top of the hill, but the only thing on the right was a modest little shanty of a house, set back from the road. Then Willard spied a saw anvil in the yard under a shade tree. So there wasn't any saw shop at all, only an anvil under a tree! Just then an old man emerged from the cabin and admitted to being Mr. Tippet.

Willard got the blade down off the truck and Old Man Tippet asked, "What do you run this blade with?"

Willard told him what kind of engine they were using.

"How fast do you run it?"

Willard told him, "Four-fifty."

Mr. Tippet stood the blade on edge, with its teeth in the grass, and holding to the top teeth with his left hand, whammed the eye with the heel of his right hand. He watched the blade vibrate, then threw it on his anvil. Mr. Tippet's saw anvil was simply a one-foot cube of steel. The old man turned the blade on the anvil as he hit it with a hammer. Turn--wham! Turn--wham! Turn--wham! Willard counted ten strikes with the hammer, and then Mr. Tippet stood the blade in the grass again. He struck the eye with the heel of his hand, and Willard heard the blade hum. Mr. Tippet said, "I think she'll run now."

Willard said, "What do I owe you?"

Mr. Tippet said, "Ten dollars," which happened to be the exact amount Willard had brought with him on the trip. Willard almost reeled with shock.

"A good pair of new leather shoes cost two dollars back in those days," Willard told me. "A ten dollar bill looked as big as a saddle blanket. Ten dollars! He charged a dollar a lick. If he'd have hit it one more time, I couldn't have paid him!"

The Stranger

Be not forgetful to entertain strangers: for
thereby some have entertained angels unawares.
~Hebrews 13:2

Our friends Jerry & Sharron Hay came from Texas years ago to live at Pea Ridge, Arkansas, about thirty miles from where we live. They were slightly younger than Judy and me and strong Christians. They had grown children and grandchildren living in the Pea Ridge area. Jerry was a draftsman by day and a square-dance caller by night. Every spring Jerry participated in a Gospel Dance, wherein all the dance songs were actually old hymns with square-dance calls added, and the callers led the singing of other hymns between dance tips.

In 2006, Jerry told us that he would have to miss the Gospel Dance, as he was going to meet his daughter—and I do mean *meet* her, as he did not know her. Jerry did not go into detail, but indicated that he had been married briefly right out of high school, the baby was born as the marriage broke up, and they gave the baby girl away for adoption. Apparently the daughter, who was now thirty-six, tracked down her birth father, and Jerry said, "I'm as nervous as a cat and quaking in my boots at what she might think of me when we meet."

Judy and I were not worried, as we knew no one sweeter than Jerry. On April 20, 2007, we went to the next year's Gospel

Dance, and when I could speak to Jerry privately, I asked him how his meeting went with his daughter last year. Jerry said, "It was wonderful. We both cried buckets of tears, and now we have a marvelous relationship. We talk on the phone all the time and email back and forth almost every day. And I got not only another daughter, but also a son-in-law and a little granddaughter."

Jerry said, "The most amazing thing happened, and I love to tell it over and over again."

This is the story: A few months after they first met, Jerry's daughter called from her home in Dallas and said, "Dad, can you come?"

It turned out that the granddaughter had been diagnosed with acute leukemia, and doctors did not think she would live. The blood platelet count apparently ought to be around 200,000, and hers was only 2,000. Jerry said he would come immediately and drove to Dallas as quick as he could, praying all the way that God would heal the little girl. By the next day, the platelet count had dropped to 500, and the little girl's death seemed imminent. Miraculously, the count bottomed out and gradually started up again. Within a couple of days the little girl was almost normal, and there was great rejoicing.

Jerry left the hospital for the drive back to Pea Ridge. As he was stopped in a line of cars on a large thoroughfare in Dallas, he saw a ragged old black man standing on the median between the lanes, near Jerry's car. Jerry thought, "Oh, I bet he'll step over to my car and ask for a hand out," but then the light changed, and the traffic started to move. Jerry's window was down, and the old man called, "God bless you, Sir, in the name of Jesus Christ, Amen!"

That made Jerry feel guilty that he had not waved a bill out the window when he had the chance.

When Jerry got back home, he called the hospital and spoke with his daughter to see how everything was going. The daughter said that the granddaughter seemed nearly normal, had gotten her appetite back. Her husband even had to go downstairs to the cafeteria for some extra food.

She said, "He was kind of taken aback when he came back with the food, because in the elevator on the way up, he was alone with this old black man that looked like a beggar, and he was afraid he would ask for a hand out. But when my husband got out on our floor, the old man stayed on the elevator. As the doors closed, the old man said, 'God bless you, Mr. Hendricks, in the name of Jesus Christ! Amen!' and my husband wasn't wearing any name tag or anything and didn't know how the old man knew his name."

Jerry said, "When was that?"

She said, "He went down for food about five minutes after you left this morning."

Jerry said, "Let me speak to him." When his son-in-law came on the line, Jerry said, "Describe that old black man for me."

"Well, he was old with grey hair and dressed kind of shabby. He had khaki pants on."

Jerry said, "Old dirty white shirt with grease stains on it?"

"Yes."

Jerry asked, "Suspenders?"

"Yes."

Jerry asked, "What about his shoes?"

The son-in-law said, "They were worn out old tennis shoes or running shoes."

"What about the right shoe?" Jerry asked.

"The right shoe was plumb open on the front so you could see his toes."

They had seen exactly the same old man in two different places at nearly the same time, and he had asked God to bless both of them, even calling one of them by name. Jerry said they both had goose-bumps, as they were certain in their hearts that the old man was an angel, who was somehow involved in healing the little girl.

Jerry told me, "You'd think that was the end of the story, wouldn't you? But there was one more thing."

The day after Jerry got back to Pea Ridge, Arkansas, several relatives were at Jerry & Sharron's house visiting them, and Jerry had told this story several times. When it was time for a meal, somebody said, "Why doesn't one of us just run down to Sonic and bring back a bunch of food?"

Jerry said, "That's a good idea, and I'll pay for it." Some time back, he had folded up a $100 bill and tucked it away in his wallet for just such an occasion. He got it out and handed it to the lady that was going for food. She unfolded it and looked surprised, saying, "Did you look at this bill?"

Jerry said, "No. A square dance club gave that to me awhile back for calling their dance, and I just shoved it in my billfold for a special occasion. Why?"

She handed it to Jerry, and in neat calligraphy across the bottom of the bill were the words, *"In the name of Jesus Christ! Amen."*

Several years later, in the fall of 2014, Sharron Hay notified us that Jerry had passed away. The Bible tells us that angels escort Christians to heaven when they die. I have a hunch that Jerry may have recognized one of the angels waiting to guide him.

Ominous Omelets

The Culinary Institute of America, *aka* C.I.A., defines an omelet as: "Beaten egg that is cooked in butter in a specialized pan or skillet and then rolled or folded into an oval. Omelets may be filled with a variety of ingredients before or after rolling."

Notice that the basic omelet has only one ingredient, eggs — though usually the cook sprinkles in a bit of salt. Omelets do not contain milk. No authoritative source I consulted listed milk as an ingredient of omelets.

Some cheeky cookbooks have recipes called "fluffy omelet" or "soufflé omelet," which are attempts at omelets using milk as an ingredient. The resultant amorphous mass of insidious egg-flavored foam is almost, but not entirely, unlike an omelet. Somehow these sinister substitutes for omelets are now abroad in the land, appearing incognito on the menu of many restaurants and cafés in the country under an assumed name. The alias they use is "Omelet!"

Common cafés usually serve small imitation omelets, and this is a good thing, since the diner has less of the offensive omelet to get rid of. Fancy restaurants serve huge imitation omelets, and that is a bad thing. I once read the title of a science fiction work called, "I Eloped With a Blob from Jupiter." I would rather have a slice of that blob than of many restaurant omelets.

It is a lucky thing that so many people do not know a good omelet from a bad one. I suspect that they are happier in this uninformed state. This may be the one situation where the old saying "Ignorance is bliss" is actually true. It is true, since ideal omelets are nearly impossible to find, but bad ones blissfully abound in many eateries across the land.

A few years ago, Judy and I visited our son Alex and his wife Rachael in their new home in Greenwood, Indiana. They generously took us to breakfast at a fancy restaurant. Judy ordered strawberry pancakes with whipped cream, and Rachael made a similar outlandish choice. I wanted to order biscuits and gravy, but Judy said, "Oh, don't be a fuddy-duddy. You have biscuits and gravy all the time at home. Get something different that you can't get at home."

Alex said, "How about splitting this western omelet with me, Dad?"

I agreed. No one ever said that I don't try to please.

The omelet arrived, split onto two plates for Alex and me. Alex, in his good-natured, Candide-like optimism, smiled and said, "This is good stuff." I smiled and thought, "This is not good stuff, but I won't say so." I ate the unhappy omelet with happy face and without complaint.

After that meal, I secretly told Judy, "If I ever order an omelet again in a restaurant, please have me committed to a mental institution, preferably one with straitjackets in its repertoire, as I may need one."

A few years and several delicious home-made omelets later, my good friend Gary Denny and I carpooled on several visits to a chiropractor some distance away. Afterward we would stop for breakfast at a restaurant. Gary looked at the menu and said, "I usually order an omelet. There's not much anyone can do to ruin an omelet."

I must be easy-going and non-argumentative to a fault. I simply choked on a swallow of my coffee and didn't say a word, as I ordered biscuits and gravy. Now every time I make an omelet, I think of Gary's remark and chuckle. Gary is the lucky one, as he can enjoy a restaurant omelet.

My friend Darrell was serving at a church dinner, and one of the diners happened to be a professional chef. Darrell, testing my veracity, asked him, "When you make an omelet, do you put milk in it?"

The chef recoiled in horror, "Put milk in an omelet? Of course not! Never!"

A church lady, who overheard and should have kept her own counsel, said, "I always put milk in omelets," which gained her a look of disdain from both the chef and Darrell.

I already mentioned how lots of restaurants make lousy omelets while the C.I.A. and I make superb ones, though I say it who shouldn't. Restaurants mix in a flood of milk, while the C.I.A. and I do not add milk. Keep the cows and hens apart! Want proof?

When Alex and Rachael visited in the summer of 2013, I made a large milkless omelet enfolding onions, peppers, ham, and cheese. Rachael, who is used to eating milk-besmirched omelets in restaurants, said, "This is the best omelet that I have ever tasted."

I thought back to that restaurant omelet that I shared with Alex years before and realized that I had done exactly what Judy asked me to do, "Get something different that you can't get at home."

I got an inferior omelet. I can't get that at home.

The Ice-Mare

The big ice storm knocked out our electric power Saturday night, January 13, 2007. We always keep lots of candles on hand — which we finally got to use. The previous big ice storm of Christmas 1987 shut off the power for over a week. Barry Electric Co-op became proactive at keeping trees cut away from the lines, so that we almost never had an outage. However, in 2007, the ice got so thick on the power lines that the sheer weight broke many of them.

This was an odd ice storm, in that the ground was warm. We received so much moisture — about three inches of freezing rain — but the highways were never icy. However, the trees, fences, in fact EVERYTHING above ground level, was heavily coated with ice. Outside we could hear the rifle-shot sound several times a minute of trees and branches in the nearby forest breaking from the weight of the ice. The trees that were not broken or uprooted were bowed down. Our yard and barn-lot became filled with fallen branches.

When we were plunged into darkness, I lit candles then went to the barn with a flashlight and got a couple of kerosene lamps, which we had not used since Jonesboro, Arkansas, about twenty-five years before. Pastor David informed us that there would be no church on Sunday, the next day.

Back in 1999, we had bought a generator at Sam's Club on account of that Y2K scare. We buried a line to the empty old well house, where we would install the generator. We bought the big switch for about $100 and had the power company install it on the pole. The big lever switches the house from "line" to "generator," so that it is impossible to fry a lineman—as people have done more than once by using their generators inappropriately. Our new generator sat out in our barn, lo these seven years, being used as a rack for saddle blankets.

Sunday morning Judy and I moved the generator from barn to old well house, cranked it up, and had power. We ran it for about an hour to pump some water, but wanted to save it mostly for night time. We threw the breaker on our water heater, which requires a large amount of current, as we knew the little generator could not run it. We had to get out our old rotary dial and touch-tone phones, as cordless ones will not work without electric power. Our first mobile phones did not have reception at our country home.

We heard that a beloved lady in nearby Aurora, Missouri, whom I knew slightly, died as a result of the power outage. Her name was Annette, and she was the wife of a close friend of one of our church elders. She was also the secretary to John Lee, a bank president. Almost everybody in Aurora knew and loved Annette. Annette's husband worked for the power company and was out on the lines, but had left her snug at home with power from a generator. Annette went into the open garage to add gasoline to the generator, was overcome by the fumes and died right there. Her father-in-law found her. She was only forty-five years old.

Our son Chris was all right so far in his powerless apartment in Springfield, Missouri, forty miles away. However, Sunday morning, we heard that the temperature was to fall down around zero on Monday and Tuesday, with more precipitation. We decided to go get Chris from his apartment. We left here around 11:00 a.m. in our old Suburban.

It was odd to drive to Springfield and see all the darkened businesses and homes. Since all the traffic signals were dark, people had to pretend crossroads were four-way stops. This took a great deal of time and confusion at big multi-lane intersections, as many people did not understand the principle of when it was their turn.

On the way home with Chris, we stopped at a Walmart, and Judy went inside to buy batteries, lamp oil, and de-icer. They were out of everything she wanted! I waited in line for about a half hour to fill the Suburban and some gasoline cans with gasoline to run the generator.

This was a year before we built our new house, which was fortunate in a way. We heated the old house with wood, so we were able to stay warm without electricity. Still, that primitive life takes a lot of time and energy. It seemed as if I spent all my time keeping water thawed, messing with the generator, carrying in wood, keeping the fire stoked and ashes cleaned out, cooking either on the gas grill or on one burner with the generator going. One time I concocted the most delicious spaghetti sauce on the gas grill, then boiled the spaghetti out there to go with it. We kept two big kettles of water on the wood heating stove, so always had hot water for dishwashing.

On Monday when I tried to start the generator, I could not get it going. I even removed the carburetor and dismantled it on the kitchen table. Our friends, the Stewards, were not connected to Barry Electric. They provided all their own power with a big generator and storage batteries, so I asked Charlie Steward's advice. He came down and said that the first thing to check is the oil level. I said, "I did check it, and it is only halfway down to the 'add' line." Charlie said that when home generators first came out, people were always ruining them by running them low on oil. So the manufacturers now install a very sensitive oil-level cut-off switch. I added oil to the "full" mark, and the generator started right up.

One afternoon, I was so exhausted that Judy told me, "You MUST lie down and take a nap."

Just then the phone rang. It was a woman at Barry Electric Co-op saying that a desperate woman named Margarita Crum had called them saying that her trucker husband was on the road, and she and her two kids could not get out, as their long driveway was blocked. She lived about two miles from us, and the Barry Electric lady asked, "Can you go help her?"

We went and saw Mrs. Crum's impassible driveway. We hooked a chain to an ice-downed tree and dragged it away with the Suburban. I used my chainsaw to cut some ice-bound limbs that were hanging in the way. We got her quarter-mile driveway opened. The lady said they had drinking water, but could not flush the toilet. We went home and got them ten gallons of water —enough for four flushes. You have no doubt heard of "four-flushers."

Tuesday, we went on a foray to Purdy to buy horse feed and then to Cassville Walmart to get a few supplies and twenty gallons of gasoline for the generator. We saw many reclining stumps where trees had fallen across the highways and been cut and carried away by road crews. As we were leaving Walmart, a neighbor stopped us and talked our ears off, distracting me. Then Chris phoned, as he was already at the gas pumps waiting for us. All this so confused me that I went off and left our groceries in the cart in the parking lot! I had to go back later and re-buy them, as someone had stolen them. Well, it was only thirty dollars worth.

Two nights we had to run the generator all night long to keep the heat-light in the well house going, so the pipes would not freeze. We were better off than our neighbors, none of whom except Stewards had generators. Several came to get water from our well. Some of the neighbors had burst pipes, since they could not keep them from freezing.

We had been hoping for over a month that Chris would get an interview for a technical writing job in St. Charles, Missouri, at the company where our son Aaron worked. In the midst of this ice and power outage, Chris got the call! Aaron urged Chris to come "while the iron was hot," so we made plans to get Chris on a bus Wednesday evening.

Wednesday morning, we left home at 10:30 a.m. and went to Kohl's in Springfield to get Chris an outfit for his job interview.

Chris hoped to get on the 5:00 p.m. bus for St. Louis, which would stop at Lambert Field, near where his brother Aaron was. He tried to buy a ticket online, but was fifteen minutes too late. When we reached the Greyhound Station, the bus guy told us that the 5:00 bus, which was now running two hours late, was sold out. It had fifty-five seats, and they had already sold sixty-four tickets. He would sell us a standby ticket, but likely Chris would have to go on the 11:00 p.m. bus, which would drop him miles from Aaron.

Judy and I were desperate to get home. Just as we were leaving Chris, he discovered that he had broken his cell phone when he dropped it while packing. He could receive calls and hear the other person, but the mike was broken, so he could not talk. He said this would be no problem, as he could dial Aaron to wake him up, and then send him a text message.

We were near Highway 44, so headed west towards home. We were astonished at the devastation around Halltown. There were miles and miles where the power poles were simply snapped off and the lines on the ground. Hundreds of the thick, heavy wooden poles were broken as if they were twigs. Crews were working at establishing new poles, but we heard it would be six weeks before all the power was on again in that locality.

As we neared home in the gathering dusk, we planned what each of us would do. Judy would go out to the barn and feed the horses. I would first start the generator, so she would have light, and the well house could warm up, and then I would stoke the fire. When we got onto our ridge, by golly, the power was on in the whole community!

Our joy was complete when Aaron called to tell us that Chris had got on the early bus. He would have his interview on Thursday afternoon, and Aaron would bring him home after work on Friday.

Even after the weather moderated and the ice melted, the aftermath of the ice lingered for months. It was astonishing to go through any town or city and see all the street margins ricked up with big windrows of branches that people had gathered from their yards. The city of Springfield had to let a contract to a company that would spend weeks or months gathering up limbs and branches and piling them to burn. I heard on the news that they had two piles seventy-five feet tall and covering several acres. It took over one thousand truckloads of branches to clean up one Missouri state park.

The fire departments were kept busy by people burning their own brush piles and letting the fires get away from them. Some people broke their own limbs while trying to clean up limbs in their yards.

When everyone at church was boasting about the trees and limbs down in their yards, one lady piped up and said, "I don't have any limbs or trees down."

"How can that be?" said the amazed group.

She said, "The tornado last spring took all my trees out."

As Yakov Smirnoff would say, "What a place!"

The Fabulous Photo

I am one of those annoying people who simply never lose things. Oh, I might misplace my keys or the checkbook temporarily, but never truly lose them the way some people do. For example, I still have my every pocket knife, even the Barlow I bought as a boy for seventy-five cents. I have not lost jackets or wallets or anything like that. Therefore I was very surprised, when a clerk asked to see my driver's license to verify a check I was cashing, and it was not in my billfold! I realized that I had not displayed the license for three or four weeks. I apparently have an honest face, so no one asked for it. Over the next week, Judy and I searched for my license in every garment I had worn and everywhere else we could think of, to no avail.

When I was in town again, I went to the License Bureau to order a replacement. The clerk said that since my license expired in less than six months, we would start from scratch and get me a new license, rather than a replacement. I had to take a vision test, identify highway signs by their shape, and so on to get a brand new license. Naturally, I had to have my picture taken afresh for the new license.

The photograph on my lost license was so bad that I was embarrassed to show it to people. In that picture, I looked as if I had been dead for two or three days after succumbing to a long and debilitating illness. By contrast, my new license picture looked wonderful! The two license bureau clerks were embarrassed that they had committed a grave photographic faux pas in taking a picture of someone that did not look nutty enough for a driver's license. They implied that they would like to take the picture over and would probably have admonished me, "Now look goofy!" I firmly insisted on retaining their first effort.

Over the next few weeks, I made a complete nuisance of myself, telling all the friends and relatives that I encountered about my great driver's license picture, making them look at it and admire it. I began to notice people stepping back into doorways or slipping around corners when they saw me coming, for fear I would make them look at my driver's license again.

Then an incident happened that made me chuckle. I thought it was just the kind of thing that would happen in a movie, after someone had made himself obnoxious by compelling people to rave about his license photo. I received validation from a perfect stranger for forcing everyone to look at my license picture.

I needed to transact some business in the bank, and the young lady at the window was a new hire who did not know me. She said, "I'm sorry, but since I don't actually know you, I'll have to ask you for a picture ID."

I handed her my new driver's license. She looked at it and exclaimed, "Wow! What a GREAT picture!"

I admit that I would have been happier, had she not looked skeptically back and forth from photo to face, as if unconvinced that this stunning picture could represent the person before her.

Scotch Shortbread

My mother got certain prized recipes from radio cooking shows, which were prevalent in the 1930s and 1940s. Mama still remembered from a high school business class, how to write in shorthand. She always had a paper and pencil handy near the radio, to take down special recipes and the words of songs she liked. She especially prized recipes that purported to be "trade secrets."

Mama was a constant cook, and our family had luscious food the year round, but Scotch shortbreads were strictly Christmastime treats. Mama made them a few weeks early and let them "ripen" in the pantry till Christmas. This recipe was a trade secret from Mama's favorite cooking show, "The Mystery Chef." The Mystery Chef's uncle was head baker for a famous old English firm, and gave him the secret recipe. The original recipe called for twenty-seven pounds of eggs! This worked out to one-half egg per shortbread, so the Mystery Chef recommended making two at a time to use a whole egg!

How we loved the sight of the Scotch shortbreads when Mama unwrapped them at Christmas! They were round, eight or nine inches across, and nearly an inch thick—a beautiful tan color, with the entire upper surface covered with holes pricked with a fork. They were too crisp to be cut, so Mama broke off a piece for each family member. The aroma was nutty, and we blessed the Mystery Chef as we enjoyed the buttery rich crunch of our portions.

Scotch shortbread and haggis are probably the most famous contributions of Scotland to the culinary art. Most people I know would prefer the shortbread, since haggis is a sheep's stomach, stuffed with its ground up heart, liver, and lungs, then boiled three hours. Scotch shortbreads travel well, and Scotsmen abroad in bygone years always hoped that wherever they might be, a kindhearted friend or relative in Scotland would send them Scotch shortbread in the yuletide season.

I knew that the Mystery Chef had a radio show Mama listened to as a young homemaker. That was all I knew about him until the 1990s, when I bought *The Mystery Chef's Own Cook Book* in a used-book store. It was copyrighted in 1934 and 1945. On a special Christmas now and then Judy and I make Scotch shortbreads, following the recipe from this cookbook. I have even given the secret recipe to a few people; I never could keep a secret.

The Mystery Chef's Story

By 1906, the young Scotsman John Macpherson had built up a successful advertising business in London, and was well off financially. That year, he decided to travel to America for a few months to find new clients. He left his father in charge of his business and boarded a steamer to cross the Atlantic. John's father, in whose veins the Scottish blood ran strong, felt that his son needed a lesson in thrift. He refused to send the liberal allowance John had arranged, but sent him only two pounds per week. John had to leave his luxuriant hotel and rent a cheap room. He taught himself to cook, in order to stretch his meager funds.

When John fell in love, the longed-for lady lamented that she could not marry him, as she could not cook. He told her, "You will never have to cook a meal if you marry me," and he was as good as his word.

Within a few years Macpherson attained renown as a chef, and famous men and women coveted invitations to his home. When he was offered a national radio show in America, he chose the sobriquet "The Mystery Chef" out of deference to his mother. John's mother considered cooking to be a task that was performed only downstairs by the household staff. She was horrified to learn that her own son cooked, and she did not wish this family skeleton to walk abroad. John and his wife made their home in the United States for the rest of their lives.

The Unfixable Clock

I have repaired a number of clocks for owners who were told by other repairers that the clock could not be repaired. My favorite "can't be repaired" story involves Dan Philbrick, whom we knew in college and again encountered here in southwest Missouri.

Dan and Anita Philbrick moved to Cassville about 1985. They visited Dan's parents fairly often at Rich Hill, Missouri, an hour and a half away from Cassville. They invited the parents to come to Cassville to see their new home and the town where they now lived. Dan's father was immovable. He was in his eighties and would not go anywhere in general, and particularly would not make a trip where he must stay away from home overnight. Dan tried his best to persuade his parents to visit them, but the old man would not make the three-hour round trip.

In 1991, Dan came across the old family clock in the garage at his parents' house. He knew that his father and aunt highly prized the clock, as they frequently reminisced about hearing that clock tick and strike as they grew up. He asked his father, "Dad, can I take the old clock home and get it fixed up. It's coming apart, and I want to glue it and get the works fixed so it will run."

His father said, "Sure, take it if you want to. You can glue it back together, but you can't get it fixed. We took it to a clock man, and he said that it can't be fixed."

Dan glued the case and then called me to fix the clock. While the clock was still in my shop, he mentioned to his aunt Rachel that he was getting it repaired, and she said, "You can't get that clock fixed. The clock man said it can't be fixed."

There was nothing especially difficult about this repair job. It was simply an Ingraham mantel clock like dozens of others I have overhauled. After I returned the repaired the clock, Dan waited till it was about to strike eleven and telephoned Aunt Rachel. He said, "Aunt Rachel, just talk to me a minute and then I want you to hear something."

When the clock struck, he held the phone close to the clock, and Aunt Rachel was excited and astonished. She could not believe that the clock was functioning again, because "it couldn't be fixed."

The next time Dan was in Rich Hill, he talked to his Dad about that clock and told him how much enjoyment he and Anita got from hearing the clock tick and strike every day. About a week later Dan's mother telephoned and said, "Can you arrange for someone to drive us down to see you? Dad wants to come for a visit."

This was after Dan had been trying unsuccessfully for six years to get them to visit, and they had not come a single time. Dan happily agreed to drive up and bring his parents to Cassville for an overnight stay. During the visit, Dan often saw his father, simply standing by the mantel looking at the clock and listening to it tick and strike.

After the ice was broken, Dan's parents came to visit another time or two, but this was the last year of his father's life. Dan felt especially grateful that I repaired the clock just in time, since it was the lure that made his parents finally come to Cassville to see his home before his father died.

Sometimes, fixing a clock that can't be fixed, fixes family problems as well.

Better is the Enemy of Good Enough

We all have our favorite old sayings or proverbs. The one our son Alex likes best is, "Better is the enemy of good enough." I found this aphorism inscrutable and mind-boggling until I thought of a personal example of the admonition in action.

Good Enough

In 1997, Judy and I bought a West Bend bread machine that made bread in two-pound, loaf-shaped loaves, rather than the up-ended pans shaped like square coffee cans, that most machines had. The bread coming out in real loaves was the reason I chose this brand. In the next eight years, until the machine wore out, we did not buy a loaf of bread, other than a couple of specialty loaves on sale. Instead, we made all our bread in our bread machine. When that machine wore out, we bought another horizontal-loaf machine and kept right on eating homemade bread.

Our normal procedure was to put the ingredients in the machine the night before, and set the timer to have the bread ready for breakfast. Throwing the ingredients into the machine took no more than five minutes, and the machine did the rest. We had hundreds of breakfasts of fresh, hot, whole-wheat bread, spread with olive oil or butter and accompanied by a slab or two of cheese. After breakfast I sliced the rest of the loaf and froze it for daily use. Between those hot-bread breakfasts we consumed the homemade bread as toast, sandwiches, French toast, and whatever else one uses bread for.

I ordered organically grown, stone-ground, whole-grain wheat flour from the food cooperative we belonged to. It came fresh from the mill, and we kept it refrigerated to preserve its nutrients. Some of our friends had flour mills and ground their flour, but mills are expensive, and for us, the flour we got was good enough.

The Enemy: Better

Our friends Findall and Clementine Crancher were exceedingly health conscious — what some people call "health nuts." Findall was an expert on health, vitamins, and holistic treatment of health problems.

Every morning Findall Crancher used his Vita-Mix machine, something like a super-blender, to make a healthful drink for Clementine and himself to consume at breakfast. At 47,000 rpm the Vita-Mix pulverized or even liquefied just about any foods one put into it and made their nutrients available for digestion. Findall used all fresh ingredients, and the drink included innumerable fruits and vegetables, plus honey and supplements. Judy and I imbibed Findall's nutritious shakes, and found them delicious.

Naturally, Findall and Clementine love hot, fresh bread, as who does not? Judy and I were so pleased with our bread machine that we encouraged Findall and Clementine to buy one. In fact, I rushed a hot loaf over to their house early one morning, so they could relish the joy of fresh bread for breakfast. They extolled the excellence of the bread, and thanked us gratefully.

Why did Findall and Clementine not buy a bread machine? It was not a question of money. Cranchers were loaded, and money was never a problem for them. So what was the roadblock? The difficulty was that the Vita-Mix machine could grind wheat berries into flour, and it also had an attachment that would knead bread dough.

248

Findall said, "The minute wheat is ground into flour, the vitamins and nutrients of the wheat begin to break down. The longer you wait after grinding it to make bread, the less nutrition the bread has. We can grind the wheat berries into flour, and make our bread dough within minutes. We can make the most nutritious bread of all with the Vita-Mix. It's no trouble at all to mix up some bread with the Vita-Mix dough hook, so we simply don't need a bread machine. We can do everything with the Vita-Mix and have the most nutritious bread possible."

Isn't that great! Can't you imagine Findall and Clementine sitting down every couple of days to a hot, fresh loaf of super-nutritious bread? Think again! Findall and Clementine did not actually grind wheat and make bread, but because they *could* grind wheat and make bread, they would not buy a bread machine. If they had a bread machine, five minutes time would get them a fresh, fairly nutritious loaf of "good enough" bread every time they wanted it. But, since they *could* grind better flour than our good-enough flour, they did not make bread with any flour. And since they *could* make better bread than our good-enough bread, they did not make any bread at all. One time we bought them a gift of ten pounds of organic wheat berries, but still no fresh bread graced their table.

Moreover, Clementine read that the so-called "wheat bread" sold in supermarkets is no more nutritious than white bread. It is called wheat bread, but is not made with whole grain, but with white flour and a little bran. After reading that, Clementine simply started buying the cheapest bread available, which is that gooey white bread I hate so much.

The conclusion is that Judy and I consumed delicious, whole-grain bread whenever we wished Yummy! It sure was good enough. On the other hand, Findall and Clementine never had fresh bread, but were forced to make do with the cheapest white bread, which most right-thinking people cannot abide. They could not have good bread, because they could make better bread.

"Better is the enemy of good enough!"

Epilogue

Clementine Crancher discussed with me many times the problem of bread in their household. She said, "Findall doesn't want me to get a bread machine, because he wants me to use that Vita-Mix to make bread, but it's more trouble to mess with that thing and clean up the dough attachment than it is just to mix bread in a bowl and knead it by hand. He doesn't want to grind wheat for bread unless I use the Vita-Mix dough hook, and I won't use the Vita-Mix, so we have always had a bread impasse."

Remember that ten-pound bag of organically grown wheat berries we bought for Findall? We hoped that it would spur him to make bread. Clementine told me that fourteen years before, when they bought the Vita-Mix machine, Findall bought a bag of whole wheat berries, so that they could grind wheat and have fresh bread. Then they had this stalemate, and the wheat stayed in the freezer. Clementine told me, "When you gave us that bag of wheat, it went into the freezer too, but Findall did get out the fourteen-year-old wheat and grind enough flour for me to make one loaf of bread, and he let me make it my way, by hand. It was very good bread, but he still wanted me to use that Vita-Mix, so we never made any more."

One day shortly after Mother's Day, 2004, Clementine Crancher was shopping in Walmart and noticed a Sunbeam bread machine on sale for thirty-eight dollars. She thought, "Hmmm! Findall didn't get me a Mother's Day present. In fact, nobody did!"

Clementine bought the bread machine. She knew that in a few days Findall would be gone most of the day, from early morning till afternoon, so she stowed the machine out of sight, planning to get it out and learn how to use it while he was away. She intended to surprise Findall with a loaf of fresh bread when he got home.

Clementine carefully read the owner's manual until she understood how to use the machine. She put all the ingredients into "the bucket," as Clementine called the vertical baking pan, and put it in the machine. "But every time I turned on the machine, the bucket jumped loose," she said.

She never could get the baking pan to stay in place, so she dumped the ingredients into a bowl, mixed them up, kneaded the dough, and baked Loaf Number One in the oven in a loaf pan.

Clementine read the manual again. She called the Sunbeam hotline, but gained no useful assistance from it. Next she called her daughter in Texas. Her daughter said, "Did you press down hard on the bucket, to make sure it snapped into place?"

Clementine said, "I didn't press down on it at all. There is not one place in the manual that says to press down on it."

To throw the ingredients for another loaf of bread into the pan was the work of a five minutes. She inserted the pan in the bread machine, pressed down, and was rewarded with a satisfying "SNAP!" This time when Clementine turned on the machine, nothing much seemed to happen. She could see slight agitation in the ingredients, but no real mixing. After several attempts to make the machine work, Clementine poured the ingredients into a bowl, mixed them up, kneaded the dough, and baked Loaf Number Two in the oven in a loaf pan.

When Findall got home that afternoon, Clementine told him, "I baked two loaves of fresh bread while you were gone."

Findall said, "Oh wonderful! Let's have some right now."

They ate three or four slices off of Loaf Number One and froze Loaf Number Two, before getting ready to go to a square dance. Their friend Vicky rode to the dance with them. Late that night, when they came back home, Clementine told Vicky, "Come inside and let me give you a couple of slices of fresh bread to take home with you."

When she cut the first slice of bread for Vicky, her knife met a hard object, and she found that she had baked the machine's mixing paddle inside Loaf Number One, which explained why the machine would not mix the second batch of ingredients.

The happy ending was that Clementine now had a bread machine and knew how to use it. Findall loved the fresh bread.

As he was munching a buttery mouthful, he commented, "Next time you want to use your bread machine, I'll grind you some fresh wheat flour, if you like."

Clementine said, "Sounds good to me!"

The Unexpected Intervention

Every Christmas season, Elm Branch Christian Church stages a live nativity near the old train depot in Aurora. We church members assume costumes as Joseph, Mary, kings, shepherds, and whatever else is needed. The Buehler family and others bring some animals to enrich the stable scene. They bring a cow and calf, a sheep, a goat, and a large donkey. These animals endure the endless petting by townspeople, both children and adults, who come to see the live nativity. All of the animals tolerate the petting, but the most tolerant of all is the donkey, which is really a "mammoth jack." Red the donkey stands docile and unflappable while an endless string of people pet him, marvel at how huge his head is, get their pictures taken with him, and generally make him a center of attention. He never moves away or threatens to bite or shows any emotion whatsoever. He is so passive and imperturbable that one sometimes questions the keenness of his intellect.

A month after Christmas, Bill Buehler, the patriarch of the family told a tale of an adventure which happened that week. Bill's daughter-in-law, Erin Buehler, drove out on a four-wheeler to check on the cattle. She disembarked from the machine and was strolling among the cattle, when the bull took exception to her presence. He pawed the ground threateningly, then put his head down and ran at Erin to butt her. Erin, who is lithe and athletic, sprinted across the field with the bull's hot breath on her heels. "Any port in a storm," she thought, as she surveyed the landscape for some safe haven. The only possible refuge she could see was a big round hay bale. Erin ran to it, barely ahead of the bull, and jumped and scrambled up on top of the bale.

The bull began butting and bashing the bale with his head, trying to get at Erin, and she knew that time was on his side. If the bull kept up his assault, her fortress would crumble, and she would be at his mercy, unless she could outrun him. As Erin pondered her hopeless situation, the cavalry arrived in an unexpected form.

Here came Red, the donkey, looking as serene and pleasant as ever, but surprisingly, this time he was no more Mister Nice Donkey. Red put his ears back and threatened the bull, then began biting him. When this tactic did not quell the nefarious work of the bull, Red turned around and gave the bull both barrels with his rear hooves. The bull finally admitted that the jig was up and went running back to his herd. Erin quickly clambered down, ran to her four-wheeler and sped back to the house.

Bill concluded, "I don't know if that donkey was really trying to protect Erin, or if he just wanted to drive the bull away so he could eat some hay."

Pastor David said, "We can run a test at the next live nativity. We'll all start being mean to Erin and study the reaction of the donkey."

Everyone relished this idea—except possibly Erin, who preferred to test whether the donkey's long association with the nativity scene would induce him to protect a Christian clergyman under attack from his flock.

Ish to Indy with a Smidgeon of Einstein

I was a frugal child and always had a hoard of money in a cigar box in my drawer. I did not get my hands on much money, but what I got I kept, unlike some of my peers. I acquired my possessions by starting with almost nothing and trading it for something a little better, then exchanging that for something even better. By this method I worked my way into ownership of some pretty nifty property. One of my favorite types of chattel was the radio, and I had a number of trendy, old-fashioned examples in my early years.

In our kitchen at home I installed a shelf and placed thereon a favorite radio, one made of maroon-colored Bakelite. My mother and I were early risers, and we turned on that radio to listen to the morning news and the "Lum & Abner Show" as she fixed breakfast.

In April 1955, when I was eleven, I heard on the red Bakelite radio the startling news that Dr. Albert Einstein had died at Princeton, New Jersey. This news was comparable to hearing that the Washington Monument has blasted into outer space or the Statue of Liberty had danced a jig. It was impossible news, as Albert Einstein had seemed a permanent part of life. I thought to myself, "I will always remember that I heard about Albert Einstein's death on this red radio." Up till now I have, and it has been nearly seventy years.

Ish and Wanda Bowling were long-time friends of our family. During World War II, when certain items were rationed, Ish had access to excess goods, possibly from some sort of black market connections, and he gave my parents bags of sugar and some other commodities to help feed our large family.

Sometime during the year or two after Einstein died, I heard that Ish Bowling had an old clock out in his chicken house. I do not remember how I learned this intelligence. Possibly someone on the school bus told me. Suffice it to say that I was simply perishing to have my own antique clock, but what did I have to trade for it? I certainly did not wish to let go of any cash from my cigar box. The only thing I had of sufficient value was the maroon Bakelite radio. I hated to betray Albert Einstein, but what else could I do?

Since I was too young to drive, I persuaded Mama to haul me and the radio to the home of Ish Bowling in the country south of Aurora, Missouri. There I told Ish, "I heard you have an old clock in your chicken house. I was wondering if you might want to trade it off."

Ish was big, heavy, and smiling. He was even more smiling in his amusement at a young boy wishing to deal for a clock. He replied, "I'll go get it, and we can look it over."

He went to the chicken house and brought back a long-drop wall clock with octagon façade for the big dial. He knocked dust and chicken manure off the clock as he carried it to the driveway where Mama and I stood near our car. The clock looked dirty, disreputable, and encrusted, having served as a roost for chickens. Still, it *was* an antique clock. I thought of Albert Einstein, swallowed hard, and produced my radio from the back seat, saying hopefully, "Would you want to trade that dirty, old clock for this nice radio. It's a good one and plays real well. We listen to it every day."

Ish looked at the radio and said, "If you'd rather have this clock than that radio, why just go ahead and take it."

I never did believe that he wanted the radio, but have believed from that day to this that Ish was merely being kind to a young boy. He likely would have traded the clock for a yoyo or anything else I might have offered. I was in seventh heaven, finally owning my first clock, but tried not to act too exuberant as I stowed the clock in the back seat of our 1950 Chevy. On the way home I twisted around and looked at the clock a hundred times.

Back home I put a lesser radio on the shelf in the kitchen. I used paint remover on the clock to take off the old varnish finish, including the chicken manure. The public television series "Antiques Road Show" has taught us that I should have kept that old varnish, but I innocently removed it and rubbed down the oak case with linseed oil. It looked beautiful. The upper round brass bezel contained no glass crystal, but I learned that Gilbert Wolf Glass Company in Aurora would cut a round glass for me. Mr. Wolf cut the glass for seventy-five cents, and I soldered it in the bezel.

I cleaned and oiled the movement and assembled the refinished clock. I hung it in the living room of my parents' house where it stayed for decades. My father worked hauling new Studebakers from a forwarding company in Indiana in those days. He was surprised and delighted when he returned home in a week or two and saw the clock.

When Judy and I moved back to Missouri in the 1980s I brought the clock home from my parents' house and hung it in the bedroom of our sons, Aaron and Alex. In 2005, Alex and his wife Rachael bought their first house and moved to the Broad Ripple section of Indianapolis. I asked Alex which clock he would like to have for their new home. He said, "I sure like the clock that used to hang in our bedroom."

I replied, "You've got it!"

The Ish Bowling clock is a Waterbury "Regent." The original painted dial is in excellent condition, and so is the label on the back of the case, things that are important to collectors. This dial contains a cunning intertwined monogram of WCCo, a logo for Waterbury Clock Company, which I have never seen on any other clock. Judy and I owned a clock glass and dial company in the 1980s, and I copied that ingenious monogram photographically to use on our line of Waterbury dials. The lower glass originally had the word "REGULATOR" in stylish gold letters, but this word was never extant in the years I had the clock.

In June 2005, I cut a bottom glass from authentically flawed, antique clock glass and reverse painted the golden word in the original style. I also cut a new top glass to replace the one Gilbert Wolf cut. He cut it from window glass, which is about 30% thicker than the type I use. I cleaned and bushed the movement.

On June 8, 2005, we went to Chicago to see Rachael receive her Doctor of Medicine degree and transported the Waterbury clock to its new home in Indianapolis. We hung it on the east wall of the kitchen, a spot Rachael chose. It wagged its shiny brass pendulum happily and looked so at home there that it might have come with the house.

Juggling Knives

I have noticed that life has more difficult moments than it used to.

One day I was out working in the yard and decided to step into my workshop to make a telephone call on my way to the house. My cordless phone wasn't on the cradle, and I couldn't spot it. I pushed the page button, which caused this phone to play a little song. I heard the music, but couldn't zero in on which direction it was coming from. I pushed the button and ran into another part of my shop. I could hear the music, but still couldn't pinpoint the direction it came from. I tried four or five more times, running to different parts of the shop each time I pressed the button. Finally I gave up and went in the house.

I said to my wife Judy, "Will you go out to the shop with me and help me locate my phone? I hear the tones, but can't tell where they are coming from."

She replied, "Let me finish this first. Just sit and rest a minute."

I sat down, leaned back, and felt the phone press against my back! I forgot that I had hooked it to the back of my belt in case I got a phone call while I was working in the yard. I needed a vacation.

The next day began Labor Day weekend, and we planned to haul two horses to one of the large conservation areas nearby for a day of riding in our beautiful Ozark Mountains. When we ride in the forest, I hook on my belt a large Schrade knife in a leather pouch, as well as my Leatherman tool in its leather pouch.

Judy was already waiting out by the Suburban and horse trailer. I quickly grabbed my belt and Schrade from one room, ran to another room, and got the Leatherman from the top of our dresser. When I reached the Suburban and started to put on the belt, I saw I had the Schrade, but I had picked up, not the Leatherman, but a pair of reading glasses in a case that was lying right next to it. I didn't even want the glasses, just the two knives. "Just a minute, Honey, I've got to run back inside," I said.

I hurried back inside, my half-inserted belt flapping like a monkey's tail behind me. I laid down the reading glasses, got the Leatherman, and dashed to the Suburban, only to suffer another disappointment. In my haste, I had laid down the Schrade and picked up the Leatherman. Now I had the Leatherman and the reading glasses, but not the Schrade!

"Don't move till I get back!" Judy exclaimed indignantly, as she marched towards the house with the reading glasses in her hand.

When Life Gives You Oranges

Late in the eighteenth century a wounded Spanish ship took refuge from a storm in the shelter of Dundee Harbor, the Firth of Tay. After the storm, her captain offered his cargo of oranges at a cheap price, in order to empty his ship for repairs. The Scottish grocer James Keiller, ever after a bargain, bought the oranges, only to find that he had outsmarted himself. No one would buy the extremely bitter Seville oranges. The thrifty Mrs. Keiller, not wanting the fruit to spoil, began chopping up the oranges, rind and all, and boiling them with sugar to make a jam she christened "marmalade." The stuff started selling like proverbial hotcakes, and the news of this marmalade spread—if I may put it that way. Keiller decided to import Seville oranges on purpose and give up his grocery store to devote full time to making marmalade. The factory he founded is still making Dundee orange marmalade over 200 years later.

When I was a college boy in Columbia, Missouri, in the early 1960s I discovered Dundee marmalade. It was still made in Scotland, under license from Her Majesty the Queen, and was the most marvelous marmalade ever to cross the tongue, chiefly due to its bittersweet taste. I later learned that the bitterness comes from those Seville oranges. Smuckers, Kraft, and other American jelly makers cannot make good orange marmalade, as they do not use Seville oranges. Their marmalade is only sweet, not bittersweet.

I ogled the Dundee marmalade in the grocery market for years, drawn by the exotic appeal of the packaging, my hand stayed by the expense of the product and my own poverty. Finally I took the plunge, and after the first taste, I knew that I must evermore indulge. The earliest jars of Dundee marmalade I bought were wrapped in sturdy white paper, printed in black with the company's crest and licensing information. Inside the paper was a pint-sized white glazed crock with the crest repeated in black under the glaze: "Est. 1797. James Keiller & Son Ltd. Dundee Orange Marmalade, Made from sugar syrup and Seville oranges." The crock was covered by a little white paper cap, and there was a disk of waxed paper lying right on the surface of the marmalade. Before the 1960s were spent, Keiller modernized by switching to an unwrapped milk-glass jar designed to look like the crock, but vacuum sealed with a screw lid.

Part of my charm, after I discovered Dundee orange marmalade, was offering tea, English muffins, cream cheese, and marmalade to the unwary young lady who was willing to sit with me for a few minutes in a tiny kitchen at the huge Missouri Methodist Church, where I lived. I got a bedroom rent-free to turn it into an "occupied building" for insurance purposes. In fact, it may have been Dundee orange marmalade, more than my personal magnetism, which won for me as wife the most enthralling young lady of all.

After Judy and I left Columbia in 1970, we were never able to find Dundee marmalade again. We stopped having marmalade of any kind, since American versions are pale, sweet ghosts compared with Dundee. During the long marmaladeless years, we occasionally bought English muffins or made our own. And whenever we shared those muffins, we would get an orange gleam in our eyes, as we discussed the days that were no more, and the marmalade that embellished those days.

During the 1970s, I worked in the library at Arkansas State University. Each year, a book remainder company would bring several boxes of attractive, coffee-table-style books as a book fair for the university professors and staff. Library employees could select books for the library collection and also had the opportunity to buy personal copies. I bought a beautiful British book called *Preserves & Pickles* by Alison Burt (Octopus Books, London, 1973).

The book has a number of excellent recipes. For example, lemon curd is nothing to turn up one's nose at. But the reason I bought the book was for the marmalade recipes. It is true that the recipe for Seville Orange Marmalade is of little practical use to me, since I cannot obtain Seville oranges. However, the recipe for Three-Fruit Marmalade has been a blessing. The three fruits are grapefruits, lemons, and oranges, and the grapefruit gives the marmalade a bitterness not unlike that of Seville oranges.

Since we had used up our last jar of marmalade some time before, I decided to make a new batch one Sunday afternoon in the winter of 2003-2004. Mercifully, I forget from one time till the next what a long and tedious undertaking it is to make marmalade. First I sliced the fruit in half and squeezed the juice into a large cooking pot. I removed all the membranes and much of the white pith from the rinds and tied all this unwanted stuff up in a muslin bag, along with the seeds, to be boiled in the juice for extra bitterness. By the way, the British cookbook author refers to the rinds of citrus fruit as "the skins." After this preliminary wrangle comes the truly tedious part. All those rinds (or skins) must be cut into tiny slivers the size of matchsticks or smaller. Judy remembered how wearisome was this work and wisely suggested that I watch a movie while slivering those rinds.

I chose *Silver Streak*, starring Gene Wilder and Jill Clayburgh. In the early 1980s, when we got our first VCR, my sister Shirley very kindly taped several movies for us from her movie channel. We appreciated her effort so much that we did not decry occasional defects in her taping techniques. For example, when she recorded *Silver Streak*, she was not quite fast enough on the trigger, so missed the opening credits. At the end, she did not record the closing credits, in order to save tape and squeeze in one more film. We loved the movie, but for years we did not know the name of it. We called it "the train movie." Finally one of our sons bought us a copy of *Silver Streak*, and when we watched it, we exclaimed, "Hey! This is the train movie!"

As it turned out, the train movie . . . er, I mean *Silver Streak* . . . was exactly the right length. While the final credits played, I sliced the last sliver of rind. Then all the rind slices, the juice, water, and bag of membranes had to be boiled for two hours, to soften the rinds and impart bitterness to the liquid. At that point, I removed and squeezed the bag, added a quantity of sugar, and boiled the mixture for over one and one-half hours longer, until the marmalade reached the jell stage. Then I ladled the marmalade into clean pint jars, and Judy sealed them. The recipe makes seven American pints. For the first time, I added some commercial canning pectin to assist in the jelling. In the past I have boiled it a bit longer and found that critical point when the fruit would jell naturally, using some of the five tests imparted in the book.

Making marmalade left me so exhausted, I fell onto the bed in a deep and dreamless sleep for an hour before leaping up and having some toast and marmalade. Yum! Yum!

A month or so after making this particular batch of marmalade, I ordered a couple of jars of genuine Dundee marmalade through the Internet at a dear price. Judy and I were surprised to find it not as good as my three-fruit marmalade. Upon examining the label I noted that the Keiller Company has changed its formula. The stuff still includes sugar and Seville oranges, as of old, but now also contains fruit pectin, citric acid, and sodium citrate as well. I suppose the addition of pectin and acids enables them to squeeze a bit more marmalade from a certain quantity of oranges. They monkeyed with Mrs. Keiller's recipe and now produce a not-nearly-as-good-as-it-used-to-be marmalade, which is a testament to that profound commandment: "If it ain't broke, don't fix it."

Three-Fruit Marmalade
From Preserves & Pickles by Alison Burt

The total weight of the three fruits should be about three pounds.

2 grapefruits	4 lemons
2 sweet oranges	15 cups water
6 lb. (12 cups) white sugar	

Scrub all the fruit thoroughly in warm water and remove the stalks. Cut fruit in half, squeeze out the juices, remove and reserve the pips (seeds). Cut excess pith off the skins and slice skins into thin matchstick strips. Tie the pips, pith, and membranes loosely in a muslin bag and place in the cooking pan with the sliced fruit skins, the juices, and the water. Bring to a boil, then reduce the heat and simmer gently until the skins are tender, about two hours. Remove the muslin bag and squeeze out any liquid.

Add the sugar, bring to a boil again, stirring until the sugar is dissolved. Boil rapidly until setting point[*] is reached.

Pour into hot, clean jars, and seal. Yields about seven American pints, or ten pounds.

Note: When I made the batch referred to in my story, I boiled to about 210°F and stirred in one pouch (3 oz.) of Certo brand liquid pectin before placing in jars. The consistency was perfect.

---

[*] Alison Burt's excellent book gives five tests for the setting point. The two I have used are the wrinkle test and the temperature test.

Wrinkle Test: Spoon about one teaspoon of the preserve onto a cold plate and put aside in a cold place for a few minutes. If setting point has been reached, the surface will have set and will wrinkle when pushed gently with finger.

Temperature Test: Hold a candy thermometer in the center of the boiling jam, not touching the bottom, to get an accurate reading. Temperature should be 220-222°F (104-106°C) if setting point has been reached.

Why Verona Has No Water Tower

When we were passing through the hilly little village of Verona, Missouri, I told Judy, "It just occurred to me that Verona does not have a water tower. Wonder how they furnish water to the residents."

Judy said, "You could ask Jerry Pinkly. The Pinklys are an old Verona family."

Next time I saw Jerry, I did ask him, and this is what he told me: Verona was settled in the early 1860s, but formally laid out in 1868. Today, if you head west from Verona on what is called Powerline Road, you cross the railroad tracks and then a little bridge just outside Verona. That bridge was called Wagon Wheel Bridge, because iron wagon wheels were embedded in the cement on each side of the bridge to form railings. When the bridge was replaced in recent times, the wagon wheels were omitted. Just near that bridge is a spring, which used to gush out huge quantities of water, before modern industry and agriculture lowered the water table. That spring near Wagon Wheel Bridge supplied all the water needs for the residents of Verona in the early days.

In the meantime another small village was beginning five miles away to the east. Aurora was actually laid out in 1870 and was a little Podunk village like Verona. Small local springs supplied the water needs of the small settlement. However, in 1885, a farmer just east of Aurora decided to dig a well. In those days this would be a shaft about three-feet square and deep enough to reach a flow of water. As he dug, the farmer discovered galena and zinc ore! Very shortly, Aurora became a mining boom town. Even in the twenty-first century, there may be an occasional sinkhole in the city, when an old mine collapses.

The new growth consisted of a tent city of miners at first, followed by brick-and-mortar homes and stores. There was not sufficient water to supply the tent city and the growing town. The solution?

Aurora and Verona reached an agreement to build a five-mile pipeline so that Verona could supply Aurora with water from its big spring at Wagon Wheel Bridge. So Verona pumped water east to Aurora for several decades. Aurora reached a peak population of 10,000 in 1900. Today its population is around 7,500, and Verona's is about 650.

At some point, Aurora grew to the point that it needed its own water system. The city drilled deep wells and erected a water tower for the water needs of its citizens. As the years rolled by, the water table lowered, and springs either dried up or reduced the quantity of their flow. Eventually the Wagon Wheel Spring could no longer supply sufficient water for the citizens of Verona. The solution?

Verona and Aurora reactivated the old pipeline, but this time the water was flowing west from the Aurora water tower to Verona. The citizens of Verona even today are on the Aurora water system. Jerry told us that the old pipeline from the 1880's was replaced with a brand new one in 2012. He said, "It goes right past our house, and we could be on the city water if we wanted to, but we have our own well."

This is why Verona has no water tower: a historic example of "You scratch my back, and I'll scratch yours."

Held Up at Heathrow

In May 2005, I was visiting my friend Lamont. He showed me some clocks he had purchased at an auction, and my eye caught one that I liked, an English fusee dial clock with an eighteen-inch dial. I told Lamont, "If you decide to sell that English dial, I would be interested in buying it."

Lamont said, "You and Judy have a fortieth anniversary coming up next month, don't you?"

I said, "No, it's only our thirty-ninth."

"Close enough," said Lamont. "The clock's yours!"

I was very grateful for this large clock, although it did have a few problems. The round brass bezel that should hold the glass was missing, as was the pendulum.

My friend Tom Jago in England had the exact pendulum bob I needed in his clock parts boxes, and he sent it to me at no charge. No pendulum rod of the right size was available in the supply catalogs, so I had to make one. I cut a rectangular brass rod to the correct length, turned a screw on one end for the rating nut, which I also made, and slit a slot for the suspension spring.

The typical English dial case is held together by four removable, tapered, hardwood pegs. This clock had an assortment of pegs, no two of which were alike. I made four new and identical pegs on a lathe.

The clock was made long before the coronation of Queen Elizabeth II, but in 1953, many government offices had the logo of the beautiful, young queen painted on the dials of their clocks. Our clock said "G.P.O." on the dial below the hands, which showed that it was a post office clock. Above the hands was the logo QIIE, the motto of the queen. I liked having Her Majesty's logo on my clock dial, but unfortunately it was too close to the center shaft, so that the hands covered it up! I sent the dial to The Dial House in Dallas, Georgia, to have the logo repainted higher on the dial and the old one removed.

The next problem was the bezel. No clock parts supplier in the United States carried so large a brass bezel; however, one company, Cousins in England, did stock this size. It was rather pricy at over £100. I believe it came to about $175 in American currency. Still, it would be worth it, especially since we got the clock as a gift. I emailed Cousins and asked the procedure for ordering the bezel. I forget the details now, but in this negotiation, the man from Cousins revealed that shipping the bezel would cost over £200 or around $350!

I emailed back to that English cousin at Cousins and said, "I just want you to ship the bezel, not deliver it in person."

He replied, "The Royal Mail will not carry a package this large, and that price is simply what our contract carrier will charge to deliver it to the United States.

I emailed back, "Forget it then! I will have to find an alternate method of obtaining the bezel."

So the clock hung idle in my shop with no bezel or glass crystal. Two or three years passed, and our son Alex told me that he had to go to England on business and would be willing to bring home a bezel if I could arrange it.

I emailed my friend Tom Jago in England, and he agreed to obtain the bezel from Cousins, so that Alex could pick it up at his house. When this was done, I sent Tom a check that he could somehow convert into pounds when he cashed it.

After Alex's business was accomplished, Tom picked him up at Oxford and drove him to the Jago home at Arlesey, Bedfordshire. Tom was a widower by this time, and welcomed a visit from Alex. Both men are charming and engaging, and they had an enjoyable visit. Tom served Alex various comestibles, including tea in the English style with milk in it. Alex stayed overnight, and the next morning Tom drove him to Heathrow Airport for his flight back to America.

The eighteen-inch, brass bezel was too fragile to be checked through in the baggage compartment, and it was not boxed. It was wrapped in bubble-wrap and taped into a package nearly as big as a sofa cushion, which Alex carried under his arm. As he approached the airport security gate, Alex was extremely apprehensive as to whether the airport officials would allow him to bring this unwieldy item onboard. If they did not, it would create a problem, since the bezel was valuable, and not something he would wish to jettison.

Alex stood with the zaftig package under his arm and sent his carry-on luggage through the X-ray machine. His worst fears were realized when he was surrounded by airport police, who escorted Alex and his suitcase to a station at one side. Alex thought the jig was up, and the airport bobbies would seize his bezel.

About twenty-five years prior to this encounter, when our three sons were children, someone gave those happy, energetic boys three plastic potato guns. We furnished them a potato apiece and sent them outdoors. They would chase each other around the house and outbuildings shooting potato pellets at each other. What fun!

While poking about in British stores on this trip to England, Alex came upon potato guns for sale. He thought, "Why, I haven't seen one of these since I was a kid!"

Alex was excited to find that these potato guns were made of pot metal and much higher quality than the plastic ones of his youth. He plunked down ten nostalgic pounds and made one of the potato guns his own. When packing for the trip home, he intended to put the potato gun in his checked luggage destined for the baggage hold, but accidentally got it in his carry-on bag. It was the ominous X-ray of this innocent weapon that almost had the airport police doing handsprings. All their lives they had longed for the day when they might catch a terrorist boarding a plane with a gun, and they thought their day had come. After years of drudgery, here was the culmination that might get them all promotions.

Alex stood with the puffy package still under his arm as a security officer gleefully dug into his suitcase. The first item he pulled from among the clothing was a mechanical hand. He held it aloft with the air of one who had found the Holy Grail, and asked Alex accusingly, "And what might this be?"

Alex said, "That's the hand for a robot. It's rather valuable, and I would like to keep it, so be careful with it!"

Finally the officious officer dramatically withdrew the potato gun from under the undies and asked severely, "And may I ask you, Sir, why you are taking a weapon onboard an airliner?"

Alex said, "Weapon? That's not a weapon! It's a toy potato gun that shoots potato pellets. I had one when I was a kid, so I bought that one for old times' sake."

He explained to the disappointed cops his inadvertent error in putting the potato gun in the wrong grip.

The glum gumshoe who acted as spokesman, borrowed his last reprimand from the late Queen Victoria, rebuking Alex, "We are not amused."

The disconsolate officers gave up their quarry, but kept the potato gun, probably planning to nip down to the airport cafeteria to try and obtain a raw potato.

During this entire episode, no one examined or asked about the bulbous bundle under Alex's arm. It could have contained a bomb, a kilo of heroin, or dozens of other forbidden items, but the potato gun so unmanned the officials that they were too distracted even to notice the package. Alex and I have always credited his potato gun dodge with getting the bezel safely on the plane and on its way to America. I should buy Alex a potato gun!

When I reached the age of seventy in 2013, it dawned on me that the next knock on the door might be the Grim Reaper, a grin on his ageless face and a gleam on the keen edge of his scythe.

Several of our own clocks were like the shoemaker's children. They had been waiting for my attention for years while I devoted myself to repairing other people's clocks. One of those neglected clocks was the big English dial. I decided that now was the time to work our clocks in between customers' clocks before I heard that knock on the door.

The new bezel was a perfect fit. I cut a round glass and soldered it in place. I dismantled and repaired the movement. Ever since, the clock has held an honored place on the landing of our staircase. And Alex has the reward of telling friends his story of petrifying the police force at Heathrow with his potato gun.

Our Pink Cadillac

Judy and I thought we had stepped in something good in 1969, when we obtained a pink and black 1956 Cadillac Sedan deVille. This was a big, heavy, four-door car, but it got over twenty miles per gallon of gasoline on the highway, and was surprisingly light on its feet. A friend asked me to haul his new lawn mower home in the capacious trunk. He was astonished as he darted quickly and deftly through narrow alleys and sharp turns in his Volkswagen bug, to see the pink and black giant always filling his rear-view mirror, as I followed him home with his mower.

The Caddy had power seats and windows. It had the only automatic light dimmer that actually worked—an electric eye about the size of a tennis ball on the dash. The air conditioner blew from behind the back seat and was powerful enough to lift a toupée and frost the edges of a passenger's ears.

There was only one flaw in the 1956 Cadillac, but that was a serious one. The engineers who designed the engine made a mistake, and these engines invariably cracked their heads. In fact, I have never known anyone who owned a 1956 Cadillac that did not complain of this problem. After we owned ours for a short while, we found out that at least one of the heads was cracked, so had the engine overhauled. When the car was finished, the mechanic told us that both our heads were cracked, and he had removed the heads from at least a dozen cars at salvage yards before finding two that were not cracked.

I loved stopping at service stations to fill the 1956 Caddy with gasoline. Those were the days when service stations provided service. There were no self-serve stations. I would drive up to the gas pumps, and when the attendant came bounding out, I would say, "Fill 'er up with ethyl!"

The car was old enough that most of the attendants did not know that the gas cap was hidden under the left tail light, and was accessed by pressing a secret release button that allowed the tail light to hinge upward. After I gave my order, I watched in the rear-view mirrors, chuckling as the attendant optimistically took down the gasoline nozzle and examined the rear of the car. He would tug at the license plate and examine both rear fins for a filler door. Finally he would hang up the nozzle and come to my window to say, "I'm sorry, Sir, but I can't find where to put the gas."

I had a satisfying experience in 1972, while Judy and I lived in Kansas City. On the 1956 Cadillac, the speedometer cable runs from the speedometer down to the left front wheel. The hub-cover of that wheel contains a nylon disk with a stem about 3/8" in diameter that sticks inward and has a square hole in it, in which the square end of the speedometer cable seats. As the wheel spins, it turns the cable and operates the speedometer.

When our speedometer jammed, I took the car downtown to K. C. Speedometer Company—where the garages over much of the state sent in their speedometers for repair in those days. The mechanics told me, "Your speedometer has some broken parts, but we have rebuilt ones we can install." I told them to go ahead, and retired to the waiting room to read a book.

In a little while one guy brought that wheel hub cover to me in the waiting room. He said, "The end of the cable is twisted off in the nylon socket. We've been working for a half hour trying to get that cable end out, and it's impossible. We'll have to order a new hub cover. It'll cost you $26, and take a couple of weeks to get here. We'll go ahead and install the rebuilt speedometer now, and you'll have to come back when we get the hub in."

In those days twenty-six dollars was a lot of money. The Caddy was out in the garage area, but the technicians were still in the office and parts area, apparently getting a rebuilt speedometer from stock.

I went to my trunk, where I had a few rudimentary tools. Using the trailer hitch as an anvil, I took a punch and hammer and knocked the rivets out of the hub assembly, and took out the nylon part. I used a sharp awl to shove through the center of the nylon disk from the rear to poke the rear end of the square socket, forcing the broken cable-end out enough that I could pull it out with pliers. I reassembled the unit and re-riveted it back together. Only about ten minutes after the guy handed it to me, telling me it could not be repaired, I handed it back to him repaired and ready to install. He was agog and wanted a lesson on broken speedometer cable-end removal!

We enjoyed the 1956 Cadillac for several years, but eventually the two new heads cracked again, so we sold it and bought a 1965 Oldsmobile 98, another remarkable car.

Galloping Granny at the Hearing Center

My mother was kind and generous. She had a brilliant mind and was amazingly well-read. She had probably devoured close to a million books in her long lifetime. Mama was so beloved that many people still mourned her for years after her death, two months shy of 100. Was Mama perfect? No, she had one fault: she was a sprinter!

Year after year, Mama's six children tried to dampen her desire to run everywhere. For fifteen years after my father died, she lived on their 500-acre farm all alone and could run as much as she wished except when offspring were visiting. When progeny were on hand to see her run to the mailbox or run out to chase crows away from her bird feeders, they would reproach her and make her promise not to run. Mama always promised to do anything they wanted, but then did exactly what she had always done. One time Mama actually broke her ankle by running out into the yard, but this taught her nothing at all. I believe her inborn phobia of being late made her dash through life.

When Mama was eighty-nine, her children finally coaxed her to leave the farm and move to an apartment at Ozarks Methodist Manor in Marionville, Missouri. The other residents quickly gave her the nickname "Speedy," as they saw her rushing up and down the halls on her way to the cafeteria or some other destination. We children finally insisted that she use a walker to traverse the hallways, simply to slow her down a little and make her less likely to fall. But she still ran to answer the door or telephone and to go other places when she thought she would not get caught.

Mama's move to the Manor enabled Judy and me to pick her up every Sunday and take her to Elm Branch Christian Church with us. She quickly developed a new circle of fans, with her humble and humorous personality—always laughing and always friendly. Mama dressed attractively for church in dresses and sweaters. One elder told me, "Your mother always dresses with good taste. She sets a nice example. I wish some of our young ladies dressed more modestly. When I walk past their pews, I feel I should avert my eyes."

I said, "Are you saying that you look down on low-cut blouses?"

"Yes, I do," he said. "I mean NO! I DON'T!"

After attending the early service, Judy would escort Mama down the long hall to the "old ladies' Sunday school class." This job of escorting was actually the task of pulling back on Mama's arm to keep her from running down the hall and knocking people out of her way. One time when we left church, to cross the parking lot toward our car, I released Mama's arm for a moment to get my keys from my pocket. Mama, suddenly released, was ten feet away from me and widening the gap before I could even give pursuit.

As soon as we entered the Marionville city limit taking Mama home, she unhooked her seat belt, so she would be ready to leap from the car a few minutes later and go running towards the Manor—if Judy and I were not quick enough to grab her. One time when she was riding from church in the second seat of our Suburban, she unbuckled as usual, and when I made a right turn onto College Street, Mama went kerplunk! right over sideways on her side.

In spite of Mama's good physical condition, her hearing deteriorated so that she could barely hear. February 2009, the same month that Mama turned ninety-four, I took her to Enhanced Hearing in Springfield, Missouri, for a follow-up exam. It amuses me that the initials of Enhanced Hearing are "EH?"

We got to the hearing center at 8:30 a.m., a half-hour before it opened, which Mama well knew, since she constantly consulted her watch. Yet, when I got in the middle lane to turn into the shopping center where the hearing place was, she quickly undid her seat belt, snatched up her purse, and started putting on her scarf, as if getting ready for the starting gun! I said, "You might as well calm down, Mama! We'll have to sit in the car for a half-hour until they open."

I parked in one of the two reserved spaces in front of Enhanced Hearing Center, then read a Perry Mason book and chatted with Mama until the place opened.

Stan, the hearing instrument specialist, took Mama's hearing aids away to check them out. Without her hearing aids, Mama always talked loud enough to rattle the panes in the windows. I kept shushing her, but she did not believe that she was talking loud, so continued to do so. In the waiting room, after Stan took Mama's hearing aids, we were among several other patients. Mama thought she was talking to me softly, but actually bellowed in a booming voice such things as, "IS THAT OLD MAN WEARING A HEARING AID?"

That same time, Mama noticed the cover of a magazine touting an article about prostate trouble. She was always amused at the way so many people mispronounce the name of that gland, so she pointed to the article to make a little joke, shouting, "LOOK! THEY MISSPELLED PROSTRATE!" which drew skeptical looks from several other patients in the room.

Stan told Mama that he was going to put her in the sound booth and test her hearing. He said, "If you'll just come with me . . ." and Stan got up and started for the booth in the corner of the room. He looked back to find that Mama was out the door and hoofing it down the hall, having thought he was releasing her. He caught her, dragged her back to the room, and put her in the booth.

Stan hooked earphones to her ears, and gave her a hand-held button on a wire to press when she heard certain sounds. As Stan was getting everything set up and adjusted, he would ask her questions about the level of sound, and Mama would hold that hand-held button up to her mouth and talk into it to give the answer. Stan finally said, "Lorene, that thing you're holding is NOT a microphone. The microphone is fastened to the wall of the booth. That thing in your hand is a push-button that I want you to press when you hear certain sounds. Look at the end of the device, and I think you will see a push button."

She said, "Oh yes, I see it."

When Mama first got the new digital hearing aids, she could practically hear the ants walking in the trees, just like Tarzan. But after she had them for a couple of years, her favorite expression was, "How's that?" I got tired of repeating everything I said, as most of what I said was barely worth saying one time, let alone repeating two to four times.

After Stan did the tests, he said, "Her hearing test results are EXACTLY the same as they were two years ago, when she first got these digital hearing aids. Her reception of the various sounds is exactly the same, and her cognition of the list of words I spoke is exactly the same."

Stan said that he did not know why she would have trouble hearing now, when she didn't two years ago, when the hearing aids were new. He said, "One thing is sure; the hearing aids have not changed, so any change is within your mother. Sometimes the brain starts having more trouble interpreting the sounds."

He also coached her on being sure to leave her hearing aid in when talking on the phone. Yet always, the first thing Mama did when answering the phone was to snatch out her hearing aid. Stan gave her the free three-month supply of batteries, and we were out the door.

It was hard to outwit Mama and predict what unexpected thing she would do next. Enhanced Hearing was in a strip mall on South Campbell. This strip mall had a covered colonnade, so one could go from one store to another without getting wet on a rainy day, which that day was. Two stores south of Enhanced Hearing was a Panera Bread Company. As we left Enhanced Hearing, I asked Mama, "How would you like to go to Panera Bread and have a cup of coffee and a roll?"

She said, "Oh, I'd love that!"

I was parked in a space reserved for Enhanced Hearing. I took Mama's arm and led her two stores down where there were sidewalk tables and chairs outside the Panera Bread store. I laid my book on a table—I don't know why, as I should have taken it to the car, but was always a bit distracted when trying to corral Mama. I told Mama, "I have to move the car out of that reserved space. I will be right back. YOU STAY RIGHT HERE! Do you understand?"

She said, "Oh, yes! That will give me time to put the batteries in my purse."

I went to the car, backed out, and had to drive a few stores farther than Panera Bread to find a parking place. As I drove along looking for a parking space, I happened to glance over to my right, and there was Mama, her long green coat flapping behind her, galloping along in the colonnade, trying to stay up with my car! I do not know how she even spotted me backing out or recognized the car as I went by in the rain. I parked, got out, and scolded her roundly for not doing what I told her. Then I had to lead her all the way back to Panera Bread and inside to get our cheese pastry and coffee. When we came out, I happened to glance over at the sidewalk tables, and there was my Perry Mason book where I had left it. I had been so upset by Mama running down the colonnade at age ninety-four that I had forgotten all about it.

If only those chairs would have had seatbelts. I know it would have slowed her down a bit to run down the sidewalk while strapped in a chair!

Correcting the Strike

A lady called me from Golden, Missouri, about thirty-five miles away, to tell me she had let her clock run down, so that the strike did not agree with the hands. She said, "When it's six o'clock, the clock strikes two times.

I told her, "That should be easy enough for you to correct."

My first several questions were to find out exactly what kind of clock she had. I then said, "It's two-thirty now, so just wait a half-hour, till the clock strikes at three o'clock. It will strike eleven times. Then you move the minute hand backward to 8. You'll hear a little click. Move it forward to 12 again, and it will strike twelve times. Move the hand back and forth from 8 to 12 until it strikes three times, and you'll be all set."

She: I don't have my clock running right now, and it says 1:15 on the dial.

I: Then simply move the minute hand forward to 12, and the clock will say two o'clock, but will strike ten times. You then do just as I told you until the clock strikes two times, then set it forward to the correct time.

She: This is so complicated. Do you have time for me to get a pencil and paper and write this down?

I: Certainly, go ahead.

She: I'm ready now.

I: Move the minute hand forward to 12 and let the clock strike.

She: Okay, I have that down.

I: Move minute hand backward to 8.

She: Do you mean that I should move the hand backward till the clock says eight o'clock?

I: No. Let me put it this way. Did you ever notice that a clock dial has twelve numbers from one to twelve on it?

She: Yes.

I: And the number 12 is at the top?

She: Yes.

I: And the figure 8 is at the lower left?

She: Yes.

I: Well, move the minute hand forward to the number 12 at the top of the dial and let the clock strike.

She: Okay, I have that down.

I: Move the hand backward to the figure 8 at the lower left on the dial. You will hear a little click as you move it back.

She: Okay, now I have that down.

I: Move the minute hand forward to the figure 12 again and let the clock strike. Simply repeat this till the strike agrees with the hands.

She: All right. I have that down. One question, should I wind the clock first? I got tired of hearing it strike wrong, so I let it run down.

I: Yes, you have to wind it first. Otherwise it won't strike when you point the hand at 12, and if it doesn't strike we can never correct the strike.

She: Just a minute, let me write that down at the top of the page.

I: That about sums up how to correct it. It won't be hard once you get started.

She: Do you have time for me to read what I've written, to be sure it's right?

I: Certainly, go ahead.

She: Wind clock first.

I: Yes, that's right.

She: Move minute hand forward to 12 and let strike.

I: Yes, that's right.

She: Move back to 8 and hear a little click.

I: Yes, that's right.

She: Move hand forward to 12 and let strike.

I: Yes, I think you've got it.

She: Repeat till strike is correct.

I: Yes, you're in business now. That ought to take care of it.

She: I just thought of something I probably should have told you when I first called.

I: Oh dear me! What's that?

She: My clock has Roman numerals.

Things That Go Beep in the Night

From ghoulies and ghosties and long-leggety
beasties and things that go bump in the night,
Good Lord, deliver us!
~Scottish prayer

In our house we have seven smoke detectors: one in the basement, one in each bedroom or office, and one in each hallway. They are all keyed together, so that if one goes off, they all go off. This is a great idea, inasmuch as, if there were a fire in the basement and only that alarm sounded, we would never hear it upstairs. In November 2008, three months after we moved into our new house, Judy and I were sleeping upstairs, since our son Chris, with a broken leg, had to have the master bedroom on the ground floor.

At 3:15 in the stilly watches of the night, we were all awakened to the loud, piercing scream of the smoke alarms going off: BEEP-BEEP-BEEP . . . BEEP-BEEP-BEEP . . . BEEP-BEEP-BEEP!

I leapt out of bed, shouting, "Gracious sakes alive!" and donning my robe and slippers. Chris had a cold and had been making hot drinks for himself at all hours, and I thought at first he must have left a burner on. But no! I went all through every room from top to basement, but found no sign or smell of fire or smoke. Judy soon joined me, and she also found nothing untoward. Of course all the time, the BEEP-BEEP-BEEP . . . BEEP-BEEP-BEEP . . . BEEP-BEEP-BEEP! kept sounding shrilly on and on and on.

We turned off the heating system on both floors, then opened up windows all over the house and turned on the great exhaust fan in the attic to infiltrate the house with clean, outside air. After a half-hour of crisp autumn air whistling through the house and the alarms continuing to BEEP-BEEP-BEEP . . . BEEP-BEEP-BEEP . . . BEEP-BEEP-BEEP! Judy went down cellar and put Chris's two cats in a cage, so she could open the outer basement door and let clean air sweep through the basement, and up the stairs to the great fan. Still the atrocious BEEP-BEEP-BEEP . . . BEEP-BEEP-BEEP . . . BEEP-BEEP-BEEP! continued, as we wondered how long we could avoid madness.

I went around with a small stepladder and took all the batteries from the smoke alarms. They continued to BEEP-BEEP-BEEP . . . BEEP-BEEP-BEEP . . . BEEP-BEEP-BEEP! Chris rolled in with his wheelchair and said, "Dad, those batteries are simply a back-up. All the smoke alarms are powered by the house's electrical wiring."

So I went in to the big breaker box and started throwing one breaker after another SNAP-SNAP, OFF-ON. After throwing all the breakers, SNAP-SNAP, SNAP-SNAP, one at a time, the smoke alarms still kept up the BEEP-BEEP-BEEP . . . BEEP-BEEP-BEEP . . . BEEP-BEEP-BEEP!

By this time it was after 4:00 a.m. Cold air was still rushing through the windows and up the basement stairs and up the front stairs to the great fan to be exhausted, but still the BEEP-BEEP-BEEP . . . BEEP-BEEP-BEEP . . . BEEP-BEEP-BEEP! went on and on. Chris went back to bed and put a pillow over his head.

Judy said, "We'll just have to shut off all power to the house for the rest of the night." I agreed. I went to the basement, shut the door, and let the cats out of the cage. We turned off the great fan and shut all the windows, as the BEEP-BEEP-BEEP . . . BEEP-BEEP-BEEP . . . BEEP-BEEP-BEEP never let up. I told

Judy, "You go upstairs and get in bed while the lights are on, and I'll throw the master switch and come up with a flashlight."

She trundled up the stairs, and I went to the breaker box with my flashlight and flipped the big red switch. Darkness pounced, and the alarms said, BEEP-BEEP-BEEP . . . BEEP-BEEP-BEEP! and then SILENCE! Blessed silence!

Naturally, even though I went back to bed, I could not get back to sleep. At 5:30, I leapt lightly from bed to start breakfast. We wondered if the alarms would all start sounding again when I turned the master switch back on, but they did not. Silence reigned. Well almost: now each alarm merely let out a periodic "Chirp" like a cricket to let me know that it missed its battery!

While we were eating a repast of fried eggs, hash brown potatoes, sausage, and toast, a piece of Judy's tooth came off! I knew that somehow this was the fault of the smoke alarms, but could not quite figure out how. I replaced all the batteries, and then after Judy left for work with a tummy full, I lay down and actually snoozed for an hour.

I telephoned our pastor David Martin for pastoral counseling about the smoke alarms, and he said that one weak battery can sometimes set off the whole gang of alarms, and that the batteries that come with them may be years old and cheap to start with. He counseled first of all to install all new batteries. Then if the problem continued, it had to be one defective alarm. Later, I called Tony the builder at Sherwood Forest Homes, and he said exactly the same thing, so it must be right. At any rate, we never had a repetition after installing the new batteries.

I wondered why such things always happen at 3:15 A.M. instead of 3:15 P.M? Well, as Frankie Valli would say, "Oh what a night!"

Chris's Version

03:37   Awakened by every fire alarm in the house going off, and the parents can't figure out why. Someday this will all seem funny.

03:39   I want to go back to sleeeeeeep . . . but I can't until the beeping stops.

03:42   Pulling the batteries didn't help. Dad is going to start flipping circuit breakers now.

03:48   Still no sleepie; lots of beepie.

03:51   Dad is going to throw the main breaker.

03:54   Darkness, and blessed silence

04:10   Guess we'll be going breaker free until morning. At least I have a flashlight.

21:18   It's kind of weird living on the ground floor of a 2 story plus basement house (because I can't do stairs with this leg).

21:21   It's like living in a stage play where you only hear about things that happen offstage when someone mentions them onstage.

Thinking like Water

After twenty-five years, my shop roof began leaking, and the old plywood eave soffits were rotten and falling apart. Jeffrey Fierce was highly recommended as a skilled carpenter and craftsman who would do a good job of installing new soffits and roof. I telephoned, and he promised to come at a certain time and survey the job to find out what I wanted done and how to do it.

When Jeffrey arrived, he proved to be a man about sixty-five years of age. I could quickly see that Jeffrey was single-mindedly serious, determined to understand the job exactly, and not given to jocularity. I thought of my late father, who described such people as "afraid to smile for fear his face might crack." In short, Jeffrey was just the opposite of me. I am something of a comedian. Many of my friends start laughing the minute they see me, believing that I am on the verge of getting off a good one. At least I hope that's why they laugh when they see me.

Jeffrey also was one of those people who stands too close to you. The "personal space" parameters vary from culture to culture. We all know exactly how close someone has to be to invade our space and make us feel uncomfortable. Well, we don't all know, and Jeffrey was one of the few who did not have that built in radar. He was short and slight, and I wondered if having to look up to most people might have caused this lack.

Jeffrey surveyed the shop with an eagle eye, moved a little closer to me, and asked, "What sort of a roof do you want me to install on this building?"

I replied, "I don't have any idea! I was hoping that you would tell me."

Jeffrey said gravely, "Oh no, no, no! I'll install whatever sort of roof you want, but I won't tell you what to do. If you don't like it, it would be my fault."

"Golly!" I said. "I don't even know what the options are."

Here is an excerpt from the conversation that ensued:

Jeffrey: Well, first you just have to think of what you want. For example, do you want metal roofing or shingles?

Mark: I don't have any idea. I thought I'd ask your advice.

Jeffrey: Well, it's completely up to you, but on a low-pitch roof like this, the metal will be a lot better and less apt to leak.

Mark: Okay! Metal it is!

Jeffrey: Do you want me to put that metal right on the old shingles or put one-by-four strips across the roof to anchor it to?

Mark: I don't have any idea. What do you think?

Jeffrey: It's your decision, but you can't anchor your metal down very well to the old decking. It would be sure to come loose, so I'd put the strips down if it was me.

Mark: All right! Let's go with the strips.

Jeffrey: Do you want gable edge trim going down the sides of the roof?

Mark: Beats me! I don't even know what gable edge trim is. What do you think?

Jeffrey: Well, I'll do whatever you decide, but if you don't have the gable trim, the rain will blow under the metal roofing and probably leak inside the building.

Mark: We'd better have that edge trim then.

Jeffrey: What about metal fascia strips at the edge of the roof? Do you want that?

Mark: Gosh! I hadn't thought about it. What would you do?

Jeffrey: Now, I don't want to influence you in any way, but if it was me, I'd want those strips, because if you don't have them, your new wood soffits will rot.

Jeffrey's method struck me as a convoluted way of coming to terms, rather than simply telling me, "You'll need to do this and that," and ordering whatever he needed to do the job right.

As Jeffrey asked me question after question about the job at hand, he stood too close and stared up directly into my eyes with his piercing blue eyes. His gaze never wavered, and he had a serious demeanor, his lips never twitching in the slightest hint of a smile.

Such unwanted solemnity began to wear on my constitution, and I felt determined to instill some mirth into the situation. Between answering these questions, I made a number of jokes and witty comments in an attempt to make Jeffrey laugh, or at least crack a smile, but to no avail. Eventually, Jeffrey got a color chart from his pickup, so I could choose the color for my new metal roof. One color was described as "Ocean Blue." I commented, "I'd better not choose Ocean Blue. You might get seasick and fall off the roof."

Jeffrey looked at me intently for some time with a dead serious, puzzled, blue gaze, his gimlet eyes boring into my eyes, to try and read some serious anxiety into my comment. It was as if his brain were churning over my remark and concluding, "Does not compute! Does not compute!"

Jeffrey finally gave up and went out to his pickup to fetch a tape measure. Ten minutes later he returned with the tape, and suddenly he threw back his head and laughed a merry, side-splitting laugh that shook his whole frame. "Hahaha! Ocean Blue! Seasick! Oh, hahaha!" It was some seconds before he could reclaim his sober demeanor.

When Jeffrey regained his composure, he borrowed my ladder, climbed up on the roof and measured this way and that with a metal tape. He made an inscrutable list of materials he would need and left, saying he would be back in a few days. A couple of days later trucks from the lumber company and metal roofing company delivered goods to the yard near the shop building. The next day Jeffrey and his helper Jeff arrived to begin work. It took them only two days to finish the job completely, and the bill for labor was only a small fraction of the job, thanks to their efficiency. I was impressed that Jeffrey had figured so exactly what materials were needed that there was simply nothing left after the job—only a few little tag ends and scraps that amounted to an armload.

It is ironic that Jeffrey's helper was named Jeff. Jeffrey never stopped talking, albeit earnestly and seriously. But he talked all the time. Jeff was almost totally silent. I never heard him say a single word except, "Howdy" when we were introduced. Of course Jeffrey drew down a higher wage than Jeff, since Jeffrey owned all the equipment and ran the business. Jeffrey got $16 per hour; while paying Jeff a mere $15.

A few days after Jeffrey and Jeff finished the new roof, it rained cats and dogs and pitchforks! Unfortunately the new shop roof leaked around the chimney, so I had to telephone Jeffrey to tell him about it.

When I telephoned Jeffrey about the leak at the chimney, he was astonished, as was I, as he had done such a skillful job of installing flashing around that chimney. He promised to come later that very day to examine it and was as good as his word, even though he had to go a long way around, thanks to a rain-flooded bridge at McDowell, Missouri.

When Jeffrey arrived, he stood close, his sharp eyes pinning me, as a lepidopterist might pin a hapless butterfly, then said grimly, "You don't need to devote a bit of worry to that roof. When I put on a roof, I'll do whatever is necessary to keep the flippin thing from leaking, so don't you worry. I guarantee I'll find the problem. Let me get my ladder. All I have to do is climb up there and examine that chimney and think like water."

I chuckled at what I thought was a jocular comment, but Jeffrey eyed me severely and said sternly, "Now that's the absolute truth! I'm not joking. I just have to think like water."

Jeffrey mounted the roof, and his imagination successfully transformed himself into a flood of raindrops, which pondered how they could gain ingress through the roof, thus quickly spotting a flaw. Back in human form, Jeffrey made the necessary corrections, and after the next wave of rain storms I found my shop still snug and dry. The water had met its match in an old carpenter who knew its thought processes.

Time Lost is Never Found

So the little minutes, humble though they be,
Make the mighty ages of eternity.
~Julia Carney

In July 2012, I received a call from an elderly Dutch lady living in Springfield, Missouri. Another Dutch immigrant in Shell Knob, Missouri, for whom I once repaired a clock, had referred her to me. The problem was: How could she get her clock to me and back again to Springfield after it was repaired? As it happened, Gisla Thompson lived a few blocks from our son Chris, whom we were about to visit, so we agreed to pick up the clock and deliver it back at no extra charge. We were to learn that Gisla was charming, friendly, and likable—but also exasperating.

Judy and I stopped by her house on Karla Lane, expecting to be there five minutes, grabbing the clock, and departing. Gisla's house was the most over-decorated house we have ever seen. Every wall was totally covered with paintings, hangings, and decorations ranging in size from a mammoth painting the size of a door showing a Dutch windmill on one wall of the vaulted living room down to tiny Dutch delft tiles twice as big as your thumbnail. In between there were paintings and photos of all sizes. Gisla's taste was eclectic. The windmill painting was realistic. There was an African wall hanging of aboriginal dancers and an impressionistic oil of a bright lady with oversized sunglasses. To complete the décor, every level surface was laden with figurines, ginger jars, framed photos, and doodads. In a week one might be able to examine the entire collection.

The clock turned out to be a reproduction Zaandam clock, a Dutch style wall clock powered by pear-shaped, shiny, brass weights on chains. I packed the clock in two minutes and was turning to the door, when Gisla said, "Oh no! You must seet and chat viss me for a leetle beet."

Gisla introduced Judy and me to her son and grandson who were visiting from Georgia, then took us into a small parlor and seated us on a couch. She talked of many things, not exactly "shoes and ships and sealing wax," but almost everything else. She wanted to know how long we had been married, how many children we had, which church we went to, whether it was a legalistic church, what our parents had done for a living, how I learned to repair clocks, where we had been born, and many other things. Judy and I kept starting to get up, but could never quite make our escape, for Gisla asking us another question.

As I looked through the door into the living room, I could see that Gisla's son was a highly nervous fellow. He paced back and forth, walked into another room and came back into the living room. He was in constant motion during our whole visit with his mother. Finally he plunged into the parlor and blurted, "I don't mean to be rude, and I'm sorry to chase you off, but I drove 2,000 miles to visit with my father, and I MUST take Mother and go to the rest home to see him!"

Judy and I skedaddled!

I received two or three emails from Gisla over the next six weeks, wanting to know when she could have her clock back. I told her the clock was ready, but that I had to find a time when we were coming to Springfield on other business, so I could drop it off.

In September, we finally had our chance. I called Gisla and told her that we would be driving our friend Kelley to the doctor on Tuesday, September 11, so could bring the clock to her. She replied, "Oh, zatt ees a problem. Tuesdays and Fridays I take zee OATS bus to zee Quail Creek Nursing Home to visit viss my husband.

I knew that the Quail Creek Nursing Home was in the south part of town, not far from Ferrell-Duncan Clinic where we were dropping Kelley. I decided that we could be at Gisla's home on Karla Lane at 9:30 a.m. with the clock, and that we would take her to the nursing home on our way back to pick up our friend at the doctor's office. Gisla emailed to confirm, "I will expect you at 9:30 Tuesday morning."

On the appointed day we dropped off Kelley at the Ferrell-Duncan Clinic in the south part of town—for a surgery follow up. We left her just before 9:00 and sped north, then out on East Grand Avenue to Karla Lane where the old lady lived.

We arrived at Gisla's home at 9:20, and Judy kept ringing the doorbell while I held the heavy clock. I was just ready to put the clock down and telephone Gisla, thinking her doorbell might not work, when we heard her rattling inside the door. She opened the door clad in a bathrobe! When we entered, she made no move to go get dressed, but was prepared to stand around in her robe and watch me set up the clock, so I said, "If you will go and get dressed, we will take you to the nursing home."

She said, "Vell, I hope zo, since I haff called off zee bus for ziss morning."

I said, "Go ahead and get dressed then, while I set up the clock."

Of course it took a lot longer for her to dress than for me to set up the clock. She finally emerged, dressed and pushing a wheelchair laden with some canvas carry-all bags to take with her to the nursing home. She said, "I use ziss veelchair to carry schtuff around zee house."

Then she said, "Oh, I haff to pay you." I followed her creeping down the hall to her office, where it took her a hair-pulling length of time rummaging and sorting to find her checkbook and write a check for my bill.

As we came back along the hallway at a snail's pace, Gisla pointed to a bar of soap on the floor outside the bathroom. She said, "Do you place sings about zee house to remind you to do somezing? Zat soap vill remind me zat my toilet keeps running, and I must call zee plumber."

I saw other inscrutable reminders of her future chores on the floor outside other doors: a little figurine of a ballerina on the floor outside one door and a bowl of spools outside another.

Back in the foyer where Judy was waiting, I was ready to snatch up Gisla's carryalls and rush impatiently to the car, when Gisla announced, "I haff not had breakfast yet. You don't mind vaiting vile I fix some breakfast, do you?"

I said, "I'm sorry, but we cannot wait. We have to leave right now to pick up our friend at the doctor's office." She said, "Oh vell, zenn I vill take viss me a banana." She was in the kitchen so long that I was about to go help her find the banana, when she emerged with a little lunchbox.

I had to wonder why Gisla wanted her clock repaired, since the passage of time seemed to have no impact on her life. She lived as if time did not exist.

We finally got Gisla out the door, hobbling slowly on a cane, and I loaded her three bags and lunch box in the car. We were barely on our way before Kelley called to say she was finished at the doctor's office and ready for us to pick her up.

On the way to Quail Creek, Gisla commented, "Zee OATS bus comes for me at 9:30 every Tuesday and Friday morning." This made us wonder: Does the OATS bus sit and wait while she gets dressed and has breakfast?

As we drove west then south to the opposite end of town, Gisla never stopped talking. She complained about the medical system in the United States and lamented the greed of penurious insurance companies. She told about her husband of sixty-three years, a brilliant man and professor. He had fallen and hit his head, causing blood to pool inside his skull, and, as she put it, "raising cane viss his mind." She told of leaving Amsterdam in

1947 as a war bride, and not visiting her home country for fifteen years, going back with four children in tow.

At Quail Creek Nursing Home, I finally was able to carry all of Gisla's paraphernalia inside, with her coming slowly behind. As we crossed the foyer, she cried out to the receptionist, loudly demanding, "Get me a veelchair, please, my schtuff viss me to carry!"

Driven by punctuality, as I am, I longed to race out the door and never see Gisla again. Meanwhile, she kept telling me amicably, "Any time venn you come to town, just pop in for a visit!"

Watching Gisla tottering unhurriedly across the waiting room with her cane, I thought of that quotation from Shakespeare: "I wasted time, and now doth time waste me."

Learning from Lorelei

I love poetry. I am not talking about those bizarre little paragraphs that people write and think they are writing poetry. I love real poetry with meter and rhyme. In the late 1990s, our friend Debbie Berger was a sixth-grade teacher at Monett, Missouri. Debbie had heard me read and recite poetry on occasion, and she asked me if I would be willing to come to the school and give a poetry reading to the sixth grade classes. This request reveals Debbie's wisdom. Poetry is an oral art and cannot be appreciated when read silently.

Always ready for the spotlight, I readily agreed. I prepared a brief introductory talk comparing poetry and prose. I selected a number of favorite poems that I thought the young students would enjoy. Debbie specifically asked me to include "To a Mouse" by Robert Burns. She said, "We've been studying that poem, and I want you to read it with your best Scottish accent."

When I arrived for my performance, I was surprised that the auditorium was filled with all the sixth-grade classes, the speech classes, and a number of teachers.

The students were very well behaved. Well, the teachers were too, for that matter. As I was starting to speak, one boy in the second row leaned over and whispered to his neighbor, and I said, "Better pay attention, Fella!"

The young man had the courtesy to look abashed and even to blush! Aside from this infringement, the auditorium was silent except for appropriate laughter when I made a joke. I read poems by Wordsworth, Poe, and other great poets, but as my last poem, I read one by a less-than-great poet. I read my poem "The Great Denture Adventure." Imagine my surprise, when Debbie later phoned to say that the classes had voted my poem as their favorite!

Debbie had made one other request during her original consultation. She asked me to read one poem in a foreign language, so that the students could hear the meter and rhyme, even though they could not understand the words. I decided to read the German poem "Die Lorelei" by Heinrich Heine. I felt that the students deserved a translation after listening to the original. I could not find a good translation on the Internet, so wound up writing my own.

In translating poetry, one cannot simply substitute word for word from one language to another, as it will not rhyme. The translator has to come as close as possible to the original meaning and mood. I was happy that my translation had the same meter and *abab* rhyme scheme as the original.

I received an extraordinary accolade when I gave the poem to a German lady named Alex. She told me, "I sink zat your tranzlation iss more powervul zehn zee original."

Die Lorelei

von Heinrich Heine, 1824

Ich weiß nicht, was soll es bedeuten,
Daß ich so traurig bin;
Ein Märchen aus alten Zeiten,
Das kommt mir nicht aus dem Sinn.

Die Luft is kühl, und es dunkelt,
Und ruhig fließt der Rhein;
Der Gipfel des Berges funkelt
Im Abendsonnenschein.

Die schönste Jungfrau sitzet
Dort oben wunderbar,
Ihr goldenes Geschmeide blitzet,
Sie kämmt ihr goldenes Haar.

Sie kämmt es mit goldenem Kamme
Und singt ein Lied dabei;
Das hat eine wundersame,
Gewaltige Melodei.

Den Schiffer im kleinen Schiffe
Ergreift es mit wildem Weh;
Er schaut nicht die Felsenriffe,
Er schaut nur hinauf in die Höh'.

Ich glaube die Wellen verschlingen
Am Ende Schiffer und Kahn;
Und das hat mit ihrem Singen
Die Lorelei getan.

The Lorelei

Translated by Mark D. Meadows

Why is my heart sorely saddened?
Some sorrow has taken its toll;
An old time legend has maddened
And almost enchanted my soul.

The air is cool in the twilight
And peaceful flows the Rhine;
The sun's last rays before the night
Make the stone peak twinkle and shine.

The lovely maiden sits there
High up and young and bold;
Her gold jewels glint, she combs her hair—
Long strands of radiant gold.

With golden comb she combs her hair
And sings a clear refrain;
A song of power and despair
Fills the darkening domain.

The boatman in his little skiff
Is seized by the song's savage grief;
He looks up to the lofty cliff,
Not down at the rocky reef.

I think that the waves did swallow
The boat and the boatman as one;
And this with her terrible solo
The Lorelei has done.

Printed in Great Britain
by Amazon

84250533R00180